Global Tabloid

This edited collection brings together a range of contemporary expertise to discuss the development and impact of tabloid news around the world.

In thirteen chapters, *Global Tabloid* covers tabloid developments in Asia, Africa, the Americas, Australia, and both Eastern and Western Europe. It presents innovative research from eighteen expert contributors and editors, who explore tabloidization as a phenomenon and tabloids as a news form. With an awareness of historical dynamics where tabloids played a role in national news media systems, it brings the debates around tabloids as a cultural force up to date. The book addresses important questions about the contemporary nature of popular culture, the challenges it faces in the digital era, and its impact on a political world dominated by tabloid values. Going beyond national borders to consider global developments, the editors and contributors explore how the tabloids have permeated media culture more generally, and how they are adapting to an increasingly digitalized media sphere.

This internationally focused critical study is a valuable resource for students and researchers in journalism, media, and cultural studies.

Martin Conboy is Emeritus Professor of Journalism History and the co-director of the Centre for the Study of Journalism and History at the University of Sheffield. He has produced ten books on the language and history of journalism. Specific to this project he wrote *Tabloid Britain* (2006) and, with Professor Adrian Bingham, *Tabloid Century* (2015). His 2002 book, *The Press and Popular Culture,* has recently been translated into Czech with a new introduction. He is on the editorial boards of *Journalism Studies*; *Media History; Journalism: Theory, Practice and Criticism*; and *Memory Studies.*

Scott A. Eldridge II, PhD, is an assistant professor at the Centre for Media and Journalism Studies, University of Groningen. His research addresses digital journalism and the changing journalistic field, focusing on antagonistic journalistic actors. He is the author of numerous studies on these changes, including *Online Journalism from the Periphery: Interloper Media and the Journalistic Field* (2018), and is co-editor with Bob Franklin of *The Routledge Handbook of Developments in Digital Journalism Studies* (2019) and *The Routledge Companion to Digital Journalism Studies* (2017). He is an associate editor for the journal *Digital Journalism.*

Global Tabloid

Culture and Technology

Edited by
Martin Conboy and
Scott A. Eldridge II

Routledge
Taylor & Francis Group
LONDON AND NEW YORK

First published 2021
by Routledge
2 Park Square, Milton Park, Abingdon, Oxon OX14 4RN

and by Routledge
605 Third Avenue, New York, NY 10158

Routledge is an imprint of the Taylor & Francis Group, an informa business

British Library Cataloguing-in-Publication Data
A catalogue record for this book is available from the British Library

Library of Congress Cataloging-in-Publication Data
A catalog record has been requested for this book

ISBN: 978-0-367-33625-7 (hbk)
ISBN: 978-0-367-33626-4 (pbk)
ISBN: 978-0-429-32088-0 (ebk)

Typeset in Bembo
by Taylor & Francis Books

Contents

Illustrations

Figures

Tables

Acknowledgments

This current volume was originally inspired in scope by a book edited in 2000 by Colin Sparks and the late John Tulloch: *Tabloid Tales*. The world has revolved many, many times since that publication and so we considered it appropriate to refresh consideration of this most controversial and successful media genre. Throughout most of the development of this book we have been under the influence of the COVID pandemic. The patience, expertise, camaraderie, and punctuality in delivery from all of our contributors have been a welcome source of support and distraction during these tragic, confusing, and unsettling times. It is therefore to all of those intrepid explorers in the world of the global tabloid that we dedicate this book. Thank you. We hope to meet you all in person one day when the world is a safer place.

It would be remiss of us not to also express thanks to the production team who have facilitated the project from start to finish: at Routledge, Margaret Farrelly, Priscille Biehlmann, Ruth Berry and the erudite and rigorous David Weintraub, our copy editor.

Martin Conboy, Nether Edge, Sheffield
Scott A Eldridge II, Groningen, Netherlands
December 2020

Contributors

Mine Gencel Bek is a researcher at the University of Siegen. She completed her PhD at Loughborough University in 1999 with the thesis titled "Communicating Capitalism: A Study of the Contemporary Turkish Press". She was a visiting lecturer at MIT Comparative Media Studies, Open Documentary Lab, and Civic Media Lab in 2013 and 2014. She worked at Ankara University for 26 years until she was dismissed from her position as a professor for signing the Academics for Peace petition.

Henrik Bødker, PhD, is an associate professor in the Media and Journalism Studies Department at Aarhus University (Denmark). His most recent work focuses on how digital technologies are transforming the circulation and temporality of journalism. He has just finished editing (with Hanna Morris, UPenn) *Climate Change and Journalism: Negotiating Rifts of Time* and is currently working on a monograph entitled *Journalism, Time and the Digital.* He has, among other journals, published in *Media History*; *Critical Studies in Media Communication*; *Journalism*; *Journalism Studies* and *Digital Journalism.*

Martin Conboy is Emeritus Professor of Journalism History and the co-director of the Centre for the Study of Journalism and History at the University of Sheffield. He has produced ten books on the language and history of journalism. Specific to this project he wrote *Tabloid Britain* (2006) and, with Professor Adrian Bingham, *Tabloid Century* (2015). His 2002 book, *The Press and Popular Culture,* has recently been translated into Czech with a new introduction. He is on the editorial boards of *Journalism Studies*; *Media History*; *Journalism: Theory, Practice and Criticism* and *Memory Studies.*

Scott A. Eldridge II, PhD, is an assistant professor at the Centre for Media and Journalism Studies, University of Groningen. His research addresses digital journalism and the changing journalistic field, focusing on antagonistic journalistic actors. He is the author of numerous studies on these changes, including *Online Journalism from the Periphery: Interloper Media and the Journalistic Field* (2018), and is co-editor with Bob Franklin of *The Routledge Handbook of Developments in Digital Journalism Studies* (2019) and *The Routledge*

Companion to Digital Journalism Studies (2017). He is an associate editor for the journal *Digital Journalism.*

Stephen Harrington is an associate professor in the School of Communication at the Queensland University of Technology, Australia. He has written extensively on the changing nature of journalism and the role of entertainment in the public sphere. He is the co-author of *Politics, Media and Democracy in Australia: Public and Producer Perceptions of the Political Public Sphere* (Routledge, 2017), and author of *Australian TV News: New Forms, Functions, and Futures* (Intellect, 2013).

Andrea Häuptli is a PhD Student in the Department of Communication and Media Research (IKMZ) at the University of Zurich. She holds an MA degree in political science from ETH Zurich. Her research focuses on the quality of the media and on the transnationalization of public spheres, especially in the Arab world.

Chengju Huang is a senior lecturer in the School of Media and Communication, RMIT University, Australia. His research interests include Asian/Chinese media studies, international communication, and comparative media systems. His work has appeared in *Journal of Communication; Journalism: Theory, Practice and Criticism; Journalism Studies; The International Communication Gazette* and *Global Media Journal.*

Julia Lefkowitz is a DPhil candidate and research assistant at the Oxford Internet Institute, University of Oxford. Her doctoral thesis focuses on possible shifts in journalistic values in view of the ascendance of the Internet and adjunct putative causal factors. Across projects, her work more broadly examines the relationship between the Internet and society through quantitative and qualitative, linguistic approaches.

Jairo Lugo-Ocando, PhD (Sussex) is a professor in residence and Director of Executive and Graduate Education at Northwestern University, Qatar. He is co-author of *The News Media in Puerto Rico: Journalism in Colonial Settings and in Times of Crises* (Routledge, 2020) and *Media and Governance in Latin America: Towards a Plurality of Voices* (Peter Lang, 2020); and author of *Foreign Aid and Journalism in the Global South: A Mouthpiece for Truth* (Lexington Books, 2020). He has received research grants funding from the United Kingdom's Arts and Humanities Research Council (AHRC), Qatar National Research Fund, the Leverhulme Trust and the Carnegie Trust for the Universities in Scotland, among other institutions. Before becoming an academic, he worked as a journalist, correspondent, and news editor for several media outlets in Latin America.

Melanie Magin is an associate professor in media sociology in the Department of Sociology and Political Science at the Norwegian University of Science and Technology (NTNU) in Trondheim, Norway. Her research focuses on the societal chances and risks of traditional and new media, and spans political communication, media performance, algorithm-based information intermediaries, media systems, media structures, and comparative research.

Andrea McDonnell is an associate professor of Communication and Media Studies at Emmanuel College, Boston. She is the author of *Reading Celebrity Gossip Magazines* (Polity, 2014) and, with Susan Douglas, author of *Celebrity: A History of Fame* (NYU, 2019). Dr. McDonnell's research on media, gossip, celebrity, and politics has been published in *Body Image, Celebrity Studies*, and the *Journal of Language and Politics*.

Khulekani Ndlovu recently completed his PhD in media studies at the University of Cape Town, South Africa. He is currently employed as a lecturer in the department of Media Studies at the University of Botswana. His research interests include critical media studies, journalism in the post-truth era, and new media in the global South.

Marcela Pizarro is an assistant professor in residence at Northwestern University, Qatar. She was a journalist at Al Jazeera English and the Associated Press for 20 years. She holds a PhD in Latin American Studies from the University of London, funded by the British Academy.

Sreedevi Purayannur is an independent researcher currently based in the United States. She received a PhD from the University of Sheffield in 2018 for the thesis titled "Quality in Journalism: Perceptions and Practice in an Indian context." For her doctoral research, she explored the extent of integration between quality perceptions of Indian journalists and the evidence of quality in Indian newspapers.

Birgit Stark is a full professor in the Department of Communication at the Johannes Gutenberg University, Mainz, Germany. Her work focuses on media convergence, media performance, fragmentation, and comparative media research. This includes research on algorithm-based information intermediaries like Google and Facebook, their societal impact and the chances, and risks associated with them.

Miriam Steiner is a PhD candidate in the Department of Communication at the Johannes Gutenberg University, Mainz, Germany. Her research interests focus on media performance (particularly on tabloidization and media diversity), and on current news consumption.

Lada Trifonova Price, PhD, is a senior journalism lecturer in the Department of Media, Arts and Communication, Sheffield Hallam University, UK She is a former journalist, and her current research is focused on media and journalistic practice in transitional democracies. She is currently the main editor of the forthcoming *Routledge Companion to Journalism Ethics*.

Linards Udris (Dr. phil.) is a Senior Research Associate in the Department of Communication and Media Research at the University of Zurich, and Deputy Director of Research at the Research Center for the Public Sphere and Society, Stiftung Forschungsinstitut Öffentlichkeit und Gesellschaft (fög), at the University of Zurich. His research interests lie in the quality of the media, political communication, especially during referendum campaigns, and social change.

1 Tabloid culture

Parameters and debates

Martin Conboy

Introduction

At the risk of tempting fate or even history, we suggest that there is a spectre stalking the global mediasphere. This spectre is the tabloid. Like any good spectre, it is hard to pin down. Critical neglect has played a part in this. It is a tendency we aim to correct. For a time in the 1990s, discussions of the tabloid or the broader process of tabloidization were lively and used to centre on the changing formats of newspapers. They did not, however, generate enough substance on the possibility that the tabloid had evolved not as a format or even a style of journalism but more as a communicative flow, despite the fact that historical accounts of popular content in print periodicals had illustrated as much. The tabloid even *avant la lettre* has been a spectre haunting journalism's past as well as its present since before its obvious modern-day manifestations, and we can see trends associated with it such as sensationalism, trivialization, exaggeration, and sexualization established within popular print culture well before the emergence of the daily tabloid press proper in the early twentieth century. Still further back in time, some of the earliest printed publications in Europe combined many of the elements associated with the later tabloid newspaper. Indeed, historically, we might see the triumph of the daily, predominantly political, commercial, and respectable newspapers of the bourgeois public sphere as deviations from the long-term successful trajectory of the tabloid. This success can be contrasted with most assessments of the tabloid and its associated phenomena which are negative and read like a miasma of bourgeois anxieties concerning taste, gender, class, politics, and sex. Allan claims it can amount to a "stigmatised label" (Allan, 2010: xxxix). Yet the wide variety of substance and tone we see in these examples renders simplified categories of the 'tabloid' or 'tabloidized' content problematic. These raise multiple questions about definitions of these terms that need to first be resolved if we are to be able to disentangle the conflicting accounts of tabloids' journalistic value, or the critique of the same.

Questions to ask of a global phenomenon

At this present juncture, where explicit discussion of the tabloid has become blended within broader discussion of emerging media forms and technologies, it is perhaps germane to re-assess the specific dynamics and complexities of the tabloid by asking certain indicative questions. Should we perhaps be considering the digital manifestation of the tabloid newspaper, trends of tabloidization within news media, or a broader tabloid culture that transcends individual media formats such as 'news'? Is the process of tabloidization merely a further intensification of discursive reality symptomatic of current media activity? Have we entered a golden age of tabloid culture, or, rather, can we interpret tabloid culture anew as the primary way of understanding modern journalistic culture?

Most research on the tabloid has concentrated on specific national variants, especially the Anglo-American. This introduction attempts to set the scene for a revision of that tendency. The contributors in this volume consider the state of tabloid journalism and related tabloid culture on six continents in order to reflect on whether the tabloid genre has continued to permeate contemporary culture and consolidate itself within emergent socially mediated communication forms. This book draws on the rich history of tabloid culture to emphasize continuities within popular journalism while situating it within a digital age. Such a research strategy allows us to address Rowe's astute observation that the speed of change in media and culture may be masking persistent or recurrent phenomena that indicate that contemporary societies are not as dramatically different from historically preceding societies as they might appear (Rowe, 2009: 122). While looking for evidence of continuities, at the same time, by breaking from the hitherto dominant Anglo-American lens, we will assess tabloid culture globally in order to show important differences when tabloid culture is adopted in varying environments.

Three little piggies went to market

A double-headed pig from a German sixteenth century pamphlet (Conboy, 2002), a wild hog eating a baby in an American supermarket tabloid in the 1990s (Sloan, 2001) and a pushy pig which was briefly the BBC website's top story in November 2019: each of these stories indicates that the sensational and the bizarre have always and continue to facilitate profit and reader interest for news media. Historically, critics have certainly sufficient evidence to claim that early print culture had its tabloid elements (Reeve, 2014). Publications in question share an attractive layout, they deploy images to good effect, and probe the tastes of the readership for excitement and scandal. We can see such trends well before the emergence of the daily tabloid press in the US in the 1920s and certainly some of the earliest printed publications in Europe combined all of those elements. The explosion of periodicals across seventeenth century Europe provided a combination of woodcut images and often sensational lead stories in keeping with societies in flux as news of religious and political wars, famine, and plague clamoured for the attention of readers. During these upheavals the sensational had every right to assert itself in the everyday.

Indeed, historically, we might see the triumph of the predominantly political, commercial, and respectable newspapers of the eighteenth and nineteenth centuries' bourgeois public sphere as deviations from the trajectory of the proto-tabloid genre. Within this hypothesis, the more sensationalist publications merely adopted other ways of finding their market through broadsides and illustrated ballads hawked by itinerant vendors and supplemented in the nineteenth century by execution sheets and the regular publication of heavily illustrated police gazettes that concentrated on crime. This indicates an even longer trajectory for popular periodicals than the emergence of the penny press in the US in the 1830s and the Sunday press in UK from the 1840s. Of course, the popular market is far from an ideologically neutral location. Curran and Seaton (2003: 106) observed that the tendency had always been for popular newspapers to push towards conservative political views as an incremental consequence of their requirement to fit within the logic of markets and advertising-audience share, despite their claims to represent the voice and interests of the ordinary people. This had been clear from at least the end of the stamp duties in the UK and evidenced in the shift in stance of initially radical Sunday papers like *Reynolds's Weekly News*. When these tendencies emerged in the daily press it was through the French daily *Le Petit Journal* and slightly later the American experiments that led to the competition between newspaper titans of the period, William Randolph Hearst and Joseph Pulitzer, in the 'yellow press'.

Although these tendencies became more consistently marketable and despite a clear flow across the centuries between American and British journalistic cultures (Wiener, 2011; Nicholson, 2016), linear progression or the pernicious influence of American mass culture are difficult to substantiate. For example, the Robinson-Jewitt murder case sensationally reported in Bennett's *New York Herald* in 1836 (Crouthamel, 1989) preceded the sensationalization of child prostitution by Stead's infamous "Maiden Tribute of Modern Babylon" in the *Pall Mall Gazette* by almost 50 years. The American tabloids of the 1920s with grotesque front pages designed to sell on the street, such as the notorious photograph of Ruth Snyder's execution by electric chair in 1928, gave rise in very different political circumstances to the conversion of the British *Daily Mirror* in the 1930s to what we would recognize today as the full tabloid style, and combined this with a left-leaning, commercially successful product.

In *I Watched a Wild Hog Eat My Baby* (2001), Sloan entertainingly chronicles how ex-Fleet Street tabloid journalists aided and abetted their American colleagues in the creation of the most successful supermarket tabloids. Some estimates claim that 80 per cent of the American supermarket tabloid journalists were British in their heyday (Taylor, 1992: 91).

More than simply reducing the size of the newspaper and far from being terminated by the emergence of new media formats for news and entertainment that some may claim have blunted its functions, the tabloid can, in fact, exist beyond format as a cultural phenomenon. It is to a certain extent content and style, but beyond this it is a matter of flow. This is particularly evident in the contemporary world, where the ability of tabloid culture to permeate media boundaries is becoming more evident (Conboy, 2007). Sometimes format and style can converge, while at other times they are perfectly able to function independent of each other. In Britain, the emergence of the first tabloid-sized newspaper, the *Daily Mirror* in 1903, certainly did not coincide with the first tabloid culture. Conversely, in the present day, with the decline of mass sales of tabloid newspapers, the culture they have enabled to flourish continues outside the confines of the paper page: sometimes on the web, at other times in more diffuse mediations such as television, celebrity formats, and as we will argue here, in many functions associated with social media as they mesh with journalism (Bingham and Conboy, 2015; Nunn and Biressi, 2008; Seaton, 2017).

Tabloid: analysis and moral panic

In the 1990s a febrile set of discussions emerged about the tabloid as a danger to the body of democratic journalism. These began with critiques of the tabloid newspaper as embodying the polar opposite to serious journalism in its triviality, naked populism, and sensation at all costs. What gave the debate added impetus was the awareness that tabloid values were extending to previously "quality" newspapers. It was a process christened 'tabloidization' in the early 1990s. Sparks (2000) provided an analytical survey of what he believed would be lost to public discourse if the values of the tabloid press continued to erode democratic engagement with the public. In the volume he edited with Tulloch is a chapter that provides a longitudinal analysis of how the success and popularity of the tabloids in the UK were shifting content in the quality press with fewer international news stories, more pictures in relation to text, more human interest emphasis, more entertainment-related stories, and fewer political/parliament stories (McLachlan and Golding, 2000).

Bromley had already provided an analysis of this process as more of a two-way flow:

> At first the quality press ignored the substantive issues of tabloid news; then decried them. These papers … subsequently began reporting and commenting on the behaviour of the tabloid press, which led to the vicarious reporting of the issues themselves. Finally, the broadsheet papers, too, carried the same news items.
>
> (Bromley, 1998: 31)

The term tabloidization became a mediacentric moral panic in its expression of concern for declining standards of professional behaviour. Esser provided an insight into the economic and legal drivers that shaped this trend within newsrooms in various national contexts. The comparative element of his work enabled him to conclude with confidence that "'tabloidization' is an extremely problematic term since it has different meanings in different societies. It can therefore only be analysed with reference to the respective media cultures and journalistic traditions" (Esser, 1999: 318).

This was a perspective that was endorsed in a later study by Uribe and Gunther (2004) who added that the increased presence of home news in tabloids may lead to a preponderance of local taste/generic preference within localized tabloid cultures. Furthermore, they asserted that tabloidization is a dynamic process within varied political and national contexts rather than a static concept. More recently, Lefkowitz has broadened the debate from a concentration on page size and thematic content to consider the linguistic specifics of tabloid newspapers as an integral aspect of the tabloidization process. While acknowledging the moral panic in observers of this phenomenon, she is more interested in the "underlying dynamics … the linguistic features through which these values are represented" (Lefkowitz, 2018: 353–354). Beyond the mediacentrism of the debate lie anxieties about the impact of tabloidization on the audience. The tabloid newspaper may be a conduit for commercialized popular culture and taste but it constitutes a political minefield in that it represents distinctions in reader preference that align with questions of political responsibility and even social worth.

Discussions of tabloidization were often conducted in the news media as meta-commentary, sometimes generating realistic and even positive assessments from elite newspaper editors. The notion that younger readers, even in the upmarket quality press, were increasingly tuned in to popular culture and sceptical, even mocking views of the political world redolent of the tabloid tradition, led successful editors such as Peter Preston of the *Guardian* to invest in creating a highbrow variant for such readers (Greenslade, 2003, 428). This trend was continued by his successor Alan Rusbridger who was convinced that future success for the paper depended on maintaining this association with more generalized mass popular cultural trends, with layout to match (Rusbridger, 2005). With academic discussion increasingly sceptical of certain of journalism's core claims to distinctiveness and contribution to the public good, tabloidization had become by the beginning of the twenty-first century a key professional and critical term. At the same time, and in all probability as a consequence of this cultural shift, the tabloid format was emerging as the default size for the newspaper. For some editors of the elite press, 'compact' became the evolutionary euphemism to avoid referring to the tabloid, and implicitly rejecting any suggestion that a shift in format necessarily meant a decline in quality, despite the fact that these downsized broadsheets needed more aggressive visual and rhetorical strategies to survive (Brin and Drolet, 2008: 390–391). Yet these changes in newspaper form and style may be regarded as accommodations of wider sociocultural change, rather than as "futile strategies of a moribund medium" (Rowe, 2009: 121). To emphasize this interpretation, drawing on Charron and Bonville (1996), Brin and Drolet claim more broadly that the changing nature of journalism reflects and follows changes in social structure, but also contributes to larger social change by its function of public discourse (Brin and Drolet, 2008: 387). This is of particular relevance as an observation when considering the shifts within the tabloid genre and their social implications.

From the beginning of the second decade of the twenty-first century, however, the debate, instead of intensifying, rather faded from prominence. Discussions now began to centre on the extent to which social media were threatening the ability of journalism to provide its traditional services to the public, albeit from an often highly idealized perspective on journalism's contemporary standing and recent performance. Nevertheless, enmeshed in these discussions of social media are what we might call traditional tabloid characteristics and functions that are at the centre of debate about changes in journalism itself via a use of click-bait headlines, a consistent focus on celebrity, and addressing directly the desires of the audience rather than what journalists and editors consider best for the audience. To reiterate a central theme within this volume, when we look at the tabloid, are we exploring the tabloid newspaper, trends of tabloidization within news media more generally, or a broader tabloid culture that has permeated society across the board? In this case, rather than considering the tabloid as merely a format, it may be a set of characteristics that engage with news media in different ways over time: the tabloid may be a format that is not a format.

In an Australian context that has a clearly broader application, Harrington calls for a reassessment of a broader set of concerns articulated around popular journalism in general rather than chronicling its decline. In keeping with these changing parameters, he stresses that although the tabloid has included a significant visual element, it cannot be reduced to the visual, as we need to include radio talk-show hosts and callers within our understanding of the tabloid. This is a further expression of the flow of the tabloid across genres. While acknowledging that the tabloid is a manifestation of "journalism's 'darker' side", he charts how it has moved from newspaper to broadcasting and from sideshow to the mainstream (Harrington, 2008: 269–270) meaning that it cannot be easily dismissed, and that to dismiss it would be a regrettable rejection of the appetites and interests of the majority of consumers of popular journalism and popular culture in general. He agrees with Lumby that such a tabloid turn can be interpreted as enabling "a new more open and egalitarian public sphere" (Lumby, 1999: p. 38). Changing consumption patterns privilege the desires and tastes of the public over the claims of what journalism adheres to as a set of practices on behalf of the public. This necessitates an increasingly interactive, even subservient, role for journalism within the broad mediasphere. Newspaper layout and online permutations of news are becoming ever more adapted to the browsing reader within a hypercompetitive environment. This has led to a more open-ended relationship between purveyors of information and their audiences: "Progressively, the weight of norms defining journalism as a distinct form of public discourse diminishes in favour of norms and dispositions focusing on the relationship between a medium and its public" (Charron and Bonville, 2004: 315).

Global de-differentiation: local differentiation

Globally, the trend towards tabloid journalism has displayed generic diversity across regional contexts, as demonstrated by Sparks and Tulloch (2000), with different socio-political regimes accommodating the phenomenon within a range of dynamics. Articulated across these trends there is evidence of relatively large differences in the approach and even political implications of the tabloid. Cultural differentiation means that the Netherlands has no genuine tabloid newspaper tradition, Japan has something quite different from Western norms, Mexico has produced a political manifestation within the genre, and American supermarket tabloids have been interpreted as enabling to alternative readerships.

The *Bildification* (the tendency to reduce the news media to the most obvious tabloid formats along the lines of the market-leading Western tabloid newspaper *Bild*) of eastern Germany after the fall of the Berlin Wall demonstrated the onward march of the tabloid and was extended as a commercial/cultural dynamic throughout the former communist states. This progress was remarkable, since the tabloid newspaper itself and the American supermarket variant had been in relative decline since the 1960s and 1970s, when circulation had peaked. For new owners, the tabloid seemed to offer a way of belatedly entering the market economics of Western rivals, while for readers the sensationalist, libertine, scandal-led agenda seemed to encapsulate a 'freedom' and a license that contrasted with the overall oppression of authoritarian regimes. Put simply, the tabloid newspaper in the early 1990s seemed to offer a more modern vision of what a popular press should look like.

Wasserman (2010) demonstrates that the tabloid influence not only moves to new geopolitical markets, but that its impact can show both a global export and a local incorporation into the social and political norms of new consumer societies: 'glocalization.' It is easy to underestimate the differences between the meanings of tabloid consumption in post-apartheid South Africa compared to the debates around similar products in Western societies. Wasserman, however, highlights the ways that a press so often derided in Western contexts, and often ignored as an agent within the recent evolution of democracy in South Africa, has drawn black, working-class readers to its approach at a time when newspaper readership in many other parts of the world is in decline. He concentrates on the most successful of these papers, the *Daily Sun*, and considers within a not-always-positive assessment that it is problematically "at least temporarily linked to the country's democratization process" (Wasserman, 2010: 80).

Within the US context, subtleties have been sketched that indicate the supermarket tradition is very different from the daily tabloid practices of Western Europe. From the perspective of their female readers, Britt has argued that they contain alternative narratives on celebrity, ideals, and ambitions of beauty, and a reassessment of the condition of older women:

> at the boundary between entertainment and news, unashamedly claiming to be both and pushing the boundaries of mainstream social reality in the process … the tabloids illuminate the pretensions of the mainstream press and challenge the upscale world of mainstream 'common sense', and in this way offer a small moment of resistance to the dominant consensus view of reality.
>
> (Britt, 1996: 438)

Tabloid culture

To return for a moment to our opening comments, we may consider the tabloid as less a particular product or format and more a flow between generic practices. This is born out if we think, for example, of the ways in which print tabloid features have migrated to broadcast media; how the success of television genres such as the soap opera have become staples of tabloid newspaper coverage. Just as tabloid culture enters and flourishes within the format of the televisual, so the tabloid newspaper and its online successors are linked with the tropes of televisual culture, increasingly crossing over between celebrity shows and the plotlines of TV shows. The public obsession with celebrity initially championed by the tabloid newspaper has subsequently moved across to other media formats. In this latter example, celebrity is a legitimate prism in identifying news value within particular news organisations. This incorporation of tabloid features into other media forms has been neatly characterized by Bastos as a form of "metonymic transfer" (Bastos, 2017: 217) and indicates the characteristic of flow between genres and the lack of fixity within one genre when it comes to popular appeal. The political economy of media formats also facilitates this sort of accommodation with popular genres as global trends drive towards softer and cheaper forms of news within more generic formats predicated on best value and most efficient exploitation of human and informational resources in a 24/7 mode (Clausen, 2003; Thussu, 2007a). The tabloid trend, therefore, is a form of de-differentiation that incorporates prevailing patterns and rules that dominate the field (Benson, 1999; Bourdieu, 2005).

Tabloid culture and its easy overlap with social media

Tabloid debates, because they deal at base with questions of how we evaluate the status of the highly emotive and even political areas of taste and knowledge, broaden out from media-specific to the social. Fiske's view of traditional popular culture, as produced and consumed within media formats, is that the news values of the elite press reinforce the status of the elites that consume and are informed by that news. This reinforces what Sparks later observed as the "perceived existential utility" (Sparks, 2000: 27) of elite information to elite classes, since it assists in articulating the discourses of dominance that subjugate subaltern classes. As popular media forms integrate ever more intensively with social practices, social media potentially promise a circumnavigation of such editor-driven agendas and the editorialized exclusion that they engender.

Following Langer's taxonomy of 'other news' that he uses to broaden out the definition of tabloid journalism to its characteristics rather than specific format or content, social media platforms disseminate content that is definitely 'other news', much of which can easily be encompassed within a broadening definition of tabloid culture. Mimicking the language of the everyday, as the popular press had done so successfully in the past (Conboy, 2002), becomes the actual language of the everyday with the ventriloquizing filter of formal tabloid editorial practice removed. Social media amplify enormously the existing level of verisimilitude within tabloid journalism, whatever its platform, in engaging audiences in comparable ways to the audiences of the tabloids "as much with their hearts and guts as with their brains" (Zelizer, 2010: 326).

In relation to the typical digital native news organization, Lewis concludes that it: "embraces fresh values … more compatible with the logic of digital media and culture" (Lewis, 2012: 852); yet we should acknowledge that such dynamics are not new and always tend to correspond to emerging/existing audiences' tastes in media productions, "best able to produce the needs corresponding to the new dispositions [of the audience]" (Bourdieu, 1984: 231). Such accelerating accommodation between popular and tabloid culture always represents a negotiation between "market transaction or participation" (Conboy, 2007: 8).

Wadbring and Ödmark (2016) provide a useful set of observations on the characteristics of social media as interactions with conventional news values that may well add to our appreciation of how they match many of the pre-existing tendencies within tabloid journalism and thus propel the tabloid further into broader everyday culture. Social media news values, for instance, privilege content that amplifies shared experience; the explosion of human interest; a privileging of empathy versus abstraction; humorous or even parodic elements; rumour, controversy, and, perhaps most interestingly, content that is incomplete in one way or another, all of which can involve users in a dynamic way (Wadbring and Ödmark, 2016: 136). Many of these characteristics are at their core tabloid formulae such as gossip and rumour, adapted to more open-ended technological platforms with added amplification from users within their communicative patterns. The consolidation of the tabloid in a world that appears inaccessible to political intervention from outside power/commercial elites enhances the popular appeal of both content and communication platform leading to "a golden age of tabloid culture" (Debrix, 2007: 38). These processes provide multiplying interchanges with viral sites which have in turn influenced traditional media companies so as to generate impact across broader social media. However, any definitive conclusion on the longer-term impact of such innovation and exchange remains on hold: "Will the content be important in social terms or merely amusing?… Only the future can tell." (Wadbring and Ödmark, 2016: 145)

Yet all is not a duplication or amplification of tabloid tendencies. There are discontinuities in the ways in which social media are developing from the previously successful templates of tabloid culture. Törnberg, for example, considers how social media facilitate, through disintermediation, and change the formation of public narratives in the spread of misinformation as mass circulation moves to viral communication. While still consumer-led, viral communication is far less institutional and more volatile in its associative potential. In what we might call the viral paradox:

> Technology that was purported to help weave tighter the bonds between humans instead seem to have led to a fraying of our social fabric, as we are

> torn into social groups with separate world-views … biased narratives, conspiracy theories, mistrust and paranoia.
>
> (Törnberg, 2018: 1–2)

BuzzFeed aggregates funny viral videos from elsewhere on the Web and generates listicles, yet these remain firmly within the tabloid tradition where humour, material borrowed and repurposed, and lists have provided tabloid newspapers with material for generations. More important than originality is the question for new entrants, such as Buzzfeed, posed by Tandoc: "How does BuzzFeed, as a new entrant to the journalistic field, participate in the field's transformation or preservation?" (Tandoc, 2018: 201). In a counter-move that once again indicates the centrality of flow to the tabloid tradition, the websites of traditional media outlets have refined for their own formats and platforms the listicles and memes that interloper news media (Eldridge, 2018) such as BuzzFeed have pioneered. The tabloid press had typically offered "the noisiest emotional register" (Richards, in Allan, 2010: 305) and this register – sensationalist, partisan, virally-success orientated – honed still further, to maximize appeal on social media beyond the news sites that generates it becomes the "money-driven, low-quality, highly shareable kind of content that is typically distributed on social media as clickbait" (Burger et al., 2019: 1–2).

The extension of tabloid tendencies in a digital world requires us to reengage with questions about tabloidization and decline (Rowe, 2010: 350), and consider whether the extension represents a populist and/or a technological extension in a world where journalism is one media genre amongst a proliferation of entertainment-based media alternatives, or an erosion of the linkage between information and democratic processes (McChesney, 2007).

Baym has interpreted these changes as "discursive integration" (Baym, 2005), later writing:

> In the face of rapidly changing technological, economic, and cultural contexts, we are seeing a marked proliferation in journalistic forms – professional, public, citizen, tabloid, alternative, and convergent, to name but a few – overlapping and interwoven approaches that complement, contradict, and always complicate one another.
>
> (Baym, 2010: 375)

The explanation that the tabloid has evolved culturally to incorporate itself and its features within the expectations of the new audiences of digital media would certainly match this view. Hartley (1999) had cautioned against a blanket dismissal of 'tabloidization' as a residual elitist exercise in defending traditional views of journalism and a journalism with a capital J'. Journalism has changed and will continue to change over time. Its most essential feature is its relationship with audience, not in its fixity as a product or service. Tabloid journalism and its evolution into a wider culture can be seen as indicative of that.

The tabloid has been wonderfully characterized by Serazio as the "shapeshifter bugaboo" and contrasted unhelpfully with "journalism with a capital J – gilded by collective memory" (Serazio, 2009:13). In assessing how the tabloid has expanded its populist tendencies in appealing to the cultural preferences and tastes of the present day we can ask whether this has been a tactical alignment or more an adjustment to the over-determined flow of cultural influences. Either way, if one of journalism's 'gilded' functions has been, over time, to create links between certain forms of privileged information, for example, the proceedings of parliament with the quotidian generalities of the public's knowledge and experience, it has been increasingly dominated by other mediated forms of information and social interaction. The process accelerates as technological permeation increases. Serious politics, in its turn, is becoming more populist and impacted upon by other mediatized trends such as personality, celebrity politicians, and branding. From a slightly different perspective we may ask whether the tabloid is a critique in itself of journalism's failure to maintain its appeal to audiences who are no longer attracted by mainstream media. Is the failing in the mainstream news media's inability or even disinterest in shifting from an outmoded mode of styling or delivery merely a consequence of a complacency that what had worked for hundreds of years should still work today?

Conclusion

News, by definition, cannot be boring. It must attract the attention of an otherwise occupied or distracted audience. From its social beginnings, it has been shaped by tidings from travellers, gossip about neighbours, scandal exposing the hypocrisies of social superiors, as well as by more respectable curiosity about political decision making. Sometimes these two tendencies, the sacred and the profane polarities of news, we might call them, converge. At their best, tabloid newspapers have allowed coverage of material that broaches both poles simultaneously. In addition, they do this in a language that appeals to the broadest and most democratic constituencies. Popular print and its commercial zenith, the tabloid newspaper, have perfected the appeal of this style of reporting; and so successful has this style become that it has broadened out to infiltrate large sections of related entertainment media as a part of a generalized tabloid culture. This success has thus been both commercial and cultural. The process of tabloidization has moved far from its original template in the press. Tabloidization is a complex conceptual process in that it encompasses a range of technical, economic, social, cultural, political, ideological, and ethical concerns (Rowe, 2011: 463). We assert that there has been a movement towards popular and then tabloid journalism, and beyond this to a more generalized tabloid culture; and that this is now the mainstream, not a marginal, constituency. The tabloid is a multifaceted phenomenon but one which has been eagerly incorporated within the most successful digital news media and social media developments of the contemporary world across the globe. If we still maintain with Dahlgren (2009: 147) that journalism aims to act as an integrative force and as a common forum for debate for a heterogenous citizenry that basically shares the same public culture, and within which citizens use journalism as a resource for participation in the politics and culture of society, then we need to engage more consistently with the ever-relevant contribution that the tabloid makes to that debate. The following chapters attempt to address pressing questions about the political impact of the tabloid, reassess received views on the value of tabloid journalism, and explore the cultural challenges of a world gone tabloid; beyond the technological buzz around digital media, exploring the cultural challenges of the breakdown of hierarchies of taste and control, and the loosing of popular taste. We are doing so not to provide answers or new normative statements about the forms and functions of journalism but in a spirit of open-minded enquiry about one of the most dynamic relationships in our media environment: the global interplay between the tabloid and digital cultural forms.

Bibliography

Allan, Stuart *(ed.)* (2010) *The Routledge Companion to News and Journalism*. Abingdon, Oxon: Routledge.

Bastos, Marco (2017) 'Digital Journalism and Tabloid Journalism'. Bob Franklin *and* Scott Eldridge II *(eds.) The Routledge Companion to Digital Journalism Studies*. Abingdon, Oxon: Routledge. pp. 216–225.

Baym, Geoffrey (2005) 'The Daily Show: Discursive Integration and the Reinvention of Political Journalism'. *Political Communication*. 22. pp. 259–276.

Baym, Geoffrey (2010) 'Real News/Fake News: Beyond the News/Entertainment Divide'. Stuart Allan (ed.) *The Routledge Companion to News and Journalism*. Abingdon, Oxon: Routledge. pp. 376–383.

Benson, Rodney (1999) 'Field theory in comparative context: A new paradigm for media studies'. *Theory and Society*. 28 (3). pp. 463–498.

Bingham, Adrian and Martin Conboy (2015) *Tabloid Century: The Popular Press in Britain, 1896 to the Present Day*. Oxford: Peter Lang.

Bourdieu, Pierre (1984) *Distinction: A Social Critique of the Judgement of Taste*. Cambridge: Harvard University Press.

Bourdieu, Pierre (2005) 'The political field, the social science field and the journalistic field'. Rodney Benson and Eric Neveu (eds.) *Bourdieu and the Journalistic Field*. Malden, MA: Polity Press. pp. 29–47.

Brin, Colette and Geneviève Drolet (2008) 'Tabloid nouveau genre'. *Journalism Practice*. 2 (3). pp. 386–401.

Britt, Theron (1996) 'Reversing the romance: Class and gender in the supermarket tabloid'. *Prospects: An Annual Journal of American Cultural Studies*. 21. pp. 435–451.

Bromley, Michael (1998) 'The "tabloiding of Britain": "Quality" Newspapers in the 1990s'. Hugh Stephenson and Michael Bromley (eds.) *Sex, Lies and Democracy*. Harlow: Longman. pp. 24–38.

Burger, Peter, Soeradi Kanhai, Alexander Pieijter, and Suzan Verberne (2019) 'The reach of commercially motivated junk news on Facebook'. *PLoSONE*. 14 (8). pp. 1–15.

Canter, Lily (2018) 'It's Not All Cat Videos: Moving beyond legacy media and tackling the challenges of mapping news values on digital native websites'. *Digital Journalism*. 6 (8). pp. 1101–1112.

Champagne, Patrick (2005) '"The double-dependency": The journalistic field between politics and markets'. Rodney Benson and Eric Neveu (eds.) *Bourdieu and the Journalistic Field*. Malden, MA: Polity Press. pp. 48–64.

Charron, Jean and Jean de Bonville (1996) "Le paradigme du journalisme de communication: essai de définition", *Communication*. 17 (2). pp. 51–97.

Charron Jean and Jean de Bonville (2004) 'Le journalisme et le marché: de la concurrence à la hyperconcurrence'. Colette Brin, Jean Charron, and Jean de Bonville (eds.) *Nature et Transformation du Journalisme. Théorie et Recherches Empiriques*. Québec: Les Presses de L'Université Laval. pp. 87–120.

Clausen, Lisbeth (2003) *Global News Production*. Copenhagen: CBS Press.

Conboy, Martin (2002) *The Press and Popular Culture*. London: Sage.

Conboy, Martin (2006) *Tabloid Britain: Constructing a Community Through Language*. Abingdon, Oxon: Routledge.

Conboy, Martin. (2007) 'Permeation and Profusion: Popular Journalism in the New Millennium'. *Journalism Studies*. 8 (1). pp. 1–12.

Conboy, Martin and John Steel (2010) 'From "We" to "Me": The Changing Construction of Popular Tabloid Journalism'. *Journalism Studies*. 11 (4). pp. 500–511.

Crouthamel, James L. (1989) *Bennett's New York Herald and the Rise of the Popular Press*. Syracuse: Syracuse University Press.

Curran, James and Jean Seaton (2003) *Power Without Responsibility: Press, Broadcasting and the Internet in Britain*. 6th Edition. Abingdon, Oxon: Routledge.

Dahlgren, Peter (2009) 'The troubling evolution of journalism'. Barbie Zelizer (ed.) *The Changing Faces of Journalism: Tabloidization, Technology and Truthiness*. Abingdon, Oxon: Routledge. pp. 146–161.

Debrix, François (2007) *Tabloid Terror: War, Culture and Geopolitics*. Abingdon, Oxon: Routledge.

Ehrlich, Matthew C. (2016) 'Taking animal news seriously: Cat tales in the New York Times'. *Journalism: Theory, Practice, and Criticism*. 17 (3). pp. 366–381.

Eldridge II, Scott (2018) *Online Journalism from the Periphery: Interloper Media and the Journalistic Field*. Abingdon, Oxon: Routledge.

Esser, Frank (1999) '"Tabloidization" of news: A comparative analysis of Anglo-American and German press journalism'. *European Journal of Communication*. 14 (3). pp. 291–324.

Glynn, Kevin (2000) *Tabloid Culture*. Durham, NC: Duke University Press.

Greenslade, Roy (2003) *Press Gang: How Newspapers Make Profits from Propaganda*. Basingstoke: Macmillan.

Harrington, Stephen (2008) 'Popular news in the 21st century: Time for a new critical approach?' *Journalism: Theory, Practice, and Criticism*. 9 (3). pp. 266–284.

Hartley, John (1999) *Uses of Television*. London: Routledge.

Hartley, John (2010) 'Journalism, History and the Politics of Popular Culture'. Stuart Allan (ed.) *The Routledge Companion to News and Journalism*. Abingdon, Oxon: Routledge. pp. 13–24.

Küng, Lucy (2015) *Innovators in Digital News*. New York: I.B. Taurus and Co. Ltd.

Langer, John (1998) *Tabloid Television: Popular Journalism and 'the Other News'*. London: Routledge.

Lefkowitz, Julia (2018) '"Tabloidization" or dual-convergence'. *Journalism Studies*. 19 (3). pp. 353–375.

Lewis, Seth, C. (2012) 'The tension between professional control and open participation'. *Information, Communication and Society*. 15 (6). pp. 836–866.

Lichterman, Joseph (2014) 'In Sweden, Traditional Tabloid Rivals Are Taking Their Battle to Viral Sites'. NiemanLab.org, December 1.

Lumby, Catharine (1999) *Gotcha: Life in a Tabloid World*. Sydney: Allen and Unwin.

McChesney, Robert (2007) *Communication Revolution: Critical Junctures and the Future of Media*. New York: The New Press.

McLachlan, Shelley and Peter Golding (2000) 'Tabloidization in the British Press: A Quantitative Investigation into Changes in British Newspapers, 1952–1997'. Colin Sparks and John Tulloch (eds.) *Tabloid Tales: Global Debates on Media Standards*. Oxford: Rowman and Littlefield. pp. 75–90.

Nicholson, Bob (2016) 'Transatlantic Connections'. Andrew King, Alexis Easley, and John Morton (eds.) *The Routledge Handbook to Nineteenth-Century British Periodicals and Newspapers*. Abingdon, Oxon: Routledge. pp. 175–184.

Nunn, Heather and Anita Biressi, eds. (2008) *The Tabloid Culture Reader*. Maidenhead: Open University Press.

Reeve, Eileen (2014) *Evening News: Optics, Astronomy and Journalism in Early Modern Europe*. Philadelphia, PA: University of Pennsylvania Press.

Richards, Barry (2010) 'News and the Emotional Public Sphere'. Stuart Allan (ed.) *The Routledge Companion to News and Journalism*. Abingdon, Oxon: Routledge. pp. 301–311.

Rowe, David (2010) 'Tabloidization: Form, Style and Sociocultural Change'. Verica Rupar (ed.) *Journalism and Meaning-Making: Reading the Newspaper*. Cresskill, NJ: Hampton Press. pp. 146–169.

Rowe, David (2010) 'Tabloidization of News'. Stuart Allan (ed.) *The Routledge Companion to News and Journalism*. Abingdon, Oxon: Routledge. pp. 350–361.

Rowe, David (2011) 'Obituary for the Newspaper: Tracking the Tabloid'. *Journalism: Theory, Practice, and Criticism*. 12 (4). pp. 449–466.

Rusbridger, Alan (2005) 'The Hugo Young Memorial Lecture', at the University of Sheffield. March 9.

Seaton, Jean. (2017) 'Review of Tabloid Century' *Twentieth Century British History*. 28 (3). pp. 477–479.

Serazio, Michael (2009) 'Rethinking a villain, redeeming a format: The crisis and cure in tabloidization'. Barbie Zelizer (ed.) *The Changing Faces of Journalism: Tabloidization, Technology and Truthiness*. Abingdon, Oxon: Routledge. pp. 13–16.

Sloan, Bill (2001) *I Watched a Wild Hog Eat My Baby: A Colourful History of the Tabloids and Their Cultural Impact*. New York: Prometheus Books.

Sparks, Colin (2000) 'Introduction: The Panic over Tabloid News'. Colin Sparks and John Tulloch (eds.) *Tabloid Tales: Global Debates on Media Standards*. Oxford: Rowman and Littlefield. pp. 1–40.

Sparks, Colin and John Tulloch (eds.) (2000) *Tabloid Tales: Global Debates on Media Standards*. Oxford: Rowman and Littlefield.

Steensen, Steen (2016) 'The intimization of journalism'. Tamara Witschge, Chris W. Anderson, David Domingo, and Alfred Hermida (eds.) *The SAGE Handbook of Digital Journalism*. London: Sage. pp. 113–128.

Stringer, Paul (2018) 'Finding a place in the journalistic field'. *Journalism Studies*. 19 (13). pp. 1991–2000.

Tandoc, Edson C.Jr. (2018) 'Five ways BuzzFeed is preserving (or transforming) the journalistic field'. *Journalism: Theory, Practice, and Criticism*. 19 (2). pp. 200–216.

Taylor, Sally J. (1992) *Shock! Horror!: The Tabloids in Action*. London: Black Swan.

Thussu, Daya Kishan (2007a) *News as Entertainment: The Rise of Global Infotainment*. London: Sage.

Thussu, Daya Kishan (2007b) 'Mapping Global Media Flow and Contra-Flow'. Daya Kishan Thussu (ed.) *Global Flow and Contra-Flow*. Abingdon, Oxon: Routledge.

Thussu, Daya Kishan on 'soft' news within television and ideological incorporation of neo-liberal values (in Allan p. 371); cf. Jacques Ellul (1965) *Propaganda: The Formation of Men's Attitudes*. New York: Knopf.

Törnberg, Petter (2018) 'Echo chambers and viral information: Modelling fake news as complex contagion'. *PLoSONE*. 13 (9). pp. 1–21.

Uribe, Rodrigo and Barrie Gunter (2004) 'Research Note: The tabloidization of the British tabloids'. *European Journal of Communication*. 19 (3). pp. 387–402.

Wadbring, Ingela and Sara Ödmark (2016) 'Going viral: News sharing and shared news in social media'. *Observario Journal*. 10 (4). pp. 132–149.

Wang, Hung-Chun (2009) 'Language and ideology: gender stereotypes of female and male artists in Taiwanese tabloids'. *Discourse and Society*. 20 (6). pp. 747–774.

Wasserman, Herman (2010) *Tabloid Journalism in South Africa: True Story!*Bloomington and Indianapolis: Indiana University Press.

Wiener, Joel H. (2011) *The Americanization of the British Press, 1830s-1914: Speed in the Age of Transatlantic Journalism*. Basingstoke: Palgrave Macmillan.

Zelizer, Barbie (ed.) (2009) *The Changing Faces of Journalism: Tabloidization, Technology and Truthiness*. Abingdon, Oxon: Routledge.

Zelizer, Barbie (2010) *About to Die: How News Images Move the Public*. Oxford: Oxford University Press.

2 Digital impacts on the tabloid sphere

Blurring and diffusion of a popular form and its power

Scott A. Eldridge II

Introduction

"How Things Work". This was the headline of the final post on *Gawker.com*, a farewell to *Gawker*'s 14-year run as an outlet which "followed the century-old tabloid cynicism about human nature, reinforced by instant data about what people actually wanted to read" (Denton, 2016). Its end, more or less, was brought about by a very 'tabloid' story of sex and scandal, made all the more sensational by the celebrity status of those involved. In this case, it involved a clip of a sex tape featuring professional wrestler Hulk Hogan and the wife of radio personality Bubba the Love Sponge. The clip was published, Hogan sued unrelentingly for invasion of privacy, and the jury agreed. *Gawker* was shuttered, and founder Nick Denton filed for bankruptcy, unable to pay the $140 million awarded.

At first glance, this could be written up as another tabloid story of scandals and repercussions. After all, similar intrusions brought down the *News of the World* in 2011 after it crept too closely and too creepily into the private lives of public figures. From that perspective, the story of *Gawker* and its downfall is simply a tabloid tale retold for the digital age. However, this chapter will argue that it is more than that, and that there is something about the digital age that has complicated our discussions of tabloids as a specific genre. It shows the characteristics which had set tabloids apart in an analogue era have now become so widespread they have diffused the very distinction that made the tabloid a once-formidable genre of popular media. "How Things Work" was itself a reflection on both *Gawker*'s ambition to uncover the real story of how society works, in all its messiness, and how *Gawker* went out on a limb to publish scandalous stories of people and power. In doing so, it shows how digital tabloids could give their publics a picture of how things really are that is unvarnished and honest, and with sensation well to the fore.

This chapter explores the evolution of the tabloid in a digital age, in order to conceptualize tabloidization through cases of digital media that mix the print tabloid legacy with new digital opportunities and a liberated web culture. It shows how digital media have worked the distinction which once separated popular tabloids from the elite press into a new genre that blurs these previous boundaries. It draws from analysis of sites which mixed the serious and the salacious in their offerings, alongside insights from interviews with journalists working on these sites.[1] On the surface, these media reflect the familiar mix of 'soft' news and prurient content which tabloids made familiar. But scratch a layer deeper and extend this discussion over time, and this chapter will show the tabloidization of the digital sphere has meant not simply the borrowing of subject matter, but a more complex diffusion of the cultural form of tabloids.

Situating the digital turn in tabloid scholarship

It is important to position this discussion in the wider body of scholarship on tabloids. This largely breaks into two camps. One has taken a normative, critical, view of the popular press, seeing tabloids as in conflict with the public service ethos of the 'Fourth Estate', and the trends of tabloidization as a development further along that path (see discussions in: Donsbach, 2010: 43; Hampton, 2010). This concern is not entirely misplaced. Practices ranging from the 'hacking' of private voicemails by British tabloid reporters (Keeble and Mair, 2012) to the 'catch and kill' practices of US tabloids buying up stories to either help or blackmail their powerful allies (Farrow, 2019) show there remain cases of tabloids breaking both journalistic ethical and wider societal norms (Chadwick, Vaccari, and O'Loughlin, 2018).

Yet placing particular emphasis on tabloids as something unserious or even detrimental to society risks treating problematic cases of tabloid missteps as emblematic of tabloids as a whole, dismissing the genre for provoking "moral panics" (see McRobbie and Thornton, 1995) or as a journalistic bogeyman responsible for all that ails journalism (Bishop, 1999). This hyper-attention to tabloid misdeeds misses a larger narrative of what the tabloids as a genre have offered both then and now, having carried over into digital space (c.f. Bastos, 2017; Tandoc and Jenkins, 2018). First, such arguments tend to ignore broader contributions to public discourse which tabloids have made, including historically making private domestic concerns acceptable for public discussion (Bingham, 2007), and more recently recognizing a public demand for entertaining online content which both amuses and informs (Epstein, 2011: 86). Second, whether in the twentieth century or the twenty-first, a dismissive view of tabloids reinforces a paternalistic discourse found in 'broadsheet' journalism that contributed to the rise of tabloids as a popular cultural form in the first place (Conboy, 2006). This paternalism has not gone away in a digital age. Rather, it has sparked specific reactions by digital media actors who see such haughtiness as a reflection of mainstream media being entrenched in positions of power, pushing against this perceived arrogance through antagonistic, sometimes sensational, news content (Eldridge, 2018: 32).

Drawing further on this line of argument, this chapter adopts a view that tabloids and tabloidization reflect a cultural pushback against normative paternalism in both journalism and journalism scholarship that dictates how news and journalism *should* be. It extends a thread of research which focuses on tabloids as reaching audiences where they live, and speaking to them as they are. As Bingham and Conboy (2015: 20) have shown, the tabloid gained its foothold with a wide swathe of the public not by dumbing down *per se* but by developing a medium of "cultural and political significance" around a middle-market interest in news about public life beyond politics. Or, as Feeley (2012: 470) notes:

> Hand wringing and condemnation aside, the enduring success of the tabloid in its many forms as well as the transformative impact of the tabloid style – including gossip reporting – on journalistic practice writ large has begun to receive much-needed careful and close analysis.

While tabloids, in print, are often treated as an *en masse* genre, Sparks (2000) shows different types of newspapers embraced these characteristics differently. Charting these, we can see the tabloid as a differentiated global phenomenon, spread across diverse media systems – a typology we will return to later in this chapter (Figure 2.1). This shows that tabloids range in the ways they separate out the 'serious' from the 'popular' more or less, and how this differs in different cultural contexts.

To explore this, and to examine the degree to which digital media model what supermarket tabloids (Bird, 2000), newsstand tabloids (Sparks, 2000), and other popular newspapers (Conboy, 2006) presented in an analogue era, it is important to present a rough outline of the implications of tabloidization for digital media.

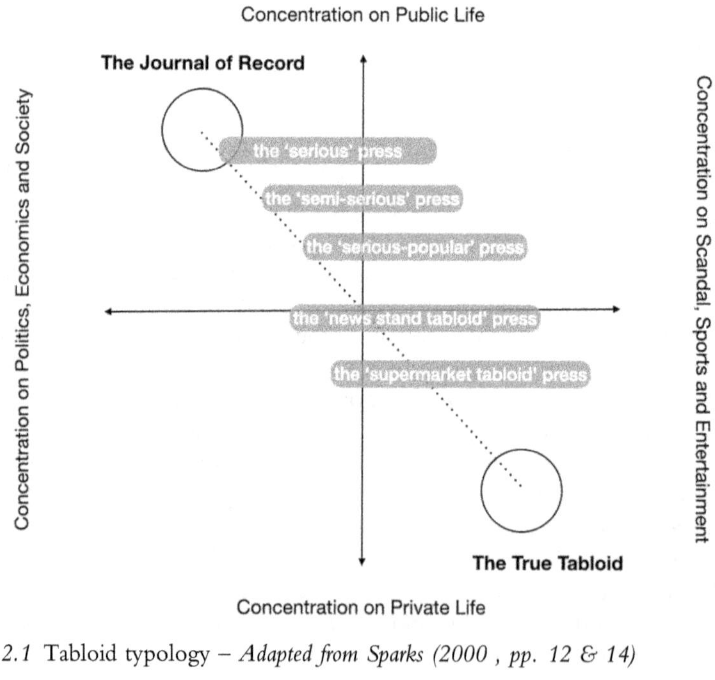

Figure 2.1 Tabloid typology – *Adapted from Sparks (2000 , pp. 12 & 14)*

Digital tabloidization and the early digital tabloid

Moving from tabloids as a specific print genre towards the cultural force of tabloidization, we can look at the degree to which the characteristics of the tabloid swing across media, particularly media eager to find profitable ways to present their content. For the argument here, tabloidization refers to a process wherein media incorporate content features borrowed from the tabloid as a popular newspaper, including sensational news, the private lives of public figures, and human-interest angles to public concerns. These characteristics helped tabloid newspapers in the twentieth century secure a mass audience (and therefore revenue), further defining the tabloid as a popular newspaper (Conboy, 2006: 11). The tabloidization of television offers a useful encapsulation of this dynamic. When TV news 'tabloidized', it did so by adopting the print-tabloid attention to images, graphics, bold type, and sensational content (Bird, 2000: 214). In doing so, it was also met with the same derision that tabloid newspapers routinely experienced, and was criticized as serving up 'low-brow', unserious content: a debate outlined in Brants (1998) and Glynn (2000). Online, digital tabloidization proceeded similarly, albeit with some diversions. Digital tabloidization in the first few years of the twenty-first century can be largely understood through two dynamics. The first is the digitization of the analogue tabloid; the second is the emergence of tabloidization in digital media. This chapter focuses primarily on the latter dynamic, but to establish for comparison a case of the former, we can look to the UK's *Daily Mail Online.*

In the early years of the digital age, the online tabloid was not terribly different than it was in an analogue era, and as such, early digital tabloidization reflected a transference of analogue approaches to sensational content that could "expose sexual misconduct and explore conservative and iconoclast topical interests, with strong commercial emphasis and populist vernacular" (Bastos 2017: 217) onto the web. The *Daily Mail Online* is consistently ranked the most-read English language news site globally, having drawn in readers in large part through its popular and sensational headlines, and its celebrity-laden "sidebar of shame" (Garde-Hansen and Gorton, 2013). This feature runs as a long sidebar down the right-hand side of the site, featuring a simple headline-plus-photo link to a story of celebrity excess or scandal. It is, for our purposes, a replication of what tabloids made popular, amplified and digitized in a way that triggers high rankings in search results using Search Engine Optimization (SEO), and luring in readers with catchy clickable headlines and photos (Dick, 2011: 464). The *Daily Mail* offers a clear case of a print newspaper adapting its content to a digital space. It also reflects the first, and sometimes last, framework for discussing digital tabloidization and, as with the broad brushes applied to print tabloids, offers a crude model by which all digital tabloids are defined. We can follow from Sparks (Figure 2.1) to position such sites as a version of what we already understood tabloids to be, in the middle of the axes (Figure 2.2).

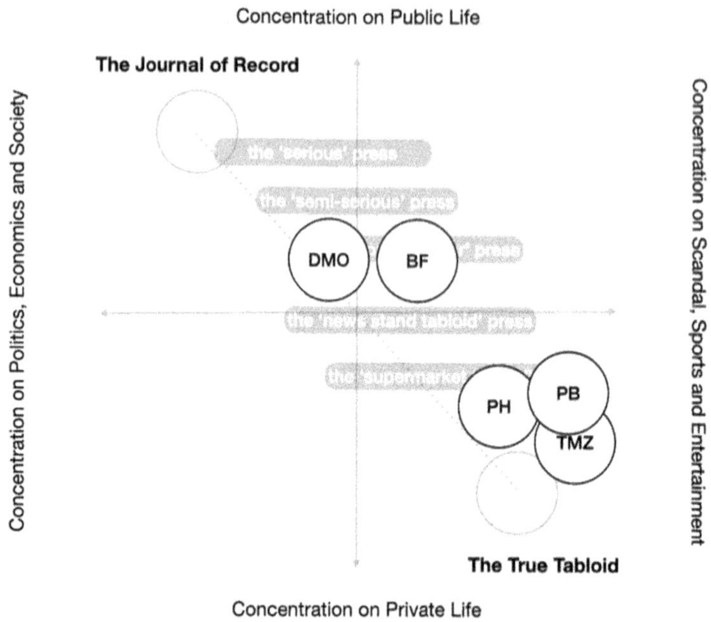

Figure 2.2 Early digital tabloids. Key: DMO, *Daily Mail Online*; BF, *BuzzFeed*; PH, *PerezHilton*; PB, *PopBitch*; TMZ, *TMZ*.

Crude as it is, this first picture of digital tabloidization offers a model for understanding other early 'digital tabloids'; and early scholarly discussions of a 'digital tabloid sphere' used such a framework to make sense of popular sites like *BuzzFeed* or *TMZ*, as they rather directly combined analogue traits of tabloids' sensational celebrity news with digital affordances (Bastos, 2017; Feeley, 2012). To these sites, we could add those digital-only media sites in the US and UK that exclusively focused on celebrity news. These include *PopBitch*, which describes itself as "the internet's longest-running, deepest-digging gossipmongers" (PopBitch, 2020), and the pseudo-eponymous site *Perez Hilton*, (quoting the *LA Times*' description of himself and his site), as a mixture of the supermarket tabloid magazines "*US Weekly*, the *Star*, the *Enquirer* and *Life & Style* all rolled into one sweet yet snarky, sagacious yet salacious gay man" (PerezHilton, 2020).

These sites were unique in being unaffiliated with analogue counterparts. But they are also similar, in a manner of speaking, to the supermarket variety of print tabloids, trading on celebrity content rather than anything public oriented or political. They saw tabloidization as a means to replicate the print tabloid model in an accelerated manner online, producing popular material more quickly than traditional newsroom routines could (Bastos, 2017: 219).

These sites enrich the mapping of tabloids as a genre in a digital arena, showing distinctions between two types of Early Digital Tabloid (EDT): 'digitized tabloids', e.g. *Daily Mail Online* (EDT, 1), which broadly replicated content approaches of print tabloids online; and digital natives like *PerezHilton*, focusing more narrowly on celebrity (EDT, 2) (Figure 2.3).

The digital tabloid: The further evolution of a (sub)popular form

Were we to leave the discussion here, we could conclude with a neat transference of the tabloid as a cultural form established in print onto a digital era, identifying where both newer and older media had picked up the mantle of tabloid journalism for their own ends. These parallels to an analogue era start to fall apart, however, when we consider that even the most celebrity-focused digital tabloid sites emerged alongside other developments of a nascent mediated web culture. In particular, they came at a time – the early 2000s – when both DIY news and gossip blogs, along with more sophisticated outlets, were eyeing the potential for a more participatory mode of publishing online (Stevenson, 2016). This was also a time when those who chose to start and sustain a digital media presence were fueled in part by interest, in part by commercial opportunity, and in large part by an ideological response to corporate, mainstream media that made a popular approach to digital news media an attractive option (Eldridge, 2018: 109). Digital news culture has been defined, to an extent, by an aversion to the objective "view from nowhere" (Rosen, 1997) of main-stream news, and the detached voice of formal news speak (Carlson, 2017: 59).

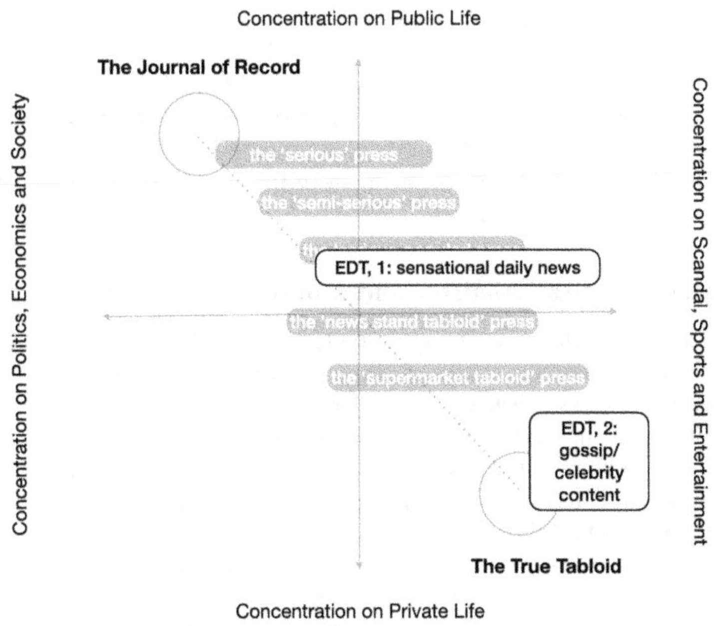

Figure 2.3 Early digital tabloid (EDT) types

What was once considered 'proper' journalistic writing was no longer sufficient, both for a public that had become cynical of such down-the-middle discourse and also for journalists tired of the established media environment.

Many digital news media launching at this time embraced a radical vision of what the web could be. As Denton, the founder of *Gawker*, described, the culture of the time shaped the ways these media imagined their place in the field: "As a group of journalists who had grown up on the web, [*Gawker*] also subscribed to the internet's most radical ideology, that information wants to be free, and that the truth shall set us free" (Denton, 2016). Or, at least, these journalists embedded this ideology in the ways in which they put themselves out there.

As we'll see below in the discussions of *Gawker, Guido Fawkes*, and *GeenStijl*, these media alongside others invite us to consider tabloidization in a specific, digital, cultural context that is radical in ideology, with content that is sensational in appeal. Linking tabloidization to this more freewheeling digital culture, we can look to the "heirs" to the tabloid legacy (Uberti, 2014), the so-called "rude press" (Pareene, 2019), for examples of this overlap. These sites have defined their contributions to public discourse around an unflinchingly antagonistic, honest, sensationalist, but unabashedly journalistic voice (Eldridge, 2019a).

In the following sections, I argue that sites that bridge a low-brow style with a hard news focus help us expand our understanding of digital tabloidization to include media that embrace the tabloid genre in form and style, while simultaneously departing from tabloids' main focus on prurient 'soft' news. In doing so, these media have blurred the soft news/hard news distinction which might have suited a previous era (Reinemann et al., 2012). Factor in a more nuanced (often data-driven) understanding of online audiences, and these sites also reflect the joining up of the appeal of a tabloid style with a better understanding of the news interests of these sites' specific publics (Conboy and Eldridge, 2018); and so we can see theirs is not a mass public but a (sub)public which is both well-known and catered to. As a critical reflection on the ways these dynamics have played out, these cases force us to ask whether, in these spaces, we can reimagine what a tabloid *could* be in a digital age.

Irreverence, sensationalism, and a public relationship

Translated as 'no style', *GeenStijl* was founded in 2003. Regularly ranking among top news sites in the Netherlands, it promises "tendentious, unfounded & needlessly offensive" news (GeenStijl, 2020a).[2] Navigating through the site, one finds a mix of independent news content written primarily by *GeenStijl*'s editors, commentary on news from other sites, and a mix of wider content ranging from recaps of television shows to celebrity gossip and more substantive political discussions. As a flavour of its approach, take March 13, 2020, when the site published both a critical discussion of Dutch Prime Minister Mark Rutte's latest policy to deal with the Coronavirus pandemic. This ran alongside a 'Coronapoll', where readers could vote for 'Which [Dutch] celebrity gets corona first?' (GeenStijl, 2020a). The following Monday, the lead story was: "'Waar is Willem?" ["Where's Willem?"], with a mock illustration from a *Where's Waldo?* book, altered to include a picture of the Dutch king, Willem-Alexander.

In a parallel to the case at the outset of this chapter, *GeenStijl* has had its own tabloidesque scandals, and like *Gawker* was found liable for disseminating explicit private content of a Dutch celebrity in 2018 (van Til, 2018). It has also been derided – in a manner akin to its tabloid peers – as "the apex of right-wing irony and nihilism in the Dutch public sphere" (Mepschen, 2016: 153). As for their ambitions to speak directly with their public, however, they attest to a knowing awareness of this match: "On *GeenStijl*, news facts, shameful revelations and journalistic research alternate with light-hearted subjects and pleasantly insane nonsense. The editors inform over 230,000 visitors every day about the other side of the news" (GeenStijl, 2020b). In the tradition of tabloids, they do so with a sensationalist's flair.

Stories on *GeenStijl* are presented within the context of an irreverent "social conversation" (Conboy, 2006: 10) with its specific public, one which they seek to order and maintain, according to their "House Rules" (GeenStijl, 2020c). These outline how *GeenStijl* embraces 'open discussion' within limits. Unwelcome commenters are categorized as: 'Kaalkoopjes' [baldheads] posting racist comments, 'Vervelios' who post enflaming comments, the 'Seksueel Gefrustreerden' [sexually frustrated] who harass women, and various other 'Dombo's [dumbos]' who post meaningless content. The comment space is actively policed for these intruders. This allows *GeenStijl* to establish a specific media/public relationship typical of digital entrants to the journalistic field, as they engage in "real and imaginary dialogue between each other" (Eldridge, 2018: 93).

While 'below the line' comment sections are often seen as something to be avoided for journalists and readers alike due to their caustic content (Frischlich, Boberg, and Quandt, 2019), on sites like *GeenStijl* these are important spaces for engagement with readers. To the extent that we can see comments as a manifestation of part of *GeenStijl's* public, they can be read as dialogues within the (sub)text of the original post. This conversation takes place within the familiar post-plus-comment format of websites, where the extension of the conversation between media and their publics into comment sections performs much of the socio-informative journalistic work of these outlets (see: Eldridge, 2018, pp. 93–95). This dialogue is apparent first in the topics and style of individual stories, and then in the community of commenters engaging with each post.

On *GeenStijl*, posts themselves are discursive and easily digestible. They mix sarcasm and wry commentary into their content, often with pictures or videos leading the post. The comments 'below the line' replicate this tone from the audience side, while extending the dialogue with everything from further links to further news to sarcastic analysis of the original post. In the article 'Waar is Willem?', the authors list options lettered 'A' to 'I'. In reply, commenters respond specifically using the letters, or their own improvised explanations for his absence from public view (e.g., "He'll be back in London again, the family's usual reaction when things get a little exciting here", a not-so-subtle reference to the Dutch monarchy escaping to the UK during World War II).

By mixing the familiar bits of gossip that have been constants in discussions of tabloids with further attention to current news agendas and a proactive engagement with their audience, *GeenStijl* embraces a style of writing that mixes a non-sober voice to recount the day's news with a brusque insensitivity towards hard news topics and an appeal towards its *own* public. It doesn't pretend to be for all; even as the most popular blog in the Netherlands, its audience of 230,000 is a relatively small audience compared to popular newspapers. While *GeenStijl* reflects the same successful appropriation of *some aspects* of a print tabloid style which brought tabloids mass appeal, bringing these aspects into a digital site, *GeenStijl* also departs from the dynamics of print popular newspapers through a seemingly conscious decision to prioritize news and public affairs discussion alongside its more salacious fare. It does so while delivering this content with a contrarian and deliberately antagonistic voice, and with a specific appeal to its own specific public.

A metajournalistic tabloid

Where *GeenStijl* replicates a tabloid approach by lampooning political figures and mixing a sharp commentary into news stories, *Gawker* offers an example of one of the most outspoken adherents to the potential of a digital tabloid as something which can be reimagined to report on hard-hitting news stories with metajournalistic commentary (Carlson, 2014). It also presents one of its more tragic tales. *Gawker* showed for more than a decade that there was an opportunity for publishing news that used sensationalist and human-interest frames to break hard news stories while pushing back against a mainstream complacency in journalism. As former *Gawker* editor Max Read said of *Gawker* founder Nick Denton, he was "a dark prophet who had appeared at the twilight of journalism to reveal a new path" (Read, 2016).

Gawker started in New York City as a blog reporting on gossip among media professionals that called the city home. It later realized media gossip was but one of many things audiences were clamouring for, and on *Gawker* and other Gawker Media sites they could find more 'honest' imaginations of what news could provide for the public. As with their tabloid forebears, they were not beyond reproach, with missteps (including with Hogan), such as not taking seriously enough the risks posed to their own journalists when embracing a cavalier attitude towards publishing certain information (see discussion in Eldridge, 2018: 87). To the detriment of the publication, their tabloid sensationalism sometimes overshadowed their more serious journalistic endeavours. Over its run, *Gawker* published many hard-hitting investigations, revealing the closeness between political journalists and the US government, the right-wing alignment of Fox News, and, years ahead of their peers, opened the doors to what would become a torrent of allegations of sexual assault against the comedian Bill Cosby (cf. Eldridge, 2018: 85–88).

Gawker offers an exemplar of a hybrid digital tabloid potential, presenting hard-news journalistic investigations on a site that also embraced sensationalism.

Gossip continued to feature in the site's content, as its traffic data showed this was something people still sought out (Denton, 2016). Yet with such a plethora of opportunities for gossip content across the web – e.g., *Daily Mail Online* and *Perez Hilton* – gossip for gossip's sake offered limited avenues for distinction in the digital environment. So *Gawker* styled itself as more than a "gossip rag" (Schofield, 2006) by focusing on: "Not just juicy, populist, tabloid stories – juicy, populist, tabloid stories with panache, and a point," according to Read (2016). "Gawker wasn't the first publication to treat gossip as an intellectual pursuit," Read added,

> [b]ut it was the first to do so in the format that now seems completely natural for it: an endlessly scrolling, eternally accessible record of prattle and wit and venom that felt less like a publication than like a place.

This allowed *Gawker* to be both swashbuckling and serious, joining up the pugnacious style of H.L. Mencken, the early-twentieth century US journalist known for his unabashed criticism, with an attention towards a watchdog role: "*Gawker* still thought of itself as a pirate ship, but a very big pirate ship, ballasted by semi-respectable journalism" (Read, 2016).[3] This was critical to its ambitions of holding power to account: "We believed that broader access to confidential information, to the real story, would constrain the powerful and liberate the oppressed" (Denton, 2016).

Timothy Burke, interviewed while at the *Gawker*-affiliated site *Deadspin,* said this helped their audience see *Gawker* content as trustworthy, particularly after it pulled itself back from self-induced scandals. Online, he said, "there is an opportunity for a sort of trust arbitrage in portraying yourself as being free and independent, regardless of whether you are or not" (personal communication, 2018). This was part of *Gawker*'s specific appeal, and Denton (2016) boasted how "*Gawker*'s web-literate journalists picked up more story ideas from anonymous email tips, obscure web forums or hacker data dumps than they did from interviews or parties. They scorned access."

Or, as Ashley Feinberg, formerly of Gawker Media, said, "I had it drilled into me that the more established outlets look down on you, the better it is." She went on to say:

> The manner in which I do my job is different than other journalists, but I think that the end result is the same … I mean if I had different aspirations, I would probably try to aim more towards mimicking whatever serious journalism is supposed to look like but, ugh, I am perfectly happy sort of right now.
>
> (Personal communication, 2018)

Among outsider sites positioning themselves as outlets to be trusted for their bluntness and their honesty, it was *Gawker*'s criticism of the failings of a wider journalistic field that became a key feature of their content. They called out journalists covering political conventions under headlines like: "Here's all the free shit journalists get at the DNC", in a style that allowed them to 'nudge' the political conversation, among journalists at least (Eldridge, 2018: 128). Enabled in part by separating itself from the familiar journalistic 'in-groups' and social circles co-occupied by political actors, the site evolved into one which embraced a metajournalistic commentary as a way to speak critically about how (primarily mainstream) journalism carried out its societal roles, embedding this critique within *Gawker*'s own media reporting. Burke said this allowed *Gawker* journalists to establish a rapport with their readers, "free as an independent media to do things outside of a manner in which traditional media has been operating for decades – or centuries – and that freedom is, in itself, a form of access" (personal communication, 2018).

Explosively political, no punches pulled

The same choices made by *Gawker* to mix a tabloid style and a sharp metacommentary on journalism writ large is imagined quite differently across the Atlantic in the UK at *Guido Fawkes*. For founder Paul Staines, the digital age brought with it an opportunity to cover policy-oriented political news in a tabloid style, and a chance to blend the speed and brevity of blogging as a way to "move the dial" (personal communication, 2018), with an open disregard for the traditional ways of doing journalism in the UK, much like its tabloid peers. Where *Gawker* and its journalists embraced their lack-of-access as access, those writing for *Guido Fawkes* specifically embrace their proximity to power as a way to unsettle the dominant media narrative by openly favouring certain political agendas, and by poking political elites towards *Guido*'s own priorities.

Founded in 2004 by Staines, 'Guido Fawkes' is both the name of the site and the catch-all *nom de guerre* first used by Staines and now by all the journalists writing on the website at Order-Order.com. At the time, "there was no real competition apart from the diary columns" in the UK for a site that blended attention to both gossip and hard political news. *Guido Fawkes* came before the political blogging scene in the UK really took off (in Staines' estimation it still has not caught up to what he started with the exception of the new left-wing site *theCanary.co*).

Guido Fawkes offers an example of a narrow reimagination of the tabloid through a specific lens. Its remit is almost exclusively politics, taking a decidedly conservative position on the debates of the day (e.g., pro-Brexit, anti-Labour). While political biases are nothing new for tabloids, particularly in the UK (Conboy, 2002: 142), *Guido*'s focus is more 'in the weeds' of Westminster debates, and the minutiae of policy disagreements. *Guido* is, at the same time, ardently tabloid: "I deliberately, consciously, set out in the beginning to do it in a tabloid accessible way. To cover somewhat high-brow subjects, somewhat complicated political subjects, in an accessible short form" (personal communication, 2018). We "do all the gossip and everything," Staines said. Coverage of policy appears alongside reports on British MP's hypocrisies and scandals; as one of many examples, *Guido* published a list kept by a Tory aide of those MPs considered 'sex pests' (Guido Fawkes, 2017).

Guido carved its niche by mixing close access to those in power – "spads", or special advisors, are well-established readers of the site, Staines said – with independence. By publishing online in short, sharp, posts, it could churn news out quickly. This has allowed Staines to be more brutally honest in what he was reporting, and to set news agendas by outpacing rival news media. Like Denton with *Gawker*, Staines regularly calls out both journalistic peers and political 'allies', as he's personally not looking for his next job: "I was never worried about fucking up someone and that I would not get a job because I did not want a job, and that is great freedom for me". In January 2020, *Guido* made waves by live-tweeting a government briefing to the Westminster Lobby, a semi-independent group of journalists reporting on UK politics. Live reporting was something that was officially banned by the Lobby, but as this is a group to which the *Fawkes* journalists did not belong, they argued they were not bound by its rules. Arguing the Westminster Lobby was a relic, Staines said it was acting as a "cartel", and that breaking from such a ban was "a better service for the readers at the end of the day" (Mayhew, 2020). The Lobby protested, and then relented, permitting live-reporting thereafter.

Its independence has also been reflected in its unrelenting attacks on both liberals and conservatives, including the former UK prime minister:

> What we are prepared to do is we are prepared to kick over the bucket. And Downing Street will ring us up screaming some time saying 'why are you doing this!?'. And it's no secret, we can't stand Theresa May. We have our agenda like everybody else, but we're not beholden.
>
> (Personal communication, 2018)

This willingness to kick over the bucket is reflected in the way *Guido Fawkes* continues to prod established notions of how political reporting should be done. Staines said: "There's always an underlying agenda. The same with Matt Drudge, the same with *Instapundit*, there are a few of us about … We do it a little bit differently, including a bit more gung ho" (personal communication, 2018). Is it abrupt? Yes. Biting? Often. Sensational? Sometimes. At times underhanded? "Yes", Staines acknowledges, "but mostly I think people know what they are getting". And in large terms, that is the advancement of a specific conservative libertarian politics, including where that factors into the way the press operates.

Unlike *GeenStijl* or *Gawker, Guido*'s political agenda drives much of its coverage. Prominently covering allegations of antisemitism in the British Labour Party, which Staines takes proud ownership of, he remarks: "That is our story, we have been plugging that for two years", adding: "We started on that as early as 2016" (personal communication, 2018). While their campaign was met by a flood of criticism by media saying it was "just our way of having a go with Jeremy Corbyn", Staines sees this differently, as other journalists reacting to their being "caught out by us". To Staines, it is all part of his approach. "We will do a drip drip sort of a strategy, we will drip drip drip on an issue but we need to do 50 of them over two years", Staines said, adding: "What tends to happen after we do it half a dozen times, the newspapers will say well this is a real issue and some people pick it up" (personal communication, 2018).

This captures what *Guido Fawkes* is to many observers: iconoclastic and persistent and with a clear political agenda. Over the years, it has been a thorn in the side of those it reports on, notably successful in uncovering new stories, and a player among the rest of the UK press. As a result, it has also found for itself the reputation of the best of its tabloid analogue forbears: a mixed bag. Or, as Staines commented on the way his reporters are seen by peers, "my perception is they are respected among reporters. Me, I'm seen as a bit more of a maligned force, but that's just the way it is" (personal communication, 2018).

The digital tabloid: a media-critical media

The image of a digital tabloid that begins to emerge from these examples is something more complex than we might have seen in their print predecessors. Across the discussions of tabloidization in the digital age, one through line is the way digital media are able to present their own content in contrast to the work of mainstream media, whether articulating mainstream media as too far right, too far left, or too aligned to corporate interests. For Burke and *Deadspin/ Gawker*, this listed towards critique of conservative media and the mainstream (Burke made headlines when he creatively reported news of a conservative US media mogul forcing local TV news reporters to read a politicized script (Eldridge, 2019b)). For *Guido Fawkes*, the way they contrast mainstream media is wrapped in a criticism of a naïve perspective which other news media espouse when insisting their work can somehow be objective, presenting news with an openly conservative viewpoint instead. For *GeenStijl,* it positions its content as presenting the 'other side' of the news, with traditional content providing fodder to comment upon.

These sites show how the digital era has brought about a way to imagine the tabloid possibilities of news media differently and successfully, by moving quickly and thoroughly within the digital cultures of the web. "I do think it is important that you have different voices … blogs can talk a little bit louder than [traditional] publications. They are a little bit more fluent," said one (anonymized) US freelance journalist writing across a number of the sites referenced here. She added, "it is good to have sharp elbows" (personal communication, 2018).

It is this fluency and this sharpness which return our discussion to the social conversation between digital tabloids and their audiences, recognizing that for *their* specific public there is an expectation of a certain style, a pointed news agenda, and an irreverent approach to news content. Add to this, that these sites can report hard news alongside soft, and the scandal and sensationalism that gave tabloids a distinct voice on the newsstands can now be diffused among blogs and independent websites which see this as part of their remit. This has allowed the sites discussed here and their peers to embrace a final point of similarity with their print predecessors: they are honest, and honest-to-goodness, journalists.

The digital journalists interviewed here, and the sites they write for, describe themselves as better and even more honest journalists than their mainstream peers, precisely due to their irreverence and their unashamed pursuit of both prurient and political news. It is *because* they operate this way, unencumbered by the niceties of traditional, mainstream approaches, that they have found success. And in doing so, they adopt a journalistic identity that was also held by print tabloid reporters (Sparks, 2000: 6). As the anonymous journalist quoted above remarked about reactions to their work and the criticism of mainstream media within it, "I would imagine that if *The [New York] Times* read that, they will be like 'well this is stupid', but you know … they are allowed to say that" (personal communication, 2018). Or, as Ashley Feinberg said:

> Among other journalists who are working mostly online, they would see something you do and say 'yup, that is Ashley at it again, **this is something we want to latch onto**' but maybe in the mainstream they would maybe poo poo it as whatever, you know, something **like a legacy of *Gawker* gang** or whatever.
>
> (Personal communication, 2018; emphasis added)

These sites have demonstrated successes in bringing new information into the public sphere, and thus have been able to position themselves within a dynamic, mixed journalistic field. However, to do so is to enter a fray where online and traditional media are often at odds (Eldridge, 2019b). They also call on us to refocus the lens of tabloidization, to see where we might begin with the criteria for selecting hard news which had hitherto been applied by popular newspapers.

Tabloids, as noted in Figure 2.1, have historically been more likely to focus on personal popular topics (e.g., celebrity news) than hard news on politics (e.g., policy and legislation). When tabloids broke from that tendency, it was only "when it concerns major issues which can be covered in sensational fashion", and when it could "serve to maintain a relationship with a particular readership articulated within the accepted public idiom of the tabloids" (Conboy, 2006: 10). For digital tabloidization, these criteria have not totally been abandoned. However, the media that adopt them move more fluidly across serious and less-serious fare, focusing more on serious content (in the case of *Guido Fawkes)* or less so (in the case of *GeenStijl*), while not fitting strictly within either domain. This more amorphous sense of tabloids is reflected in Figure 2.4, below. This maps how sites like *Gawker* have extended tabloidization dynamics by incorporating an array of harder and softer stories, pushing forward discussions of public import alongside gossip. It also reflects *Guido Fawkes*' narrower political/policy agenda, with its low-brow style and attention to scandal. Finally, it shows where *GeenStijl*, sits

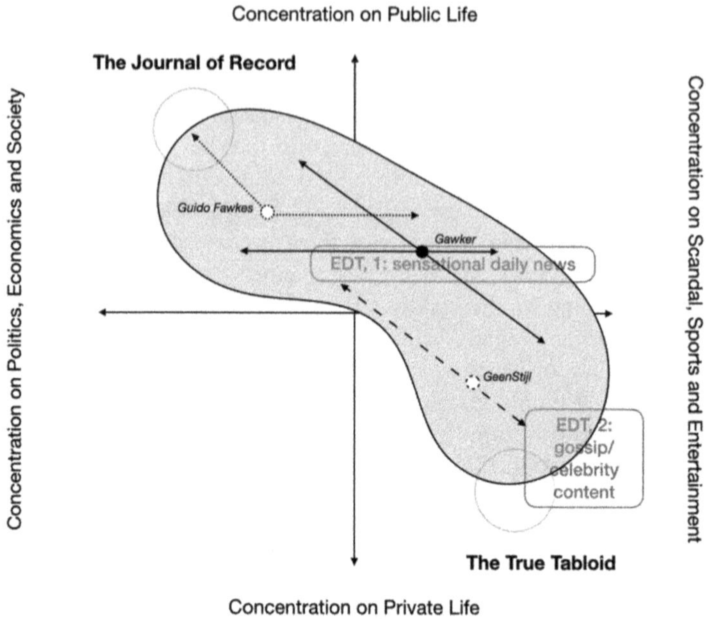

Figure 2.4 Digital tabloidization

closer to the familiar tabloid form by joining celebrity scandal and ribald commentary with a public appeal, even as it also puts forward public- and politically oriented content.

Reckless, or revolutionary? A closing discussion of digital tabloidization

This discussion of digital tabloidization offers a new reflection on a tabloid legacy that is now found online. On the one hand it reflects "the latest permutation of the language of the people in periodical form" (Conboy, 2006: 1). On the other, it shows how this has played out differently in a dynamic digital space where the popular nature of tabloids can be reimagined by sites that meet their public with a range of hard and soft news content; more or less serious at times, but nevertheless building on a tabloid legacy. They also reflect the "textual bridge" which tabloids have offered, drawing a link for audiences

> between their own experience of the culture in which they live, and their own attitudes and beliefs within a range of language which is a close approximation to what they imagine themselves to be using when they speak of these things themselves.
>
> (Conboy, 2006: 11)

As such, the cases here help us surface key aspects in the transition from the tabloid as a mass market popular media to the digital manifestations of the tabloid as a (sub)popular form with narrower agendas and focused understanding of their audiences, enveloped in an emerging digital media culture. As this chapter has shown, in the digital era the primacy of tabloids as a counter-punching popular media form is alive and well, just reimagined to reach beyond the sensational appeal of prurient content which print tabloids popularized. From this discussion, digital tabloidization emerges not as a straightforward expansion of a popular cultural media form online, but in the development of a (sub)popular form in the context of a more fluid digital culture which crosses journalistic boundaries.

As we began, we can conclude by turning to *Gawker* and its demise. Now bankrupt, *Gawker* met its end when Hogan sued them and won. But underlying that lawsuit, and subsidizing its persistence, was the tech capitalist, Peter Thiel. A scourge of the left and a darling of the right, Thiel is best known now for two things: founding the e-payment service PayPal, and secretly financing Hogan as a way to get back at *Gawker* for publicly outing Thiel as gay in 2007. As far as *Gawker* went into an unbridled new digital culture, embracing the opportunity to liberate knowledge freely online with a tabloid zeal, Thiel returned the favour with an unrelenting traditional power – financial power – to fight back against his media enemies. "It's difficult to recall now, but at Gawker's founding there was a sense that the internet was a free space, where anything can be said", Denton (2016) wrote. "But when you try to make a business out of that freedom, the system will fight you."

And so, Denton's reflections on "how things are" offer a sobering commentary on the ability of tabloidization to take new shape in a digital age, and its limits. Digital tabloidization, as a dynamic, calls to our attention the ways in which new media, drawing on a tabloid legacy, can report aggressively, quickly, and with an eye towards using popular appeal to advance public discourse. Yet, it also sits within a longer legacy, where tabloid-style reporting, and the inclination to report on the scandals of celebrity life, continue to rankle public sensibilities. It offers a reminder of the ups and downs, and the inherent messiness, of a changing and dynamic cultural force within a news media environment. We are still in the early decades of seeing how this transpires online, and it is unclear in which direction the trend line is pointing. But what remains likely is the human desire for news with a popular sensational touch that made tabloids a global phenomenon will likely persist, regardless what form it takes. And if so, a digital era for a reimagined tabloid may just be beginning.

Notes

1 These were conducted as part of the Interrogating Antagonists project, funded by a University of Groningen, Faculty of Arts, start-up grant and carried out in 2018 and 2019.

2 Quotes of *GeenStijl* content are originally in Dutch, with the author's translation provided.

3 Mencken described his style as 'hoisting the black flag', to further the pirate analogy.

References

Bastos, Marco Toledo (2017) "Digital Journalism and Tabloid Journalism", in Bob Franklin and Scott Eldridge (eds.) *The Routledge Companion to Digital Journalism Studies*. Abingdon: Routledge, pp. 217–225.

Bingham, Adrian (2007) "Representing the people? The Daily Mirror, class and political culture in inter-war Britain", in Laura Beers and Geraint Thomas (eds.) *Brave New World*. London: University of London Press, pp. 109–128.

Bingham, Adrian and Conboy, Martin (2015) *Tabloid Century*. London: Peter Lang.

Bird, Sue E. (2000) "Audience Demands in a Murderous Market", in Colin Sparks and John Tulloch (eds.) *Tabloid Tales*. Oxford: Rowman & Littlefield, pp. 213–228.

Bishop, Ronald (1999) "From Behind the Walls", *Journal of Communication Inquiry* 23 (1): 90–112.

Brants, Kees (1998) "Who's Afraid of Infotainment?", *European Journal of Communication*, 13 (3): 315–335.

Carlson, Matt (2017) *Journalistic Authority*. New York: Columbia University Press.

Carlson, Matt (2014) "Gone, But Not Forgotten", *Journalism Studies* 15 (1): 33–47.

Chadwick, Andrew, Vaccari, Cristian, and O'Loughlin, Benjamin (2018) "Do tabloids poison the well of social media?", *New Media & Society* 20 (11): 4255–4274.

Conboy, Martin (2006) *Tabloid Britain*. Abingdon: Routledge.

Conboy, Martin (2002) *The Press and Popular Culture*. London: SAGE.

Conboy, Martin and Eldridge, Scott (2018) "Journalism and Public Discourse", in Colleen Cotter and Daniel Perrin (eds.) *Handbook of Language and Media*. Abingdon: Routledge, pp. 164–177.

Denton, Nick (2016) "How Things Work", *Gawker*, Available at: https://gawker.com/how-things-work-1785604699.

Dick, Murray (2011) "Search Engine Optimisation in UK News Production", *Journalism Practice* 5 (4): 462–477.

Donsbach, Wolfgang (2010) "Journalists and their Professional Identities", in Stuart Allan (ed.) *The Routledge Companion to News and Journalism*. Abingdon: Routledge, pp. 38–59.

Eldridge, Scott (2019a) "Where do we draw the line? Interlopers, (ant)agonists, and an unbounded journalistic field", *Media and Communication*, 7 (4): 8–18.

Eldridge, Scott (2019b) "'Thank god for Deadspin': Interlopers, metajournalistic commentary, and fake news through the lens of 'journalistic realization,'" *New Media & Society* 21 (4): 856–878.

Eldridge, Scott (2018) *Online Journalism from the Periphery*. Abingdon: Routledge.

Epstein, Joseph (2011) *Gossip*. Boston: Houghton Mifflin Harcourt.

Farrow, Ronan (2019) *Catch and Kill*. London: Little Brown.

Feeley, Kathleen (2012) "Gossip as News: On Modern U.S. Celebrity Culture and Journalism", *History Compass*, 10 (6): 467–482.

Frischlich, Lena; Boberg, Svenja, and Quandt, Thorsten (2019) "Comment Sections as Targets of Dark Participation? Journalists' Evaluation and Moderation of Deviant User Comments", *Journalism Studies*, 20 (14): 2014–2033.

Garde-Hansen, Joanne and Gorton, Kristyn (2013) *Emotion Online*, London: Palgrave Macmillan.

GeenStijl (2020a) "GeenStijl ". Available at: https://www.geenstijl.nl/contact/.

GeenStijl (2020b) "Contact". Available at: https://www.geenstijl.nl/contact/.

GeenStijl (2020c) "Huisregels". Available at: https://www.geenstijl.nl/huisregels/.

Glynn, Kevin (2000) *Tabloid Culture*. Durham, NC: Duke University Press.

Guido Fawkes (2017) "Tory Aides' Spreadsheet Names 36 Sex Pest MPs". Available at: https://order-order.com/2017/10/29/tory-aides-spreadsheet-names-36-sex-pest-mps/.

Hampton, Mark (2010) "The Fourth Estate Ideal in Journalism History", in S. Allan (ed.) *The Routledge Companion to News and Journalism*. Abingdon: Routledge, pp. 3–12.

Keeble, Richard Lance and Mair, John (2012) *The Phone Hacking Scandal*. London: Abramis.

Mayhew, Freddy (2020) "Lobby allows live reporting from Government briefing after *Guido Fawkes* tweets", *Press Gazette*, 23 January. Available at: https://www.pressgazette.co.uk/lobby-allows-live-reporting-government-briefing-guido-fawkes-tweets/.

McRobbie, Angela and Thornton, Sarah (1995) "Rethinking 'Moral Panic' for Multi-Mediated Social Worlds", *The British Journal of Sociology*, 46 (4): 559–574.

Mepschen, Paul (2016) "Sexual democracy, cultural alterity and the politics of everyday life in Amsterdam", *Patterns of Prejudice*, 50 (2): 150–167.

Pareene, Alex (2019) "The Death of the Rude Press", *The New Republic*, 7 November. Available at: https://newrepublic.com/article/155627/death-rude-press-deadspin-splinter-blogs.

PerezHilton (2020) "About". Available at: https://perezhilton.com/about-perez-hilton/.

PopBitch (2020) "About". Available at: https://popbitch.com/about-us.

Read, Max (2016) "Did I Kill Gawker?", *New York Magazine*, 22 August. Available at: https://nymag.com/intelligencer/2016/08/did-i-kill-gawker.html.

Reinemann, Carsten, Stanyer, James; Scherr, Sebastian, and Legnante, Guido (2012) "Hard and soft news: A review of concepts, operationalizations and key findings", *Journalism* 13 (2): 221–239.

Sparks, Colin (2000) "Introduction: The Panic over Tabloid news", in Colin Sparks and John Tulloch (eds.) *Tabloid Tales*. Oxford: Rowman & Littlefield. pp. 1–40.

Stevenson, Michael (2016) "The cybercultural moment and the new media field", *New Media & Society*, 18 (7): 1088–1102.

Tandoc, Edson and Jenkins, Joy (2018) "Out of bounds? How *Gawker*'s outing a married man fits into the boundaries of journalism", *New Media & Society*, 20 (2): 581–598.

Uberti, David (2014) "In a tabloidized world, tabloids struggle", *CJR*, 29 July.

van Til, Gijs (2018) "NL-Netherlands: Twitter user and Dutch website liable for disseminating explicit content of well-known TV personality", *IRIS*, 8 (1): 35.

3 Tabloidization in the Internet age

Julia Lefkowitz

Introduction

Claims of a decline in 'quality' newspaper standards are not new, dating back to the rise of the penny press in the US during the 1830s. However, with the ascendance of the Internet, such charges have proliferated. Throughout the nineteenth and twentieth centuries, and now in the twenty-first century, these claims have been particularly salient in the British context, where tabloid newspapers have historically enjoyed strong popularity. Despite this, claims asserting a tabloidization of British newspapers have been made largely on the basis of intuition rather than empirical data, and it is unclear whether or not a tabloidization of newspapers may have commenced during or before the Internet era, or whether or not such a process has taken place at all.

This chapter assesses the extent to which a tabloidization of British newspapers may or may not have occurred during the period from 1968 to 2016, a time before, and in the wake of, the rise and widespread use of the Internet. Furthermore, this study examines change in the journalistic values of British tabloid and 'quality' newspapers longitudinally and on the basis of a large body of newspaper texts. It uses diachronic linguistic data to examine the possible tabloidizing impact the rise and widespread use of the Internet has had on British newspapers.

An overview of key journalism and media concepts pertinent to notions of tabloidization and its significance are discussed in the first section of this chapter. Following this, putative causal factors of tabloidization, namely economic and technological ones, are reviewed. An explanation of the study's methods subsequently precedes the findings, with conclusions considered in the final section.

Key concepts: tabloidization and the public sphere

In media studies research, tabloidization has often been seen to operate as an umbrella term through which scholars have conveyed a spectrum of assumptions and opinions (e.g. Bird 2009; Esser 1999; Magin 2017; Magin and Stark 2014; Sparks 1998, 2000; Uribe and Gunter 2004). It can be noted that recent references to the phenomenon by media scholars and commentators often tap into contemporary debates regarding the changing nature of mass media, the role of journalism in democratic societies, and the shifting public sphere. Upon examining the tabloidization scholarship more closely, it becomes clear that tabloidization has often been understood in terms of a reconfiguration of the journalistic values and/or content traditionally seen as characteristic of tabloid and 'quality' newspapers respectively (e.g. Bird 2009; Bromley 1998; Esser 1999; Magin 2017; Skovsgaard 2014; Sparks 2000). In view of space limitations within the chapter and the overarching role of journalistic values in shaping newspaper content, this chapter focuses on journalistic values as the core constitutive element of 'tabloidization.' Drawing from the work of Galtung and Ruge (1965) and Deuze (2005), journalistic values can be understood as the ideals or standards according to which journalists make decisions and define themselves as professionals. Those values regularly identified in media scholarship include truth, objectivity, fairness, neutrality, impartiality, balance, accuracy, independence, partisanship, literary value, emotionalism, personalization, and sensationalism (e.g. Boykoff and Boykoff 2004; Conboy 2004, 2011; Esser 1999; Hampton 2008; Sambrook 2012; Schudson 1978; Skovsgaard 2014; Streckfuss 1990; Tuchman 1972;). In the British context, specific values associated with 'quality' newspapers have been identified as truth, fairness, and independence (Conboy 2011; Hampton 2008). Interestingly, while values identified as characteristic of 'quality' news publications tend to vary on a nation by nation basis – for example, with literary values seen as characteristic of French 'quality' journalism (e.g. Chalaby 1996), and objectivity identified as characteristic of 'quality' journalism in the US (e.g. Schudson 1978) – those values identified as characteristic of tabloids tend to remain the same across national contexts.

In journalism studies research, discussions of 'tabloidization' often depict a 'spillover' of tabloid values and content into 'quality' press (e.g. Bromley 1998; Esser 1999; Franklin 1997; Magin 2017; Skovsgaard 2014; Sparks 2000). Words such as "infected" (Conboy 2011, 117) and "contaminated" (Esser 1999, 293) are deployed, to highlight the perceived negative societal implications of these ostensible shifts. Some scholars describe these critical reactions to 'tabloidization' of 'quality' newspapers as a "moral panic" in their own right (e.g. Conboy 2011; MacDonald 2000; Örnebring and Jönsson 2007). Across the media cited in the relevant debates, 'tabloidization' is principally represented as a phenomenon which affects the 'quality' press (Bingham and Conboy 2015; Esser 1999; Franklin 1997; Magin and Stark 2014; Skovsgaard 2014). A deterioration of the public sphere is implied, through which citizens are deprived of the information necessary to inform their participation in processes crucial to democracy. While the relevant literature tends to focus on ostensible shifts in 'quality' journalism, several studies also identify a recent increase of tabloid values and content within tabloids (Bingham and Conboy 2015; Magin and Stark 2014; Uribe and Gunter 2004). This suggests that it is important to subject both tabloid and 'quality' outlets to empirical study.

Beyond attention to the negative implications of 'tabloidization,' media scholars have also identified virtues in the ascendance of tabloid characteristics. Bas and Grabe, for example, illustrate the capacity of "emotion-provoking personalization" (2015, 159) to enhance audiences' retention of news stories, in effect narrowing the knowledge gaps between audiences of lower and higher education levels. In a case study of British television news programs, MacDonald (2000) depicts putative increases in personalization as a welcome remedy to the restrictive, male-oriented rationalism and objectivity previously seen as characteristic of the 'quality' press. Her interpretation encourages 'tabloidization' to be seen as a form of emancipation empowering those previously marginalized by the Habermasian public sphere model. As noted by Sparks (1998), scholarly perceptions of the possible effects of an ostensible recent 'tabloidization' tend to dichotomize into camps of those in favour and those against the phenomenon.

On the basis of the above discussions and literature cited therein, a working definition for tabloidization is proposed:

> **Tabloidization** is the convergence of 'quality' newspapers towards the journalistic values of sensationalism and personalization characteristic of tabloid newspapers.

Similarly, and also in line with the relevant scholarship (Bennett 2012; Lefkowitz 2016; MacDonald 2000; Skovsgaard 2014; Umbricht and Esser 2016; Wang 2012), the following definitions for personalization and sensationalism are proffered:

> **Personalization** can be understood as journalistic focus on an individual or entity representative of a larger theme or topic, in which emphasis on the personal and/or emotional often supersedes the emphasis on fact or public affairs-oriented information.

> **Sensationalism** can be understood as journalistic deployment of content and/or language that stands to provoke sensory and emotional reactions from readers as a result of emphasis placed on drama, magnitude, salaciousness, and/or the unexpected.

In this chapter, the term 'information-orientation' is used in place of other values which have been identified as characteristic of 'quality' British newspapers, with a view towards operationalizing these values (Lefkowitz 2016). Truth and impartiality, for example, would require intensive qualitative analysis in which features such as agency and metaphor could be examined in depth. By contrast, 'information-orientation' is a term which captures the quantitatively operationalizable components of the multiple values depicted as traditionally characteristic of 'quality' British newspapers.

The scholarship either indirectly or directly associates tabloidization with a range of factors both endogenous and exogenous to the journalistic field. For example, while the emergence of editorial analytics can be seen as a development more specific to the journalism industry, certain cultural factors, such as the increasing salience of popular culture, might have developed more externally from newspapers. The following section discusses these putative causal forces, consideration of which will serve to facilitate synchronic and longitudinal analysis of the study's data collection.

Historical trajectory

Journalism and media scholarship have traditionally depicted economic and technological factors as agents of tabloidization. While cultural factors have also been identified as possible enabling forces, the relevant literature tends to rely on narrow, qualitive case studies, and in some cases lack empirical data altogether. This section of the chapter focuses on economic and technological references in the scholarship, and in a final subsection, discusses pertinent cultural considerations and frameworks.

Regarding economic forces, scholars including Esser (1999) and Skovsgaard (2014) identify the "beginnings" (Esser 1999, 294) of tabloidization with the rise of the penny press in the US, in which "scandals, crime, celebrities and gossip" were the focus of publications such as the *Illustrated Daily News* in the US, and the *Daily Mirror* and the *News of the World* in the UK. In the 1830s, when US newspapers costing one penny emerged as competitors to the traditional six-penny papers, the latter issued "charges of sensationalism" against their more popular counterparts (Schudson 1978, 23). A mass appeal of sensationalism is implied, which is depicted as at odds with the conventions of the traditional, 'quality' newspapers of the era.

An 'Americanization' of the UK press in the 1890s has been associated with an increase in tabloid elements in the country (Conboy 2004). This happened when tabloid journalism faded out in the US after the brief heyday of Yellow Journalism; as competition augmented, British newspapers became increasingly commercially oriented (Conboy 2004, 2011). Conboy highlights a growth in crime, entertainment, and sports content, and a decline in political stories, alongside a more colourful presentation, as "therefore more profitable" (2011, 16), suggesting the often-conveyed notion of a juxtaposition between the public interest and interesting to the public. While the source(s) of increased profits are not explicitly identified, this implies a process through which certain tabloid elements subsequently increase circulation and/or advertising figures.

Between the 1920s and 1940s, US advertisers moved their investments from tabloids to radio, due to both the nascent commercialism of the latter and the shift of audiences from tabloid newspapers to radio in the 1930s (Picard 1998). By contrast, in the UK, advertisers continued to buy advertising space from tabloids, as radio was from its inception a public service broadcasting medium (Esser 1999; Picard 1998). This broader political-economic context contributed to the increased competition seen in the British newspaper market during the first half of the twentieth century. During this period, the development of numerous new technologies stood to have an impact on journalism. Scholarship attributes several shifts in newspaper journalism to the emergence of broadcast journalism, first through the medium of radio, starting in the 1920s. Research further depicts a subsequent flourishing of partisan and popular speech in print journalism which, in contrast to the broadcast medium, remained unconstrained by public service and impartiality mandates (Conboy 2011).

The rise of television, starting in the 1950s, has been linked to a rise of television and entertainment-centric content in newspapers in the UK (Conboy and Steel 2010; Rooney 2000), despite variation across tabloid and 'quality' newspapers as well as on a publication-to-publication basis (Belson 1965). In response to increased competition for advertising posed by the rise of television, Conboy and Steel (2010, 653) cite an increase in "feminized content", particularly in the *Daily Mail*, as well as an augmentation of "lifestyle and consumer journalism" (ibid.) in the *Guardian*, suggesting a growth in consumption-oriented content which might serve to attract augmented attention from advertisers and readers in a cross-fertilizing manner. This is to say that perceptions of a supposed tabloidizing impact of new media technologies on newspapers pre-date the rise of the web.

One key moment in this history is the Wapping Revolution of 1986, which has been implicated in initiating a sea change in the British newspaper industry (Conboy 2011; Curran and Seaton 2003). This 'revolution' kicked off when Rupert Murdoch moved his stable of British newspapers to facilities equipped with computerized printing technologies located in Wapping, East London. The move to Wapping introduced a streamlining of printing and production processes, resulting in mass layoffs and significantly changed material properties for the printed newspaper products, including increases in pagination and colour printing. Shortly thereafter, other major UK titles replicated Murdoch's approach, carrying out a revolutionary shift in the country's newspaper industry.

The introduction of computerized printing technologies led directly to layoffs, "new industrial relationships" (Conboy 2011, 94), and facilitated increases in pagination, colour printing, and entertainment-focused content. Unpacking each of these shifts, the surge in individual contracts entailed in the new relationships resulted in a decline in job stability, benefits, and working conditions, threatening to decrease the commitment of newspaper staffs, including journalists', to their respective newspapers and the standard of work produced (Van Aerden et al. 2015). Furthermore, simultaneous growth in pagination suggests an increased demand for journalistic content, despite the thinning out of journalists. Added to this, an increase in colour printing was seen as suggesting a heightened emphasis on literal and figurative elements of 'colour', while growth in entertainment-focused content directly indicates an augmentation in tabloid-like 'soft' news content.

Beginning in the mid-1990s, the emergence of the web as a new avenue towards accessing media content, as with the Wapping Revolution, was accompanied by new newspaper production platforms and technologies. It also brought about fundamental shifts in the economics of the newspaper industry. Such shifts have often been associated with increased pressures in newsrooms and upon journalists, as advertising revenue declined while the speed of publishing newer and newer content increased. Within the Internet era more broadly, the aforementioned shifts have in particular been associated with the rise of Web 2.0,[1] starting in the early 2000s, and the rise of the Web 3.0[2] in the early 2010s (Allen 2012).

Speed and interactivity have been depicted as principle affordances of Internet-powered technologies (Lewis et al. 2010; O'Sullivan and Heinonan 2008; Witschge and Nygren 2009). Similar to the effects attributed to the technological shifts of the Wapping Revolution, the lower cost and ease of content production available through the Internet, and the rise of Web 2.0 and Web 3.0, amongst other changes, are implicated in a range of negative effects on the newspaper industry. Most directly, each has been seen as contributing to newsroom layoffs made by media owners unable to maintain revenue streams, meaning that as a consequence, reduced editorial staffs have had to learn new skills and produce more content (Örnebring 2010). Furthermore, the profusion of news and information online has contributed to an information economy in which competition between news organizations has heightened.

With regards to interactivity, the rise of Web 2.0 and then Web 3.0, and the deployment of user generated content and social media platforms, signalled a shift in the capacity of journalists employed by professional news outlets to communicate directly with audiences outside of the temporal and professional constraints imposed by their news organization. Vis (2013), for example, illustrates the ability of legacy journalists to both reinforce and break with 'quality' journalism norms through their engagement on Twitter. Platforms such as Twitter as well as Facebook, for example, provide journalists with the ability to publish content and opinions instantaneously, enhancing their relationships with audiences and building their own personal brands, as reflected through Holton and Molyneux's concept of "brand journalism" (Holton and Molyneux 2017).

Often in conjunction with considerations of speed and interactivity, media scholarship references increased fragmentation and concerns over factual accuracy as features of this new media landscape (e.g. Hermida 2010; Lewis et al. 2010; Sambrook 2012). Microblogging and social media platforms such as Twitter and Facebook have allowed for the "instant dissemination of short fragments of data from a variety of official and unofficial sources" (Hermida 2010, 297); as Witschge and Nygren note, "News organizations with resources can also use the web for giving depth and background, but the dominant logic of the web is fast and short" (2009, 47). Extending this notion of fragmentation, Witschge and Nygren (2009, 46) assert that "constant deadlines conflict with the need for accuracy". Increasingly, the disjuncture between an emphasis on speed and the time required of journalists to ensure accuracy has become a source of tension with profound consequences for the production of public service journalism, as seen, for example, with the spate of election-related 'fake news' from 2016 (Tandoc, Ling, and Lim 2017).

Central to Web 2.0 technological developments are fundamental shifts in gatekeeping and agenda-setting dynamics (e.g. Hermida 2010; Lewis et al. 2010; O'Sullivan and Heinonan 2008). Gatekeeping in particular has been identified as a core role of journalists (e.g. Shoemaker et al. 2001; Singer 2010), and can be defined as, "the process of selecting, writing, editing, positioning, scheduling, repeating and otherwise massaging information to become news" (Shoemaker et al. 2008, 73, in Tandoc 2014, 560). Historically viewed as core functions of journalists, gatekeeping and agenda-setting have in this context increasingly become impacted by audience preferences, particularly as calculated through editorial analytics (e.g. Petre 2015; Tandoc 2014). As a consequence, a perceived ascendance in tabloid journalistic values has been associated with the increasing involvement, or democratization, of journalistic practices.

Cultural factors

Beyond the technological developments highlighted above, tabloidization is implicitly or explicitly attributed to cultural factors by journalism scholars as well, particularly in critical analysis approaches (e.g. Conboy 2002; McDonald 2000; Örnebring and Jönsson 2007; Turner 1999). Tabloidization scholarship which depicts the phenomenon principally in terms of cultural criteria, or which ascribes primary agency to cultural shifts is, however, rare.

Many of these cultural approaches to tabloidization draw heavily from the Habermasian public sphere model. MacDonald (2000), for example, depicts shifts in the Habermasian public sphere according to which recent personalization in the 'quality' press may be seen as a virtue. In line with other proponents of tabloidization, MacDonald views an increase in personal, emotional content in newspapers as representing a broader range of perspectives and values, which encourage a wider readership and subsequently contribute to an increasingly well-informed public. Accordingly, a reconfiguration of the public sphere is suggested in which previously marginalized demographics are increasingly emancipated.

When it comes to highlighting possible changes in journalistic values, shifts in so-called popular culture are also relevant. A view is often adopted that sees popular culture as an ongoing process constituted by conflicting, hierarchical forces (Fiske 1989; Conboy 2002). As an example, the rise and widespread use of television in the 1950s, which, as discussed, has been connected with a rise in entertainment and leisure content and a decline in 'hard news' stories in newspapers, can also be associated with an ascension of popular culture. Indeed, media technologies such as broadcast television have often been depicted as the resources through which popular culture is constructed (Fiske 1989); accordingly, and importantly, the ascendance of the web can thus be seen as a new means through which popular culture can be constructed.

The rise of popular culture has at times been associated with the emergence of a postmodern paradigm. Postmodernism, like tabloidization, is a somewhat fraught term: whereas adherents of a more extreme strand of postmodernism view a loss of meaning and truth as a by-product of the rise of mass production and mass media, adherents of more moderate strands of postmodernism tend to underscore the role of commercial forces in rendering a break from a modern paradigm, that was defined by values of rationality and enlightenment thought. The switch to a postmodern context is in this sense seen in the rise of claims alleging a decline in facts and truth, and an ascension of 'fake news' and misinformation in the journalism ecosystem. A reconfiguration of the Habermasian public sphere, in which a broader range of publics has gained representation, may also be seen as a postmodern reconfiguration, in that a plurality of demographics, rather than the Habermasian white, bourgeois, male, is treated as democratic citizens. Furthermore, the rise of corporations, in particular multinational ones, global financial markets, global media communications systems, as well as the "capitalist boom" (Whitley 2011, 187) of the 1980s have been seen as characteristic of the emergence of a postmodern context. The conglomeration of media companies during the 1980s can as such be understood as a key enabling featuring of a shift towards postmodernity. The move from a modern to postmodern context can thus serve as a useful framework for understanding certain shifts of key relevance to the journalistic field.

Methods

In this study, one tabloid and one 'quality' British newspaper are subject to analysis. In view of the value-laden role of language use in journalistic discourse, a corpus linguistic approach was deemed appropriate. While numerous studies have applied qualitative linguistic methods to British newspapers (e.g. Conboy 2006), extending the corpus and methods applied in Lefkowitz (2016) in which the quoted speech of tabloid and quality newspapers were examined, this study applies a corpus linguistic analysis to a large sample of two newspapers over an extended time period.

Corpus linguistics can be understood as a methodology through which computer-based methods are used to examine a large body of texts. This approach first emerged in the 1960s and its popularity has blossomed alongside developments in computational technologies. A number of studies have applied corpus linguistics to examinations of newspaper texts (e.g. Biber 1988; Biber and Finegan 1989, 2014; Clark 2013; Westin 2001). With the aim of examining the journalistic values at play and assessing a possible tabloidization of newspapers, this study introduces into media and journalism scholarship new methodological approaches for systematically comparing the language and journalistic values of tabloid and 'quality' newspapers against one another.

In this study, articles selected for analysis were extracted from the appropriate digital database,[3] converted into .txt format, and uploaded into linguistic software, AntConc, in which parts of speech (POS) tags were applied to each word in the corpus. Frequency counts of each part of speech of interest were then conducted across the newspapers and years subject to analysis.

Articles were extracted using a two-constructed-week sampling approach within each year analysed; two random dates from each day of the week – two randomly-selected Mondays, two randomly-selected Tuesdays, and so on – were subject to examination, with the exception of Sundays, which were omitted from examination. The two-constructed-week approach was selected in view of its capacity to generate a statistically representative sample of newspaper articles from the year of interest (e.g. Lacy, et al. 2001; Wang 2012).

From the 1990s to 2016, every article published on the dates and in the newspapers subject to analysis were downloaded, and constitute a new corpus, 'British Newspapers: 1968–2016.' Due to the poor OCR quality of digitized newspaper articles from the 1968–1987 period, as well as associated time and budget constraints, within this earlier part of the corpus, for each date selected, two page-one articles were chosen for examination and transcription. Articles selected from this earlier period were transcribed into .txt formatted articles by a third-party company due to the time-intensive nature of the required retyping.[4] The .txt formatted articles were then run through the part-of-speech tagger, followed by AntConc, and subjected to corpus linguistic analysis.

In order to avoid political ideology as an independet variable, one left-wing tabloid, the *Mirror*, and one left-wing 'quality,' the *Guardian*, were studied. The number of newspapers subject to analysis was limited in particular due to the lack of digital availability of other publications of interest, in particular the *Sun*, in the period preceding the 1990s, as well as the time intensive processes involved with generating .txt versions of pre-1990s articles.

The study's corpus consists of articles sampled from one year before and one year after key economic and technological events of pertinence to possible shifts in journalistic values. The events and developments selected for analysis were Rupert Murdoch's purchase of the *Sun* in 1969, the Wapping Revolution of 1986, the launch of online editions by the *Guardian* in 1999 and the *Mirror* in 2001, the introduction of social sharing functions through email and social media platforms such as Facebook and Twitter by the *Mirror* in 2007 and the *Guardian* in 2008, and the emergence of the Web 3.0 era, starting in 2012. As data collection began towards the end of 2017, and in view of the number of key technological events of potential impact on journalism taking place during this period, each year in the 2012–2016 period is subject to examination.

Those values identified as traditionally characteristic of tabloids, personalization and sensationalism, and the 'information-orientation' identified as traditionally distinctive of 'quality' British newspapers are operationalized linguistically. Subsequently, the frequencies of the linguistic proxies of each value are charted synchronically and longitudinally in order to capture possible change and/or continuity in the prominence of each value in each of the two publications over time.

Findings

Corpus linguistic findings are discussed value by value, addressing change and/or continuity in terms of each respective linguistic proxy. Of particular interest are trends seen before the rise and widespread use of the Internet, from the second half of the twentieth century through the beginning of the twenty-first century.

Personalization

Figures 3.1–3.3 display longitudinal change in the markers of personalization across the newspapers. Linguistic markers of personalization were selected on the basis of linguistics and media linguistics literature (Biber 1988; Biber and Finegan 1989, 2014; Clark 2013; Westin 2001). These linguistic markers are first person pronouns, second person pronouns, and private verbs. First person pronouns, including *I, me, we, us, myself, our, ourselves,* and *my*, express ego-involvement and are a prominent feature of interactive discourse (Biber 1988). In the context of news reporting, the feature is frequently found in quoted speech (Hundt and Mair 1999). Second person pronouns, including *you, your, yourself,* and *yourselves,* are also frequently used in interactive contexts and indicate a speaker's involvement with an addressee (Biber 1988; Westin 2001). While first person pronouns index a speaker's views directly, second person pronouns can index a speaker's views indirectly. Finally, private verbs, as noted by Quirk et al. (1985), reflect intellectual states or acts, and contrast with public verbs, which are observable speech acts. Examples of private verbs include *think* and *believe.*

Overall trends

Initially, in 1968, each of the three markers of personalization are more characteristic of the *Mirror* than the *Guardian.* In the *Mirror,* the use of first-person pronouns is 27.9% higher, second person pronouns 110% higher, and private verbs 15.7% higher than in the *Guardian.* Accordingly, personalization is shown to be more characteristic of the tabloid.

Overall during the 48-year time period, the trend is towards an increase in markers of personalization. In particular, first- and second-person pronouns increase in both newspapers, while private verbs decrease. Further, in the 2012–2016 period, a growth in first- and second-person pronouns is particularly pronounced in the tabloid, while pre-1998 and 1998–2009 data roughly mirror each other. Interestingly, between 1985 and 1987, before and after the Wapping Revolution, a convergence is seen in the prominence of first- and second-person pronouns, according to which the feature decreases in the *Mirror* and increases in the *Guardian.* It is the Web 3.0 period where personalization surges in salience.

Sensationalism

Diachronic trends in sensationalism are shown in Figures 3.4–3.6 (pp. 46–47). Drawing from literature by Quirk et al. (1985) and Bednarek and Caple (2012), degree adverbs, general adverbs, and general adjectives are used as markers of sensationalism. Quirk et al. (1985) attest to the ability of degree and general adverbs to quantify and/or compare that which they modify. Degree adverbs specify the degree to which an adverb applies; examples of this part of speech include *extremely* and *utterly.*

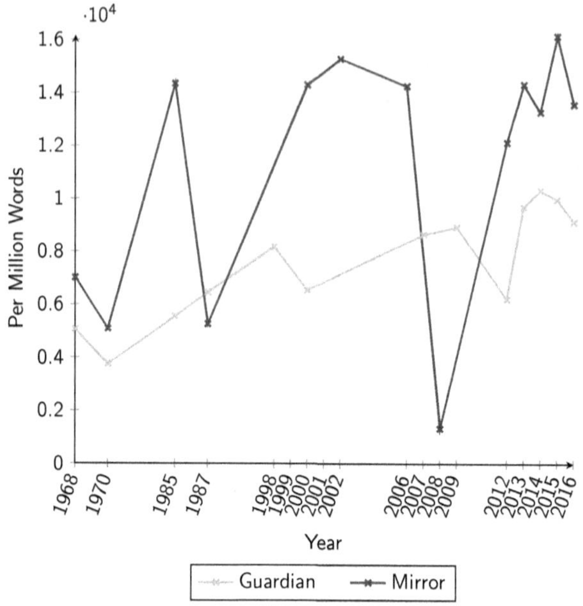

Figure 3.1 First person pronouns

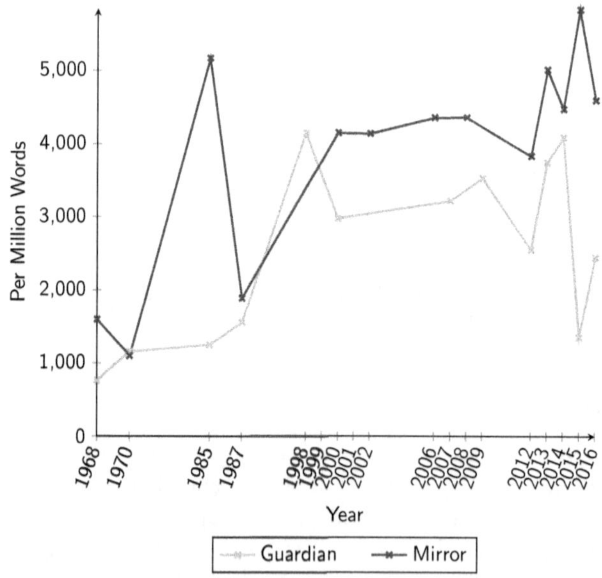

Figure 3.2 Second person pronouns

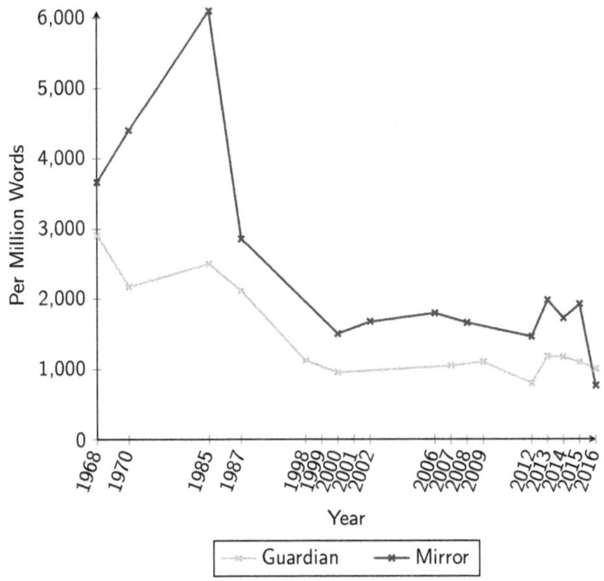

Figure 3.3 Private verbs

Overall trends

Interestingly, the proxies of sensationalism are initially more characteristic of the *Guardian* than of the *Mirror*. This configuration of adverbs and adjectives questions the traditional assumed predominance of sensationalism in tabloids referred to by the tabloidization scholarship. Furthermore, during the span of the corpus' 48-year period, the overall trend is one of flux, or a lack in stability in each of the markers. It is worth mentioning, however, that there are similarities in the fluctuations seen in degree adverbs and general adverbs before and after 1998; these two periods can be observed to roughly resemble one another in their flux. More broadly, however, there is the distinct possibility that the sensationalism referred to in the literature is constituted by other features, such as headlines or article topic.

'Information-orientation'

Shifts in the 'information-orientation' of the newspapers are displayed in Figures 3.7–3.9 (pp.48–49). Word length, sentence length, and reading difficulty level are assessed as markers of 'information-orientation' on the basis of scholarship by Westin (2001), Westin and Geisler (2002), and Lefkowitz (2016). Westin (2001) assesses word and sentence length, treating each as markers of 'information-density.' Reading difficulty level, as measured through the Flesch-Kincaid readability (FKR) metric (Table 3.1), has been examined by Lefkowitz (2016). FKR is the most reliable metric, and measures readability using the total

Figure 3.4 Degree adverbs

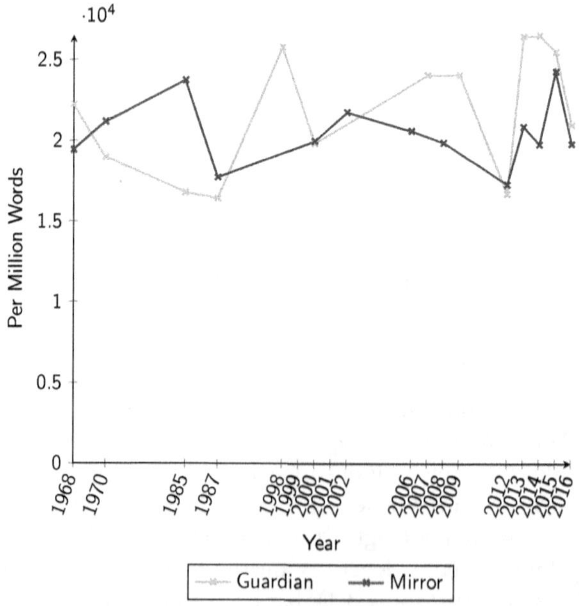

Figure 3.5 General adverbs

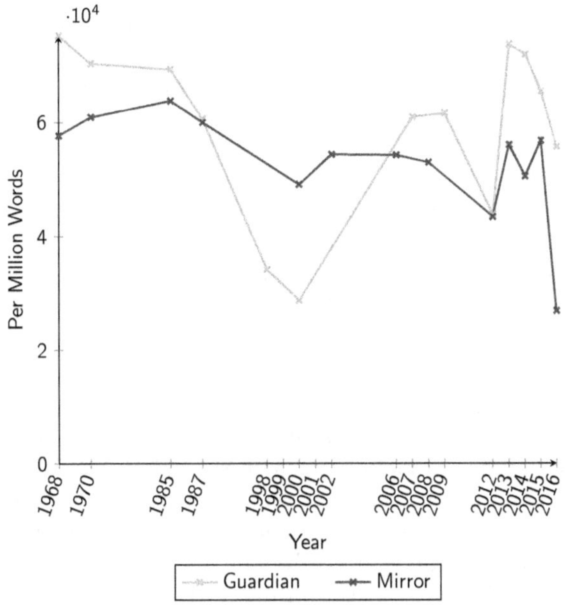

Figure 3.6 General adjectives

Table 3.1. Flesch-Kincaid readability, scale interpretation

Flesch-Kincaid readability score	*Reading level*
100.0–90.0	An average 11 year-old student
90.0–80.0	An average 12 year-old student
80.0–70.0	An average 13 year-old student
70.0–60.0	An average 13–15 year-old student
60.0–50.0	An average 15–18 year-old student
50.0–30.0	College student level
30.0–0	Graduate student level

number of sentences, words, and syllables in a given text. Lower FKR scores reflect higher reading difficulty levels.

Overall trends

Proxies indicating higher levels of 'information-orientation' are initially more prominent in the *Guardian* than in the *Mirror*, corroborating the role of each as indexical of the 'quality' newspaper journalistic value.

Over time, remarkable stability is seen with FKR levels, and in particular in word length, where only one data point, from the *Mirror* in 2000, reflects change. With regard to both sentence length and FKR level, a very slight convergence between the two publications occurs, where sentences become longer and reading difficulty becomes higher (more sophisticated) in the *Mirror*, with the reverse trend observed in the *Guardian*. The shifts seen in FKR are slight to the extent that the *Guardian*'s readability remains within the average 15- to 18-year-old difficulty level bracket, while the *Mirror* remains within the average 13- to 15-year-old difficulty level bracket. Due largely to an absence of any dramatic fluctuations, FKR level and word length trends resemble one another before and after 1998.

Quotes

Quoted speech has also been identified as an index of the more casual, familiar language characteristic of tabloid publications (Clark 2013). Indeed, quoted speech is initially more characteristic of the *Mirror* than of the *Guardian*; however, over time, the feature increases dramatically in both newspapers (Figure 3.10).

Both before and after the launch of online editions, a surge is seen in quoted speech, suggesting that the increase in quotes is not solely attributable to the emergence of online news platforms. For example, between 1985 and 1987, the use of quotes increases in both publications, suggesting that causal factors of tabloidization associated with the Wapping Revolution may have contributed to an increase in quoted speech.

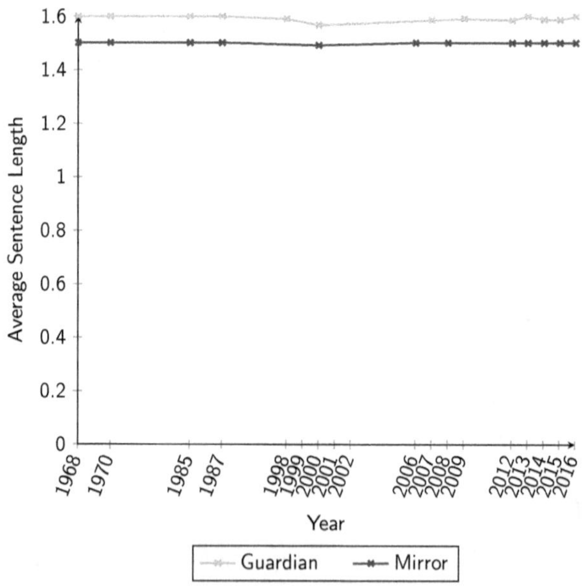

Figure 3.7 Word length

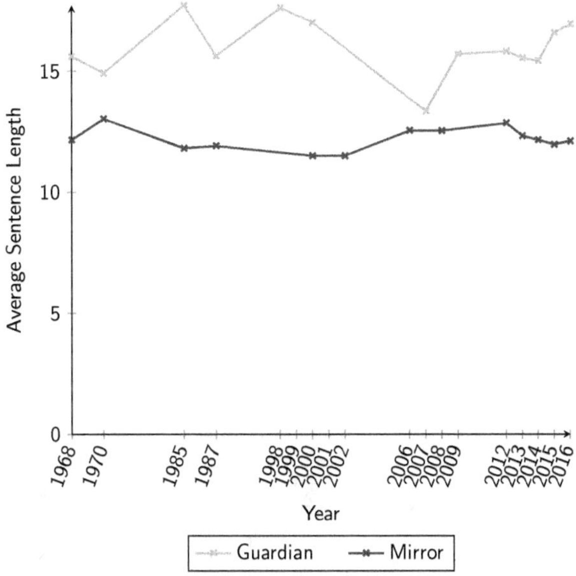

Figure 3.8 Sentence length

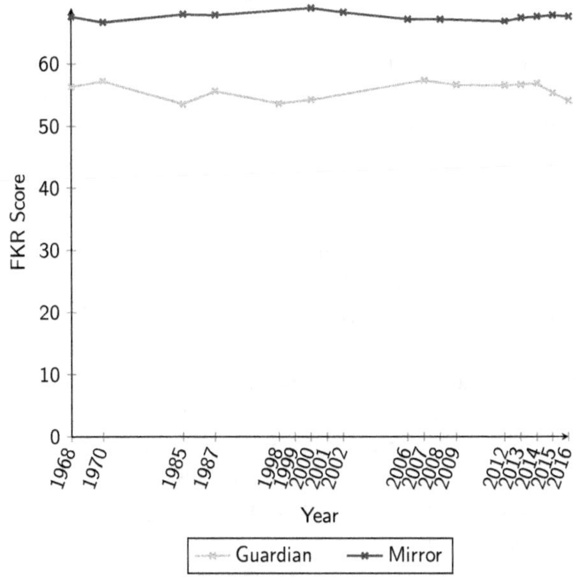

Figure 3.9 Flesch-Kincaid readability level

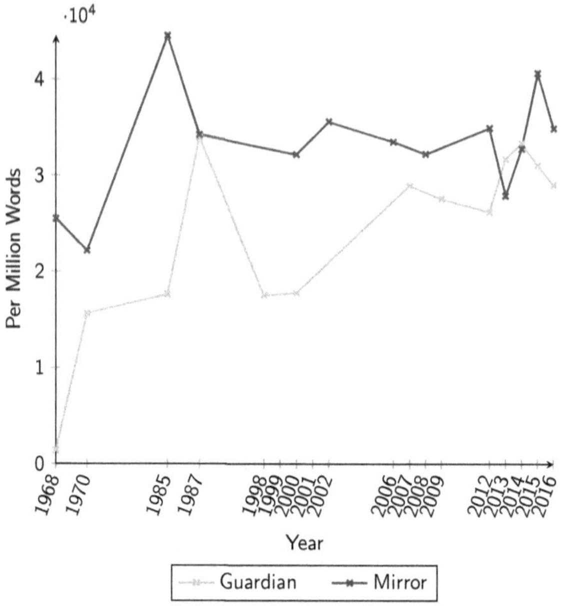

Figure 3.10 Quotes

The post-1998 trend seen in quotes, however, is markedly towards an increase in the use of quotes across publications. Between 2012 and 2014, encompassing the period of the emergence of Web 3.0, quotes become even more prevalent in *Guardian* than in the *Mirror*. Thus, possible causal agents associated with the ascendance of the Internet and its later developmental stages appear to link with a stronger augmentation in quoted speech.

Conclusions

This chapter's analysis of newspaper texts from a 48-year timespan which pre- and post-dates the ascendance of the Internet calls into question assumptions of the Internet's role as an agent of tabloidization. Contradicting popular claims, it shows that the degree of shifts in linguistic markers of journalistic values which might have been expected after 1998 largely do not occur. Only some of the linguistic proxies of tabloidization are found to have undergone major shifts in the wake of the Internet's mainstream ascendance; and in most cases, trends either resemble one another before and after the Internet's introduction, or a dynamic of tabloidization is seen to commence before the Internet era. Furthermore, the process of tabloidization that is identified takes the form of a dual-convergence between the two publication types, in which both tabloid and 'quality' newspapers are becoming more similar to one another.

Notable exceptions to the broader temporal patterns with relation to the ascendance of the Internet, however, are seen with the markers of personalization and quotes, which emerge as arenas of particular interest. Overall increases are seen in two of the three markers of personalization, as well as in quotes, in both the 'quality' and the tabloid publications; and while this trend begins before the rise of the Internet, increasing in the wake of the Wapping Revolution, a surge in these features occurs in particular between 2012 and 2016. Thus, the putative technological as well as the economic factors associated with both Wapping and with the Internet – namely, the ability to produce more content cheaply, increased competition between news organizations, a thinning out of editorial staff, and increased pressure on remaining staff – may be regarded as agents associated with tabloidization. Furthermore, the more dramatic increases in tabloid features seen in the latter part of the Internet era, or during the Web 3.0 period, corroborate the role of a growing emphasis on speed and interactivity, connecting with widespread use of editorial analytics and related shifts in gatekeeping dynamics, as forces associated with an ascendance of tabloid values. These journalistic shifts seen in the post-2012 years are likely to link with the increasingly widespread use and entrenchment of Web 2.0 and Web 3.0 technologies, through which interactivity and user-generated data functions have been dramatically enhanced.

In view of the similar shifts seen across the newspapers, the role of broader, cultural factors also merits consideration. The rising salience of popular culture, and the introduction of a new resource, the Internet, through which it may further flourish, emerges as an agent of interest. The increased prominence of quotes in particular, where the voice of more people, and of a broader cross-section of people, may be gaining representation, suggests not only shifts in, and an increase in, the salience of popular culture, but also indicates the emergence of a postmodern Habermasian public sphere, commencing in the 1980s. From this era onwards, it is possible that voices previously marginalized by the traditional Habermasian public sphere have been empowered, a development which has occurred alongside an ostensible crisis concerning traditional notions of 'truth' and 'facts.' The results reported here can be seen as contributing to scholarship both within and external to journalism studies, asserting the emergence of a postmodern context aligning with the rise of global corporations and new media technologies, particularly those facilitating greater emphasis on speed and interactivity.

These shifts have important implications for the public service function of journalism. The dual-convergence seen in personalization, markers of 'information-orientation,' and quotes not only points to an increase in a potentially emancipating reconfiguration of journalistic values, but specifically to an elevation in the values at play in tabloids which may serve to more meaningfully inform citizens. It is also important to note the importance of future research and data triangulation, such as through content analysis, to examine shifts and/or continuity in the proportional coverage of certain types of article topics, for example, in 'hard' news versus 'soft' news coverage. A substantial increase in entertainment or sports reporting, for instance, would almost certainly modify the findings discussed in this chapter. Currently such a content analysis is being conducted in the author's doctoral thesis, where additional tabloid and 'quality' British newspapers, as well as a digital-native news outlet, are also being subject to examination.

Notes

1 Web 2.0 has been understood as the second generation of the Web's development, and is marked by its interactive elements, contrasting the read-only, or static, basis of Web 1.0 (Allen 2012; Choudhury 2014).
2 Web 3.0 has been associated with the rise of the Semantic Web and a broader emphasis on machine-facilitated learning to enhance online experiences (Choudhury 2014).
3 Articles from the *Guardian* were downloaded from the *NexisUK* and the *Guardian Digital Archive*, and *Mirror* articles were extracted from *UKPressOnline*.
4 Transcription was enabled thanks to funding from the ESRC.

Bibliography

Allen, Matthew. 2012. "What was Web 2.0? Versions as the Dominant Mode of Internet History." *New Media & Society* 15 (2): 260–275..

Bas, Ozen, and Grabe, Maria Elizabeth. 2015. "Emotion-Provoking Personalization of News: Informing Citizens and Closing the Knowledge Gap?" *Communication Research* 42 (2): 159–185..

Bednarek, Monika, and Caple, Helen. 2012. "'Value-Added': Language, image and news values." *Discourse, Context & Media* 1: 103–113..

Bennett, Lance W. 2012. *News: The Politics of Illusion*. 9th ed. Glenview, Illinois: Pearson.

Biber, Douglas. 1988. *Variation Across Speech and Writing*. Cambridge: Cambridge University Press.

Biber, Douglas, and Edward Finnegan. 1989. "Drift and the Evolution of English Style: A History of Three Genres." *Language* 65 (3): 487–517.

Biber, Douglas, and Edward Finegan. 2014. "Diachronic Relations among Speech-based and Written Registers in English." In *Variation in English: Multi-Dimensional Studies*. Abingdon: Routledge, 66–83.

Bingham, Adrian, and Conboy, Martin. 2015. *Tabloid Century: The Popular Press in Britain, 1896 to the present*. Oxford: Peter Lang.

Bird, S. Elizabeth. 2009. "Tabloidization": What is it, and Does it Really Matter?" In *The Changing Faces of Journalism: Tabloidization, Technology and Truthiness*, edited by Barbie Zelizer, 40–50. Abingdon: Routledge.

Boczkowski, Pablo J. 2004. "The Processes of Adopting Multimedia and Interactivity in Three Online Newsrooms." *Journal of Communication* 54 (2): 197–213.

Boykoff, Maxwell T., and Boykoff, Jules M. 2004. "Balance as Bias: Global Warming and the U.S. Prestige Press." *Global Environmental Change* 14 (2): 125–136.

Bromley, Michael. 1998. "The 'tabloiding' of Britain: 'Quality' newspapers in the 1990s." In *Sex, Lies and Democracy*, edited by Michael Bromley and Hugh Stephenson, 25–38. London: Longman.

Chalaby, Jean. 1996. "Journalism as an Anglo-American Invention: A Comparison of the Development of French and Anglo-American Journalism, 1830–1920s." *European Journal of Communication* 11 (3): 303–326.

Choudhury, Nupur. 2014. "World Wide Web and its Journey from Web 1.0 to Web 4.0." *International Journal of Computer Science and Information Technologies* 5 (6): 8096–8100.

Clark, Caroline. 2013. "It's always the same old news! A diachronic analysis of shifting newspaper language style, 1993–2005." In *Variation and Change in Spoken and Written Discourse*, edited by Julia Bamford, Silvia C. Cavalieri, and Giuliana D. Diani, 269–282. Amsterdam: John Benjamins Publishing Company.

Conboy, Martin. 2002. *The Press and Popular Culture*. London: Sage.

Conboy, Martin. 2004. *Journalism: A Critical History*. London: Sage.

Conboy, Martin. 2006. *Tabloid Britain: Constructing a Community through Language*. London: Routledge.

Conboy, Martin. 2011. *Journalism in Britain: a Historical Introduction*. London: Sage.

Conboy, Martin, and Steel, John. 2010. "From 'We' to 'Me': The changing construction of popular tabloid journalism." *Journalism Studies*. 11 (4): 500–510.

Curran, James, and Seaton, Jean. 2003. *Power without Responsibility: The Press, broadcasting, and new media in Britain*. 6th ed. London: Routledge.

Deuze, Mark. 2005. "What is Journalism? Professional identity and ideology of journalists reconsidered." *Journalism* 6 (4): 442–464.

Esser, Frank. 1999. "'Tabloidization' of News: A Comparative Analysis of Anglo-American and German Press Journalism." *European Journal of Communication* 14 (3): 291–394.

Fiske, John. 1989. *Reading the Popular*. London: Routledge.

Franklin, Bob. 1997. *Newszak and News Media*. London: Arnold.

Galtung, Johan, and Ruge, Mari Holmboe. 1965. " The Structure of Foreign News: The Presentation of the Congo, Cuba and Cyprus Crises in Four Norwegian Newspapers." *Journal of Peace Research* 2 (1): 64–91."

Hampton, Mark. 2008. "The "objectivity" ideal and its limitations in 20th century British journalism." *Journalism Studies* 9 (4): 477–493.

Hermida, Alfred. 2010. "Twittering the News: the emergence of ambient journalism." *Journalism Practice* 4 (3): 297–308.

Holton, Avery E. and Molyneux, Logan. 2017. "Identity Lost? The personal impact of brand journalism." *Journalism* 18 (2): 195–210.

Hundt, Marianne, and Mair, Christian. 1999. "'Agile' and 'Upright' Genres: The Corpus-based Approach to Language Change in Process." *International Journal of Corpus Linguistics* 4 (2): 221–242.

Lacy, Stephen, Riffe, Daniel, Stoddard, Staci, Martin, Hugh, and Chang, Kuang-Kuo. 2001. "Sample Size for Newspaper Content Analysis in Multi-Year Studies." *Journalism & Mass Communications Quarterly* 78 (4): 836–845.

Lefkowitz, Julia. 2016. "'Tabloidization' or Dual-Convergence: Quoted Speech in Tabloid and 'Quality' British Newspapers, 1970–2010." *Journalism Studies* 19 (3): 1–23.

Lewis, Seth C., Kaufhold, Kelly, and Lasora, Dominic L. 2010. "Thinking about Citizen Journalism: The philosophical and practical challenges of user-generated content for community newspapers." *Journalism Practice* 4 (2): 163–179.

Macdonald, Myra. 2000. "Rethinking Personalization." In *Tabloid Tales: Global Debates over Media Standards*, edited by Colin Sparks and John Tulloch. Lanham, Maryland: Rowman & Littlefield Publishers, Inc.

Magin, Melanie. 2017. "Attention Please! Structural influence on campaign coverage in German and Austrian Newspapers (1949–2009)." *Journalism* 20 (12): 1704–1724.

Magin, Melanie, and Stark, Birgit. 2014. "Explaining National Differences of Tabloidisation Between Germany and Austria." *Journalism Studies* 16 (4): 1–17.

McLachlan, Shelley, and Golding, Peter. 2000. "Tabloidization in the British Press: A Quantitative Investigation into Changes in British Newspapers, 1952–1997." In *Tabloid Tales: Global Debates Over Media Standards*, edited by Colin Sparks and John Tulloch, 75–89. Lanham, Maryland: Rowman & Littlefield Publishers, Inc.

Örnebring, Henrik. 2010. "Technology and journalism-as-labour: Historical perspectives." *Journalism* 11 (1): 57–74.

Örnebring, Henrik, and Jönsson, Anna Maria. 2007. "Tabloid journalism and the public sphere: a historical perspective on tabloid journalism." *Journalism Studies*. 5 (3): 283–295.

O'Sullivan, John, and Heinonen, Ari. 2008. "Old Values, New Media: Journalism role perceptions in a changing world." *Journalism Practice* 2 (3): 357–371.

Petre, Caitlin. 2015. "The Traffic Factories: Metrics at Chartbeat, Gawker Media, and The New York Times." New York: The Tow Center for Digital Journalism. https://www.cjr.org/tow_center_reports/the_traffic_factories_metrics_at_chartbeat_gawker_media_and_the_new_york_times.php.

Picard, Robert G. 1998. "Media Concentration, Economics and Regulation." In *The Politics of News*, edited by Doris Graber, Dennis M. McQuail, and Pippa N. Noris, 193–217. Washington, DC.: Congressional Quarterly Press.

Picard, Robert G., and van Weezel, Aldo. 2008. "Capital and Control: Consequences of Different Forms of Newspaper Ownership." *The International Journal on Media Management* 10 (1): 22–31.

Picard, Robert G. 2014. "Twilight or the New Dawn of Journalism? Evidence from the changing news ecosystem." *Journalism Studies* 15 (5): 500–510.

Quirk, Randolph, Greenbaum, Sidney, Leech, Geoffrey, and Svartvik, Jan. 1985. *A Comprehensive grammar of the English Language*. London: Longman.

Rooney, Dick. 2000. "*Thirty Years of Competition in the British Tabloid Press: The Tabloid Tales: Global Debates over Media Standards*, edited by Colin Sparks and John Tulloch, 91–109. Lanham, Maryland: Rowman & Littlefield Publishers, Inc.

Rusbridger, Alan. 2018. *Breaking News: The Remaking of Journalism and Why It Matters Now*. Edinburgh: Canongate Books.

Sambrook, Richard. 2012. "Delivering Trust: Impartiality and Objectivity in the Digital Age." Report. Oxford: Reuters Institute for the Study of Journalism.

Schudson, Michael. 1978. *Discovering the News: A Social History of American Newspapers*. United States: Basic Books, Inc.

Seymour-Ure, Colin. 1991. *The British Press and Broadcasting Since 1945*. New York: Basil Blackwell, Inc.

Shoemaker, Pamela J., Eichholz, Martin, Kim, Eunyi, and Wrigley, Brenda. 2001. "Individual and Routine Forces in Gatekeeping." *Journalism & Mass Communications Quarterly* 78 (2): 233–246.

Shoemaker, Pamela J., Vos, Tim, and Reese, Stephen D. (2008) "Journalists as gatekeepers." In *Handbook of Journalism Studies*, edited by K Wahl-Jorgensen and T Hanitzsch, 73–87. New York: Routledge.

Singer, Jane B. 2010. "Quality Control: Perceived effects of user-generated content on newsroom norms, values and routines." *Journalism Practice* 4 (2): 127–142.

Singer, Jane B., and Ashman, Ian. 2009. "'Comment Is Free but Facts Are Sacred': User-generated Content and Ethical Constructs in the Guardian." *Journal of Mass Media Ethics* 24 (1): 3–21.

Skovsgaard, Morten. 2014. "A tabloid mind? Professional values and organizational pressures as explanations of tabloid journalism." *Media, Culture & Society* 36 (2): 200–218.

Sparks, Colin. 1998. Introduction to Special Issue. *Javnost – The Public: Journal of the European Institute for Communication and Culture* 5 (3) 5–10.

Sparks, Colin. 2000. "The Panic Over Tabloid News." In *Tabloid Tales: Global Debates over Media Standards*, edited by Colin Sparks and John Tulloch, 1–40. Maryland: Rowman & Littlefield Publishers, Inc.

Streckfuss, Richard. 1990. "Objectivity in Journalism: A Search and a Reassessment." *Journalism & Mass Communication Quarterly* 67 (4): 973–982.

Tandoc, Edson C.Jr. 2014. "Journalism is twerking? How web analytics is changing the process of gatekeeping." *New Media & Society* 16 (4): 559–557.

Tandoc, Edson C.Jr., Lim, Zheng Wei, and Ling, Richard. 2017. "Defining 'Fake News:' A typology of scholarly definitions. *Digital Journalism* 6 (2): 137–153.

Tuchman, Gaye. 1972. "Objectivity as Strategic Ritual: An examination of Newsmen's Notions of Objectivity." *American Journal of Sociology* 77 (4): 660–679.

Turner, Graeme. 1999. "Tabloidization, journalism and the possibility of critique." *International Journal of Cultural Studies* 2 (1): 59–76. https://doi.org/10.1177/136787799900200104.

Umbricht, Andrea, and Esser, Frank. (2016). "The Push to Popularize Politics: Understanding the Audience-Friendly Packaging of Political News in Six Media Systems since the 1960s." *Journalism Studies*, 17 (1): 100–121.

Uribe, Rodrigo, and Gunter, Barrie. 2004. "A Research Note: The Tabloidization of British Tabloids." *European Journal of Communication* 19 (3): 387–402.

Van Aerden, Karen, Moors, Guy, Levecque, Katia, and Vanroelen, Christophe. 2015. "The relationship between employment quality and work-related well-being in the European Labor Force." *The Journal of Vocational Behavior* 86: 66–76.

Vis, Farida. 2013. "Twitter as a reporting tool for breaking news: Journalists tweeting the 2011 UK riots." *Digital Journalism* (1): 27–47.

Wang, Tai-Li. 2012. Presentation and impact of market-driven journalism on sensationalism in global TV news. *International Communication Gazette* 74 (8): 711–727.

Westin, Ingrid. 2001. *Language Change in English Newspaper Editorials.* Amsterdam: Rodopi.

Westin, Ingrid, and Geisler, Christer. 2002. "A multi-dimensional study of diachronic variation in British newspaper editorials. " *ICAME Journal* 26: 133–152.

Whitley, Zoe. 2011. "Dressing Viciously: Hip-Hop Music, Fashion and Cultural Crossover." In *Postmodernism: Style and Subversion, 1970–1990*, edited by Glenn Adamson and Jane Pavitt, 186–191. London: V&A Publishing.

Witschge, Tamara, and Nygren, Gunnar. 2009. "Journalism: A Profession Under Pressure?" *Journal of Media Business Studies* 6 (1): 37–59.

4 Is Facebook driving tabloidization?

A cross-channel comparison of two German newspapers

Melanie Magin, Miriam Steiner, Andrea Häuptli, Birgit Stark and Linards Udris

Introduction

Tabloidization describes a process of convergence. Other media types, particularly quality media, are increasingly adopting characteristics of tabloid journalism as a result of increased competition in and commercialization of the news media market (Esser 1999). This theoretical concept had been developed against that growing commercialization and increasing role of tabloid newspapers in the analogue age. Currently, media markets all over the world are experiencing even stronger commercialization due to the advancing competition from the Internet and social media. In the recent past, these have become very important, both as news sources (Newman et al. 2019) and for advertising (Croteau and Hoynes 2019, 82). As a result, newspapers must compete more fiercely than ever for the attention of users and advertisers. In order to still reach their audiences, they must run both "on-site" channels such as their own websites or apps, as well as "off-site" channels provided by digital intermediaries such as Facebook pages or accounts on Twitter or Instagram (Bell and Owen 2017; Rashidian et al. 2019). These developments have led to concerns about how far they affect newspapers' democratic function to inform the public comprehensively (Steiner 2016; van Dijck and Poell 2015).

It has been assumed that social media content is particularly tabloid-like (Bastos 2017; Gran 2015; Karlsson and Clerwall 2013). Accordingly, tabloids should be even more tabloid-like online and particularly on social media compared to their printed version. However, empirical studies verifying these assumptions are so far scarce (for an exception see Lischka and Werning [2017]). This chapter contributes to closing this research gap by answering the following research question: *How far do newspaper type and distribution channel influence the degree of tabloidization of political coverage in different German newspapers?* We answer it by comparing two German newspapers of different types, the tabloid *BILD* and the quality paper *Frankfurter Allgemeine Zeitung* (*FAZ*), on three different distribution channels: their print versions, websites, and Facebook pages, since Facebook represents the most important social media platform in Germany (Newman et al. 2019).

Tabloidization as a bipolar continuum

Even though studies on tabloidization have a long tradition in political communication research, we still lack conceptual clarity and even a consistent definition of the term (Otto, Glogger, and Boukes 2017). There is consensus that tabloidization describes the adoption of characteristics of tabloid journalism[1] by other media types, but what exactly these characteristics are is the controversial issue. Tabloid journalism has often been associated with a broad range of characteristics, such as a focus on "soft news", mostly understood as specific topics such as human interest, sports, scandals, crime, and natural disasters, together with sensationalism, scandalization, emotionality, negativity, personalization, visualization, eye-catching headlines, colourful pictures, and a narrative style of reporting (Bird 2009; Klein 1998; Reinemann et al. 2012; Sparks 2000). Moreover, there is a common tendency to consider tabloids the opposite of quality newspapers (Landmeier and Daschmann 2011). These are, however, very imprecise ways of defining tabloids. Neither tabloids nor quality newspapers are uniform types in themselves but differ both cross-nationally and even within countries (Magin 2020). Both types' degree of tabloidization can both increase and decrease over time in reaction to changing framework conditions (Lefkowitz 2018). Thus, all newspaper types and outlets can and will show tabloid-like characteristics to a certain degree.

Reinemann et al. (2012) therefore suggest conceptualizing tabloidization[2] as a continuum. Their model comprises three bipolar, continuous dimensions which allow for measuring the degree of tabloidization of all kinds of news media by means of content analysis: (1) The poles of the *topic dimension* are marked by politically relevant vs. irrelevant issues. (2) The *focus dimension* ranges (a) from social to individual relevance, and (b) from thematic to episodic framing. (3) The *style dimension* reaches (a) from unemotional to emotional reporting, and (b) from impersonal to personal reporting style. According to this model, the more tabloid-like a news medium is, (1) the less politically relevant its news coverage is, (2) the more it focuses on personal, private, and individual events and examples, and (3) the more strongly it emphasizes emotions and journalists' personal views. In order to determine the overall degree of news media's tabloidization, the authors recommend combining the three dimensions into a simple additive index. Magin and Stark (2015) empirically confirm these three dimensions for German and Austrian newspapers, and show that a newspaper's degree of tabloidization is influenced by the structural conditions under which it is produced. If our study wants to explain the influence of newspaper type and distribution channel on tabloidization, we must thus take the conditions of media production into account.

How business models shape newspaper content

In principle, all newspapers operate in two interwoven markets: the audience market and the advertising market. The so-called advertising-circulation spiral describes ideal-typically how both markets are related: the larger the audience, the higher the advertising revenues – respectively, the smaller the audience, the lower the advertising revenues. The spiraling process is started up if advertising revenues start to increase or decrease. Increasing advertising revenues will be used as resources to increase an outlet's attractiveness for the readers, the audience will grow, even more advertising revenues will be generated, and so on. The other way around, declining advertising revenues will reduce attractiveness for the readers and lead to decreasing audiences and advertising revenues (Björkroth and Grönlund 2014).

However, various newspaper types differ in their dependence on large audiences. For example, quality papers are predominantly sold by subscription in Germany and have more reliable sales revenues available, combined with advertising revenues. Their target group is small (the economically strong, societal elites), expects serious, in-depth quality journalism, and is particularly attractive for financially strong advertisers (Magin 2020). By contrast, most tabloids are predominantly sold on the street, at kiosks and other public places, rather than by subscription (Leidenberger 2013, 80) and therefore must woo as many readers as possible day after day. As a consequence, they require attention-catching strategies, which explains the use of the tabloid-like characteristics described above (Magin 2019). A newspaper's degree of tabloidization is thus strongly related to its degree of commercialization (Karlsson 2016) and its orientation towards the largest possible audience (Magin 2019). In line with these considerations, previous research shows clear differences in the degree of tabloidization between quality and tabloid newspapers (Djupsund and Carlson 1998; Esser 1999; Magin and Stark 2015). This leads to our first hypothesis:

H1: The tabloid BILD is more tabloid-like than the quality paper FAZ.

Internet and social media as potential drivers of tabloidization

In principle, the relationship between type of financing and type of content is nothing new (Sparks 2000, 4). In the last two decades, however, news production has radically changed; the advent of the web has significantly intensified the commercialization of the media market (Lund, Raeymaeckers, and Trappel 2011; Palau-Sampio 2016). The migration of advertising revenues to digital media (Croteau and Hoynes 2019) and the competition with free content online, coupled with users' low willingness to pay for content (Newman et al. 2019), have increased the competitive pressures on news media (Karlsson 2016). Online metrics have made the measurement of number, attention, and interests of the users faster and more precise than ever before (Karlsson and Clerwall 2013; Palau-Sampio 2016) by means of clicks, page impressions, 'likes', 'shares', visit duration, and so forth. They determine which content generates the highest advertising revenues, generally those with the most "traffic" (Blom and Hansen 2015). High traffic, in turn, can often be generated most effectively through entertaining, emotional, sensational, shocking visual content that is, to put it simply, tabloid-like. Thus, recipients' preference for tabloid-like content is assumed to drive tabloidization of web content. One extreme form and consequence of this is clickbait (Bastos 2017; Blom and Hansen 2015). These considerations lead to our second hypothesis:

H2: Both BILD and FAZ are more tabloid-like on their websites than in their printed versions.

Most recently, social media platforms such as Facebook have further intensified the competitive pressure on newspapers. If they are to survive, newspapers must be present on social media and provide their content in a way that meets the attention criteria there (Steiner, Magin, and Stark 2019). These criteria confront newspapers with new challenges. On newspapers' own websites, they can still decide for themselves how far they select and present content in line with their journalistic standards, despite increasing commercialization pressures. On social media, however, they must adapt to the rules of providers for whom journalistic standards have no significance at all. Indeed, the selection logic of social media (Jürgens and Stark 2017) shows a strong bias towards the popular. This selection logic encourages content, raising the greatest possible attention in the form of user reactions, which is a commonality with tabloids. The mechanism behind this pattern is that social media's business model is to collect as much data about their users as possible and use it to personalize advertisements. The more reactions content evokes, the more data the platforms can select, leading to a Matthew effect: social media platforms prefer content that is already popular, and direct the attention of even more users to it (Stark and Magin 2019). The promise of reaching certain precise target groups makes social media very attractive for advertisers. This is one reason why social media's advertising revenues are growing steadily at the expense of news media and particularly print newspapers (Cornia, Sehl, and Nielsen 2016; Croteau and Hoynes 2019). This problem is aggravated by the fact that the way content is presented on social media makes it extremely difficult for users to remember which brand they received information from (Kalogeropoulos, Fletcher, and Nielsen 2019), further reducing newspapers' brand value on the advertising market. The newspapers thus need to attract the attention of as many users as possible on social media, facilitating a gateway to tabloidization (Steiner 2016). Although research in this field is still scarce, the few existing studies indicate that newspapers indeed use tabloidization as a strategy to adapt to a social media logic (Klinger and Svensson 2015) and thereby increase their reach. In their study on regional newspapers, Lischka and Werning (2017) show that journalists' selection of topics is influenced by social media algorithms and user interactions. Human interest news on Facebook is used to increase its reach, and social media editors accentuate tabloid style elements such as emotions and subjective expressions (Lischka 2018; Welbers and Opgenhaffen 2019). The effects of this can also be seen in the content. In a comparison between Swiss newspapers on their websites and Facebook pages, Häuptli and Hauser (2017) show the journalistic quality is almost consistently poorer on Facebook, with the only exception being the quality newspaper *Neue Zürcher Zeitung*. These considerations lead to our third hypothesis:

H3: Both BILD and FAZ are more tabloid-like on their Facebook pages than on their websites.

Method

To test our hypotheses, we conducted a quantitative content analysis of news coverage about domestic politics[3] within two German newspapers, the tabloid *BILD* and the quality newspaper *FAZ*, in their printed versions, on their websites, and on their Facebook pages.

The digital strategies of BILD *and* FAZ

An appropriate interpretation of our results requires some contextual information on the German newspaper market and the newspapers under investigation. Belonging to the democratic corporatist media systems (Hallin and Mancini 2004) and the newspaper-centric countries (Norris 2003), newspapers are still pivotal in Germany, even though digital and social media have become important news sources, especially for younger age groups (Newman et al. 2019). While internet penetration is 96 per cent, only 34 per cent of the population use social media for news (Hölig and Hasebrink 2019). The decentralized newspaper market is characterized by a broad range of regional newspapers, a relatively strong segment of five national quality newspapers representing the political spectrum, with *FAZ* as third largest German newspaper being one of them, and *BILD* as the only national tabloid and by far the largest German newspaper in terms of circulation. Table 4.1 compares both newspapers' distribution on all three channels under investigation, and illustrates the smaller audience and elite status of *FAZ* when compared to the size of the German population of more than 82 million. Moreover, it is apparent how important the "on-site channels" have become for the newspapers, all the more as both have been facing declining reader numbers for their printed versions during the last few years (Schröder 2019).

When it comes to the newspapers' digital strategies, they show both similarities and differences. Both have opted for paywalls on their websites and are present on Facebook with several pages: one main page each and several others dedicated

Table 4.1 Newspaper users in numbers

	FAZ	*BILD*
Offline: Copies sold[1]	190,000	1,280,000
Online: Visits[2]	67,362,590	508,086,275
Facebook: Number of likes of main Facebook page[3]	547,192	2,518,425

[1] Data from the German Audit Bureau of Circulation (IVW), 3rd quarter 2019 (Schröder, 2019).
[2] Data from the German Audit Bureau of Circulation (IVW), January 2020.
[3] Status: March 5, 2020

to special interests (e.g., *FAZ*: travel, economy, science) and niche topics (e.g., *BILD*: wrestling, mystery) with the aim of being as relevant for every individual user as possible (Rickmann, Wais, & Goesche 2016; Schütz 2017). Beyond these similarities, their strategies differ. *FAZ* tries to transfer the brand as a flagship of elite journalism online, in order to strengthen and make use of its high reputation both on the website (Lobigs and Neuberger 2018) and on Facebook (Schütz 2017). This strategy makes sense in light of Häuptli and Hauser's (2017) finding that the Swiss quality newspaper, *Neue Zürcher Zeitung*, generates user reactions on Facebook with articles of high quality, while Swiss tabloids get more user reactions to articles of low quality. In contrast to *FAZ, BILD* has opted for a mixed strategy, combining the core news brand with classified media (e.g., stepstone.de) and marketing media (e.g., idealo.de) (Lobigs and Neuberger 2018). On Facebook, *BILD* focuses strongly on community building through a broad range of Facebook groups (Lux 2019).

Sample and collection of material

Newspaper articles were collected during two periods totalling eight weeks in 2018: four weeks from the end of May to the beginning of July, and four weeks from mid-September to the end of October. Both periods included weeks when parliament was in session and when it was not. No national elections were held during the investigation periods. Relevant articles in the printed versions and on the newspaper websites were identified in a three-step process. First, we identified potentially relevant articles among all articles published during the period of investigation by means of a technical pre-filtering, using a search string including potentially relevant terms.[4] Second, three human coders decided on the actual relevance of the identified articles based on their heading and first paragraph. Third, we drew a random sample from these relevant articles. Here, each news outlet and channel was treated separately. For instance, random sampling for the printed version of *BILD* was done separately from the random sampling of both the printed version of *FAZ* and the website of *BILD*.

The relevant Facebook posts were stored by means of the tool Facepager (Jünger and Keyling 2019) which can access the posts' IDs via an API interface. The IDs enabled us to access the Facebook posts in the browser. In order to minimize loss of data, we retrieved the IDs at least every day during the period under investigation. We analyzed the articles linked by the Facebook posts, which ensures the best possible comparability with the two other distribution channels. Video reports embedded in the Facebook post were also coded, while Facebook posts not including or linking to any article were excluded from the sample. Since Facepager cannot output the text of the linked article, however, the technical pre-filtering described above was impossible. Therefore, human coders decided on the relevance of all Facebook posts based on the linked articles or the beginnings of the videos. All relevant Facebook posts were coded. Our final sample consists of 2,441 articles (*FAZ* offline: n=619, *FAZ* online: n=491, *FAZ* Facebook: n=480, *BILD* offline: n=264, *BILD* online: n=441, *BILD* Facebook: n=146).

Measurement and reliability

With reference to Reinemann et al. (2012), our operationalization comprises all three dimensions of tabloidization. On the *topic dimension*, we coded the main topic of the article. We contrast substantive policy areas (not tabloid-like) with reports on politicians (tabloid-like) (see also Magin 2019) as well as articles focusing on politicians in their political role (e.g., the political career of German Chancellor Angela Merkel; not tabloid-like) with articles focusing on politicians as private individuals (e.g., the German chancellor's skiing accident; tabloid-like).

The *focus dimension* is explored by means of two indicators. The first one refers to the difference between *episodic* and *thematic framing* (Reinemann et al. 2012; Seethaler 2015) and is measured with four variables, combined into one indicator. While episodic framing (tabloid-like) focuses solely on the event itself, thematic framing (not tabloid-like) tends to explain the event by means of (a) reasons or causes, (b) consequences and possible solutions, (c) evaluations by at least two actors, and (d) contextualizing information (e.g., reference to earlier, similar events or to the overall situation). Each of these aspects could be coded as not present at all (0), present at least to a small extent (1), or present to a significant extent (2). Based on these four values, we calculated an additive index ranging from 0 (none of these aspects mentioned, pure episodical framing; tabloid-like) to 8 (all aspects present to a significant extent, strong thematic framing; not tabloid-like). The higher the index value, the less tabloid-like an article is on the focus dimension. The second indicator on the focus dimension provides information about whether an article is *framed publicly* (articles referencing to the macro-level; e.g., society as a whole or parts thereof) or the meso-level (e.g., parties, associations, organized interest groups; not tabloid-like) *or personally* (articles referencing to the micro-level; e.g., politicians in their professional or private role, citizens; tabloid-like). Only one level (macro, meso, micro) per article could be coded.

The *style* dimension consists of two indicators. *Emotional reporting* explores how emotional an article's language is in general (e.g., depiction of emotions, dramatic and exaggerated language, emotional metaphors) by use of a 5-point-scale ranging from 1 (completely unemotional/not tabloid-like) to 5 (very emotional/tabloid-like). *Personal reporting* measures how far the journalists include their own opinions in an article on a 5-point-scale ranging from 1 (no inclusion of journalists' personal opinions/not tabloid-like) to 5 (strong inclusion of journalists' personal opinions/tabloid-like).[5]

In the last step of our analysis, we combined the three dimensions into a standardized *overall index* which does justice to the complexity of tabloidization and allows its prevalence to be measured on a continuum (Reinemann et al. 2012). Aiming at comparability between the dimensions and standardized total mean values for all newspapers and distribution channels, each single indicator described above is standardized to a value range from 0 (lowest possible degree of tabloidization) to 1 (highest possible degree of tabloidization) and calculated as a standardized index which indicates the degree of tabloidization across all dimensions. For both the focus and the style dimension, which were measured by two indicators each, we calculated the arithmetic mean between the two respective indicators (Table 4.2).

For the identification of relevant articles, the percentage of agreement (based on 283 articles from both newspapers and all three distribution channels) was satisfactory (from 77 to 95 per cent). The reliability of the manually coded variables was tested using Brennan-Prediger's kappa, which is chance-corrected and more robust than Krippendorff's alpha regarding variables with a skewed distribution (Quarfoot and Levine 2016). Reliability coefficients were good for all variables (topic: .61; societal level: .69; thematic vs. episodic framing: .75; emotional language: .77; personal reporting style: .81).

Results

To test our hypotheses, we first compared all media outlets on the three dimensions of tabloidization and the different distribution channels in detail before presenting the results of the tabloidization index.

Dimensions of tabloidization

The *topic dimension* differentiates between political hard news (i.e. policy) and soft news (i.e. coverage about politicians, and in particular about the private life

Table 4.2 Calculation of tabloidization index

Indicator	*Original values*	*Calculation of index values (0–1)*
Sub-index topic dimension		
Articles on politicians (both in political and private role)[1]	Share (0–100%)	Share of coverage on politicians / 100
Sub-index focus dimension		
Personal framing	Share (0–100%)	Share of personal framing / 100
Episodic framing	9-point scale (0–8)	Scale value / 8
Focus dimension (total)		(Personal framing + episodic framing) / 2
Sub-index style dimension		
Emotional reporting	5-point scale (0–4)	Scale value / 4
Personal reporting	5-point scale (0–4)	Scale value / 4
Style dimension (total)		(Emotional reporting + personal reporting) / 2
Overall index		
Additive index	Index values for the three dimensions	(Topic dimension + focus dimension (total) + style dimension (total)) / 3

[1] In order to reduce complexity and since coverage on politicians in their private role is negligible, we add the proportion of articles on politicians in political and private roles.

of politicians). Results show an overall high proportion of hard news in line with previous research (Magin 2019), which indicates an overall low degree of tabloidization (Table 4.3). However, comparisons among news outlets show that politics is being focused upon differently. The proportion of hard news is clearly higher in the quality newspaper *FAZ* than in the tabloid *BILD*, with the difference being strongest offline and smallest on Facebook. This is due to the fact that *BILD*'s proportion of hard news online and on Facebook is higher than offline, while the proportion of *FAZ*'s hard news is highest offline and lowest on Facebook. When it comes to coverage of politicians, all outlets publish very few articles on politicians in their private role as an extreme form of tabloid-like, relatively soft news. However, articles of that kind appear far more frequently in *BILD*, particularly offline and on the newspaper's website.

With regard to the *focus dimension*, we first explored how episodically or thematically framed the articles in each outlet are. The lower the mean values in Table 4.4, the stronger the episodic framing of articles and the higher the degree of tabloidization. Overall, the results indicate a moderate degree of tabloidization which is, however, at a significantly lower degree for *FAZ* than for *BILD* across all channels. Particularly offline, *BILD* frames its articles more as episodic rather than thematic. Less than five per cent of these articles have a value of 6 or above, compared to almost one quarter of the *FAZ* articles offline. Surprisingly, BILD online is significantly less tabloidized than *BILD* offline.[6]

The second indicator on the focus dimension refers to the question which proportion of articles displays a public or a personal frame, the latter indicating a higher degree of tabloidization. Table 4.5 shows that the vast majority of articles focus on public affairs, indicating an overall rather low degree of tabloidization,

Table 4.3 Share of topics

Share of topics (in %)	*FAZ offline (n=619)*	*FAZ website (n=491)*	*FAZ@ Facebook (n=480)*	*BILD offline (n=264)*	*BILD website (n=441)*	*BILD@ Facebook (n=146)*	*Total (n=2,441)*
Policy	94.3	91.6	89.6	85.2	85.7	87.7	89.9
Politician (political role)	5.5	8.1	9.8	12.1	11.8	11.6	9.1
Politician (private role)	0.2	0.2	0.6	2.7	2.5	0.7	1.0

χ^2 (10)=45.67; p=0.00; V=0.97

Table 4.4 Episodic vs. thematic framing

Mean values[1]	*FAZ offline (A) (n=619)*	*FAZ website (B) (n=491)*	*FAZ@ Facebook (C) (n=480)*	*BILD offline (D) (n=264)*	*BILD website (E) (n=441)*	*BILD@ Facebook (F) (n=146)*	*Total (n=2,441)*
Thematic framing	3.91^{D,E,F}	3.86 ^{D,E,F}	4.17 ^{D,E,F}	2.39	3.31 ^{D,F}	2.71	3.60

[1]Mean values range from 0 (pure episodic framing/tabloid-like) to 8 (strong thematic framing/not tabloid-like).
^{Aa} The letters behind the values indicate from which other values the respective value differs significantly (lower case letters: $p<0.05$; upper case letters: $p<0.01$).
F(5/835.7)=52.55; p=0.00; η^2=0.09

Table 4.5 Public vs. personal framing

Share of public and personal framing (in %)	*FAZ offline (n=619)*	*FAZ website (n=491)*	*FAZ@ Facebook (n=480)*	*BILD offline (n=264)*	*BILD website (n=441)*	*BILD@ Facebook (n=146)*	*Total (n=2,441)*
Public framing	85.3	83.9	80.0	65.9	72.8	71.9	78.8
Personal framing	14.7	16.1	20.0	34.1	27.2	28.1	21.2

χ^2 (5)=63.72; p=0.00; V=0.16

even in the tabloid *BILD*. However, *BILD* is again more tabloid-like than *FAZ* on all distribution channels.[7] The cross-channel differences are particularly interesting. Both newspapers' degrees of tabloidization differ most strongly offline (almost 20 percentage points) and least strongly on Facebook, resulting from the fact that *FAZ*'s public framing is slightly lower on both online channels, while we see the opposite result for *BILD*.

The *style dimension* is about (a) how emotional news is presented, and (b) to what extent it contains journalists' opinions. The more emotional the presentation and the more strongly journalists' opinions are mirrored, the higher an article's degree of tabloidization. Table 4.6 reveals quite low values of emotional reporting, which means that the political coverage in both newspapers is rather unemotional. However, there are differences between both newspapers across all distribution channels that are again largest offline. Overall, *BILD* is significantly more emotional and thus more tabloid-like than *FAZ*. Surprisingly, *BILD* is more emotional offline (with about 10 per cent of articles being rather or very emotional) than on its website and on Facebook, both of which show the same degree of emotionality. By contrast, *FAZ* shows a very similar degree of emotionality offline (with about 2 per cent rather or very emotional articles) and on its website, while the articles distributed on Facebook are slightly, but non-significantly, more emotional.

The following analysis of personal reporting (Table 4.7) excludes comments which explicitly have the function of presenting the journalist's opinion and can thus not be seen as an indicator of tabloidization. Similar to emotional style, personal reporting indicates a low degree of tabloidization of political coverage.

Table 4.6 Emotional reporting

Mean values[1]	*FAZ offline (A) (n=619)*	*FAZ website (B) (n=491)*	*FAZ@ Facebook (C) (n=480)*	*BILD off-line (D) (n=264)*	*BILD website (E) (n=441)*	*BILD@ Facebook (F) (n=146)*	*Total (n=2,441)*
Emotional reporting	1.73	1.76	1.84	2.19 [A,B,C]	2.03[A,B,C]	2.02[A,B]	1.88

[1]Mean values range from 1 (not emotional at all/not tabloid-like) to 5 (very emotional/tabloid-like).
[Aa] The letters behind the values indicate from which other values the respective value differs significantly (lower case letters: p<0.05; upper case letters: p<0.01).
F(5/816.0)=15.96; p=0.00; η^2=0.04

Table 4.7 Personal reporting

Mean values[1]	*FAZ offline (A) (n=520)*	*FAZ website (B) (n=402)*	*FAZ@ Facebook (C) (n=399)*	*BILD offline (D) (n=220)*	*BILD website (E) (n=405)*	*BILD@ Facebook (F) (n=130)*	*Total*[2] *(n=2,076)*
Personal reporting	1.46	1.34	1.41	1.59^{B}	1.52^{B}	1.55^{b}	1.46

[1]Mean values range from 1 (not opinionated at all/ not tabloid-like) to 5 (very opinionated/ tabloid-like).
[2]The lower case number in this table are explained by the exclusion of commentaries from this analysis.
[Aa] The letters behind the values indicate from which other values the respective value differs significantly (lower case letters: $p<0.05$; upper case letters: $p<0.01$).
$F(5/712.9)=5.40$; $p=0.00$; $\eta^2=0.01$

Overall, the differences between both newspapers are surprisingly small. The online coverage of the *FAZ* reveals the lowest value and represents the only example of *FAZ* being significantly less opinionated than *BILD* on all three channels. The similarities between tabloid and quality newspaper might be caused by two different reasons. As a tabloid, *BILD* tends to mix facts and opinions, while *FAZ,* as a newspaper of record with a clear editorial line, has the function of providing political standpoints in the process of public opinion formation. The slight difference between *FAZ* online and offline can be explained by the fact that *FAZ* uses more press agency material for their online articles, which in many cases do not contain any journalistic opinions.[8]

Tabloidization index

In the last step of our analysis, we finally test our hypotheses regarding the differences between quality and tabloid newspapers (*H1*) and between the three distribution channels – offline, newspaper websites, and Facebook (*H2, H3*) – by means of the tabloidization index.

According to the total index values, both newspapers as well as all three distribution channels indicate rather low levels of tabloidization of political coverage (Table 4.8). The three dimensions (topic, focus, style) contribute differently to the overall index, which confirms the multidimensionality of tabloidization. Different dimensions of tabloidization focus on different characteristics of the overall phenomenon that appear and are combined in different ways. The lowest degree of tabloidization is found on the topic dimension, the highest on the focus dimension. *H1* is clearly confirmed by the data: *BILD* shows a significantly higher degree of tabloidization both measured by the overall index and across the three dimensions, while the difference between both newspapers is largest on the focus dimension. By contrast, *H2* and *H3* are not confirmed by the data, since the mean index values are very similar across distribution channels on all three dimensions.

However, the pattern becomes clearer when comparing the two newspapers on the three distribution channels (Table 4.9). In fact, the lack of overall differences

Table 4.8 Tabloidization index by newspapers and distribution channels

Mean index values[1]	*Newspaper*			*Distribution channel*[Aa]			
	FAZ total (n=1590)	*BILD total (n=851)*		*Offline (A) (n=883)*	*Website (B) (n=932)*	*Facebook (C) (n=626)*	
Topic dimension	.08	.14**	t(2,405.2)=114.22 p=0.00	.09	.11[A,C]	.10[A]	F(2/1,383.6)=87.66; p=0.00; η^2=0.09
Focus dimension	.34	.46**	t(2,439)=25.48 p=0.00	.39[c]	.38	.37	F(2/1,521.4)=3.16; p=0.04; η^2=0.00
Style dimension[2]	.15	.20**	t(1,498.4)=8.21 p=0.00	.17	.16	.17	F(2/1,541.9)=0.49; p=0.62; η^2=0.00
Total degree of tabloidization	.19	.27**	t(1,574.8)=31.31 p=0.00	.22	.22	.21	F(2/1,555.9)=0.91; p=0.40; η^2=0.00

[1]Mean index values range from 0 (lowest possible degree of tabloidization) to 1 (highest possible degree of tabloidization)
[2]The missing values on personal reporting for the commentaries were replaced by mean values.
[Aa] The letters behind the values indicate from which other values the respective value differs significantly (lower case letters: $p<0.05$; upper case letters: $p<0.01$).

Table 4.9 Tabloidization index by single outlets

Mean index values[1]	*FAZ offline (A) (n=619)*	*FAZ website (B) (n=491)*	*FAZ@ FB (C) (n=480)*	*BILD offline (D) (n=264)*	*BILD website (E) (n=441)*	*BILD@ FB (F) (n=146)*
Topic dimension[2]	.06	.08	.10	.15	.14	.12
Focus dimension[3]	.33	.34	.34	.52[A,B,C,E,F]	.43[A,B,C]	.47[A,B,C,E]
Style dimension[4]	.15	.14	.16	.22[A,B,C]	.19[A,B,C]	.20[A,B,C]
Total degree of tabloidization[5]	.18	.19	.20[A,B]	.30[A,B,C,E,F]	.25[A,B,C]	.26[A,B,C]

[1]Mean index values range from 0 (lowest possible degree of tabloidization) to 1 (highest possible degree of tabloidization).
[2]Since the mean values reflect the percentages of the distribution, there is only one mean value per outlet. Due to the lack of variance, it is therefore not possible to make any statements about significant differences.
[3]$F(5/835.7)=177.60$; $p=0.00$; $\eta 2=0.24$
[4]$F(5/818.1)=15.38$; $p=0.00$; $\eta 2=0.03$
[5]$F(5)=245.49$; $p=0.00$; $\eta 2=0.34$
[Aa] The letters behind the values indicate from which other values the respective value differs significantly. (lower case letters: $p<0.05$; upper case letters: $p<0.01$).

between the distribution channels results from two contrary tendencies that the two newspapers show: The degrees of tabloidization for FAZ, the quality paper, increase as it goes first onto its website and then onto Facebook. Contrarily, BILD, the tabloid, shows more degrees of tabloidization offline than it does on its website and on social media.. Admittedly, this difference is rather small and only significant when taking the difference between Facebook and the other distribution channels into account (confirming *H3*, but not *H2*). By contrast, *BILD* is significantly more tabloid-like offline than on its newspaper website and on Facebook (contrary to *H2* and *H3*).

Discussion

The aim of our study was to find out to what degree the distribution channel, whether it be offline, newspaper website, or Facebook, influences how tabloid-like its political news coverage is. In doing so, we responded to general concerns about the adaptation of journalism to the logic of social media (e.g., van Dijck and Poell 2015) and corresponding tabloidization tendencies (e.g., Lischka 2018; Lischka and Werning 2017; Steiner 2016). Overall and in line with *H1*, our study reveals that the degree of tabloidization persistently differs between the tabloid *BILD* and the quality newspaper *FAZ,* even on their websites and on Facebook. This finding reflects both newspapers' digital strategies (Lobigs and Neuberger 2018; Rickmann, Wais, and Goesche 2016), but particularly *FAZ*'s focus on providing high-quality journalism (Schütz 2017): *FAZ* is most tabloid-like on Facebook, in line with *H3*, while we do not find any significant differences between its offline version and the website contrary to *H2*. In other words, *FAZ* slightly adapts its professional standards to Facebook's rules of attention, but this happens at a very low level. By contrast, *BILD* is in some respects even more tabloid-like offline than on its website and Facebook page, which runs counter *H2* and *H3*. This finding calls into question to what extent one can speak of a universal "social media logic" at all, because this logic seems to be influenced by the media brand and target audience. What we see here might be a ceiling effect, as *BILD*'s degree of tabloidization offline is already relatively high. This general strategy is continued, but not further increased, on the other channels.

Taken as a whole, our study does not confirm widespread concerns about strong tabloidization tendencies online and especially on Facebook. Can we thus give an all-clear signal that the quality of news – particularly in quality newspapers – remains at a consistently high level? Maybe yes, but there is a different interpretation that seems more likely to us: tabloids and tabloidization might take slightly different forms in social media that are not captured sufficiently by the traditional indicators which we used in this study. These are undoubtedly useful to compare different platforms, but they need to be complemented by new ones in order to measure tabloidization on social media more validly (Steiner 2019). One example is the so-called clickbait concept, which arose mainly online and particularly uses strategies of forward referencing (Blom and Hansen 2015) (e.g., "WHY THIS politician may be our future chancellor"). This strategy creates a so-called "curiosity gap", and is thus a way to attract attention and reduce a message to mere affects. Even though clickbait can thus be seen as a stylistic element of tabloidization, it has neither been incorporated in the theoretical concept of tabloids and tabloidization, nor has it been analyzed in this context yet.

Moreover, our study, as it is common practice, investigated entire articles, which neglects a very important development in the online context; news teasers on websites or Facebook posts (Welbers and Opgenhaffen 2019) can give strong indication of tabloidization. Particularly on social media, news has to compete with a lot of other content for the users' attention, and teasers are an absolutely necessary choice here. This is not least because many users only scan their newsfeeds (Steiner et al. 2019; Vraga, Bode, and Troller-Renfree 2016) rather than clicking on the actual articles. Thus, the content of the teasers is extremely relevant for the extent to which these users are informed.

Another limitation is that the small size of our sample limits the generalizability of our findings. Future studies should complement it with more media outlets and platforms. Both newspapers we investigated are typical and very important representatives of tabloids and quality newspapers respectively in Germany, but proponents of these general types can differ strongly cross-nationally (Magin 2020), which calls for comparative studies. Furthermore, although Facebook is still the most important news source on social media (Newman et al. 2019), there have been recent shifts that should be taken into account in future research.

For example, Instagram is becoming increasingly important, especially in the younger age group, which is increasingly turning away from Facebook. The majority of news providers have reacted to this trend and started to provide content on Instagram. In contrast to Facebook, they do not link to their websites in most cases due to different technological affordances. Rather, news posts usually consist only of pictures with a little text or short videos, which makes an analysis of these news posts extremely exciting and important. Recently, a few media providers have also joined the social network TikTok and distribute short news videos there. This social network seems still to be of little relevance for news consumption, but this may change over time, bearing in mind how quickly news consumption is changing. If tabloidization research focuses on media and platforms relevant to news users, it must adapt to such changes accordingly. The study at hand enriches traditional research on tabloidization – which still pays too little attention to the online world in general and particularly to social media – and provides a valuable starting point for future research in the proposed directions.

Acknowledgements

The data used in this study result from the project "Media Performance and Democracy", funded by the German Research Foundation (grant 323375807), the Austrian Science Fund (grant I 3155), and the Swiss National Science Foundation (grant 170784).

Notes

1 Originating from newspapers, the phenomenon has expanded to other highly commercial media types, above all commercial broadcasting (Bird 2008; Gripsrud 2000). This led to the more general terms of "tabloid media" and "tabloid journalism" as a specific journalistic style (Magin 2019a).
2 The authors use the term "tabloidization" as synonymous with "softening of news".
3 Our broad definition of political news coverage includes articles on national politics, articles on regional policy and foreign affairs (the latter two only when referring to national politics), and articles on issues of societal interest which are negotiated in national political institutions (e.g. employment conditions in the health sector, unemployment statistics, food pollution caused by new pesticides).
4 For example, the names of political parties (e.g., SPD, CDU) or organizations (e.g., European Union) as well as labels of political institutions, functions, and positions (e.g., government, chancellor, parliament, minister). Due to our broad definition of national politics, the search string also contains international terms and actors outside the political center (e.g. NGOs, trade unions, aid organizations).
5 In case of party newspapers, personal reporting is not necessarily an indicator of tabloidization (Magin 2019a), but our sample does not include this newspaper type, which has become extremely scarce in Germany.
6 Based on the assumption that these differences could be affected by the length of the articles or the duration of videos – since longer articles may contain more contextualizing information than very short ones –, a further analysis was run, weighted according to the size of the articles or videos. This analysis produced similar results at a generally

higher level. Only the differences between offline and Facebook disappeared completely (*FAZ*) or at least almost (*BILD*).

7 Based on the assumption that the difference between *FAZ* and *BILD* could be affected by the topics (since *BILD* reports more strongly on politicians which is assumingly more often accompanied by a personal frame, Table 4.2), the analysis was run once again for pure policy coverage, showing similar results at a generally higher level.

8 In an additional analysis that differentiated between sources, we found that the articles written by individual journalists (*FAZ* offline: 1.48, *FAZ* website: 1.74) contain more journalistic opinions than articles written by agencies (*FAZ* offline: 1.00; *FAZ* website: 1.04). The fact that the *FAZ* offline contains more articles written by individual editors (n=477/92%) than the FAZ website (n=141/35%) and less articles from agencies (*FAZ* offline: n=24/5%; *FAZ* website: n=133/33%) explains why the average value for *FAZ* offline is higher.

References

Bastos, Marco T. 2017. "Digital Journalism and Tabloid Journalism." In *The Routledge Companion to Digital Journalism Studies*, edited by Bob Franklin and Scott A. Eldridge II, 217–225. Abingdon: Routledge.

Bell, Emily and Taylor Owen. 2017. "The Platform Press: How Silicon Valley reengineered journalism." *Columbia Journalism Review*, March 29. https://www.cjr.org/tow_center_reports/platform-press-how-silicon-valley-reengineered-journalism.php.

Bird, S. Elizabeth. 2008. "Tabloidization." In *The International Encyclopedia of Communication*, edited by Wolfgang Donsbach, 4947–4952. Malden, Massachusetts: Blackwell.

Bird, S. Elizabeth. 2009. "Tabloidization: What is it, and Does it Really Matter?" In *The Changing Faces of Journalism*, edited by Barbie Zelizer, 40–50. London: Routledge.

Björkroth, Tom and Mikko Grönlund. 2014. "The Growth of Leading Regional Newspapers." *Nordicom Review* 35 (1): 115–133. doi:10.2478/nor-2014-0008.

Blom, Jonas Nygaard and Kenneth Reinecke Hansen. 2015. "Click bait: Forward-reference as lure in online news headlines." *Journal of Pragmatics* 76: 87–100.

Cornia, Alessio, Annika Sehl, and Rasmus Kleis Nielsen. 2016. *Private sector media and digital news*. Oxford: Reuters Institute for the Study of Journalism.

Croteau, David and William Hoynes. 2019. *Media/society: Industries, images, and audiences*. London: Sage.

Djupsund, Göran and Tom Carlson. 1998. "Trivial Stories and Fancy Pictures? Tabloidization Tendencies in Finnish and Swedish Regional and National Newspapers 1982–1997." *Nordicom Review* 19 (1), 101–114.

Esser, Frank. 1999. "Tabloidization of News: A Comparative Analysis of Anglo-American and German Press Journalism." *European Journal of Communication* 14 (3), 291–324.

Gran, Celine Storstad. 2015. "Tabloidisation of the Norwegian News Media: A Quantitative Analysis of Print and Online Newspaper Platforms." Dissertation for MSc in Media and Communications. London: London School of Economics and Political Science. http://www.lse.ac.uk/media@lse/research/mediaWorkingPapers/MScDissertation Series/2014/Celine-Storstad-Gran-LSE-MediaSeries-AF.pdf

Gripsrud, Jostein. 2000. "Tabloidization, Popular Journalism and Democracy." In *Tabloid Tales. Global Debates over Media Standards*, edited by Colin Sparks and John Tulloch, 285–300. Lanham, Maryland: Rowman & Littlefield.

Hallin, Daniel C. and Paolo Mancini. 2004. *Comparing Media Systems: Three Models of the Media and Politics*. Cambridge: Cambridge University Press.

Häuptli, Andrea and Lucie Hauser. 2017. "Medienqualität." In *Qualität der Medien. Schweiz – Suisse – Svizzera. Jahrbuch 2017*, edited by fög – Forschungsinstitut Öffentlichkeit und Gesellschaft/UZH, 41–60. Basel: Schwabe.

Hölig, Sascha and Uwe Hasebrink. 2019. "Germany." In *Reuters Institute Digital News Report 2019*, edited by Nic Newman, Richard Fletcher, Antonis Kalogeropoulos, and Rasmus Kleis Nielsen, 86–87. Oxford: Reuters Institute for the Study of Journalism.

Jünger, Jakob and Till Keyling. 2019. Facepager. An application for generic data retrieval through APIs. https://github.com/strohne/Facepager/.

Jürgens, Pascal and Birgit Stark. 2017. "The Power of Default on Reddit: A General Model to Measure the Influence of Information Intermediaries." *Policy & Internet* 9 (4), 395–419.

Kalogeropoulos, Antonis, Richard Fletcher, and Rasmus Kleis Nielsen. 2019. "News brand attribution in distributed environments: Do people know where they get their news?" *New Media & Society* 21 (3), 583–601.

Karlsson, Michael. 2016. "Goodbye politics, hello lifestyle Changing news topics in tabloid, quality and local newspaper websites in the U.K. and Sweden from 2002 to 2012." *Observatorio (OBS*)* 10 (4), 150–165.

Karlsson, Michael and Krister Clerwall. 2013. "Negotiating Professional News Judgment and 'Clicks': Comparing Tabloid, Broadsheet and Public Service Traditions in Sweden." *Nordicom Review* 34 (2), 65–76.

Klein, Ulrike. 1998. "Tabloidised Political Coverage in BILD-Zeitung." *Javnost – The Public* 5 (3), 79–93..

Klinger, Ulrike and Jakob Svensson. 2015. "The Emerge of Network Media Logic in Political Communication: A Theoretical Approach." *New Media & Society* 17 (8), 1241–1257.

Landmeier, Christine and Gregor Daschmann. 2011. "Im Seichten kann man nicht ertrinken? Boulevardisierung in der überregionalen deutschen Qualitätspresse." In *Krise der Leuchttürme öffentlicher Kommunikation*, edited by Roger Blum, Heinz Bonfadelli, Kurt Imhof, and Otfried Jarren, 177–191. Wiesbaden: VS Verlag.

Lefkowitz, Julia. 2018. "'Tabloidization' or Dual-Convergence: Quoted speech in tabloid and 'quality' British newspapers 1970–2010." *Journalism Studies* 19 (3), 353–375.

Leidenberger, Jakob. 2013. *Boulevardisierung von Fernsehnachrichten: Eine Inhaltsanalyse deutscher und französischer Hauptnachrichtensendungen*. Paris: Library and information sciences, Université Paris-Est.

Lischka, Juliane A. 2018. "Logics in social media news making: How social media editors marry the Facebook logic with journalistic standards." *Journalism*. Published online ahead of print. doi:10.1177/1464884918788472.

Lischka, Juliane A. and Markus Werning. 2017. "Wie Facebook den Regionaljournalismus verändert: Publikums- und Algorithmusorientierung bei der Facebook-Themenselektion von Regionalzeitungen." *Kommunikation@gesellschaft* 18, 1–25. http://nbn-resolving.de/urn:nbn:de:0168-ssoar-51469-5.

Lobigs, Frank and Christoph Neuberger. 2018. *Meinungsmacht im Internet und die Digitalstrategien von Medienunternehmen. Neue Machtverhältnisse trotz expandierender Internet-Geschäfte der traditionellen Massenmedien-Konzerne*. Leipzig: Vistas.

Lund, Anker B., Karin Raeymaeckers, and Josef Trappel. 2011. "Newspapers: Adapting and Experimenting," In *Media in Europe Today*, edited by Josef Trappel, Werner A. Meier, Leen d'Haenens, Jeannette Steemers, and Barbara Thomaß, 43–59. Bristol: Intellect.

Lux, Torben. 2019. "Wie die Bild Sport-Communitys mit Facebook-Gruppen und Club-Accounts auf Instagram aufbaut." *OMR*, June 25. https://omr.com/de/bild-sport-communitys-plattform-strategie-facebook-gruppen/.

Magin, Melanie. 2019. "Attention, please! Structural influences on tabloidization of campaign coverage in German and Austrian elite newspapers (1949–2009)." *Journalism* 20 (12), 1704–1724.

Magin, Melanie. 2020. "Elite versus Popular Press.," In *The International Encyclopedia of Journalism Studies*, edited by Tim P. Vos, Folker Hanusch, Margaretha Geertsema-Sligh, Annika Sehl, and Dimitra Dimitrakopoulou. Chichester: Wiley. Available at doi:10.1002/9781118841570.iejs0226.

Magin, Melanie and Birgit Stark. 2015. "Explaining National Differences of Tabloidisation Between Germany and Austria: Structure, conduct and performance." *Journalism Studies*, 16 (4), 577–595. doi:10.1080/1461670X.2014.921398.

Newman, Nic, Richard Fletcher, Antonis Kalogeropoulos, and Rasmus Kleis Nielsen. 2019. *Reuters Institute Digital News Report 2019*. Oxford: Reuters Institute for the Study of Journalism.

Norris, Pippa. 2003. *A virtuous circle: Political communications in postindustrial societies*. Cambridge: Cambridge University Press.

Otto, Lukas, Isabella Glogger, and Mark Boukes. 2017. "The Softening of Journalistic Political Communication: A Comprehensive Framework Model of Sensationalism, Soft News, Infotainment, and Tabloidization: Softening of Journalistic Political Communication." *Communication Theory* 27 (2), 136–155.

Palau-Sampio, Dolors. 2016. "Reference press metamorphosis in the digital context: clickbait and tabloid strategies in Elpais.com." *Communication & Society* 29 (2), 63–79.

Quarfoot, David and Richard A. Levine. 2016. "How Robust Are Multirater Interrater Reliability Indices to Changes in Frequency Distribution?" *The American Statistician* 70 (4), 373–384.

Rashidian, Nushin, George Tsiveriotis, Pete Brown, Emily Bell, and Abigail Hartstone. 2019. "Platforms and Publishers: The End of an Era." *Columbia Journalism Review*, November 22. https://www.cjr.org/tow_center_reports/platforms-and-publishers-end-of-an-era.php.

Reinemann, Carsten, James Stanyer, Sebastian Scherr, and Guido Legnante. 2012. "Hard and Soft News: A Review of Concepts, Operationalizations and Key Findings." *Journalism* 13 (2), 221–239.

Rickmann, Andreas, Jakob Wais, and Malte Goesche. 2016. "Was das Social Media-Team von BILD 2016 gelernt hat. Über Erfolg bei Facebook und Co." *Bild.de*, December 23. https://www.bild.de/corporate-site/blog/blog_bild/blog-artikel-social-media-was-wir-2016-gelernt-haben-49452102.bild.html.

Schröder, Jens. 2019. "Zeitungs-IVW: 'Bild', 'BamS', 'Welt' und 'FAS' dick im Minus, 'Handelsblatt', 'Zeit' und 'Freitag' legen zu." *Meedia*, October 21. https://meedia.de/2019/10/21/zeitungs-ivw-bild-bams-welt-und-fas-dick-im-minus-handelsblatt-zeit-und-freitag-legen-zu/.

Schütz, Volker. 2017. "'Bin dankbar, in solchen Zeiten Journalist sein zu dürfen'. FAZ-Digitalchef von Blumencron." *Horizont*, August 30. https://www.horizont.net/medien/nachrichten/FAZ-Digitalchef-von-Blumencron-Wir-werden-noch-lange-Zeitungen-auf-Papier-lesen-160649.

Seethaler, Josef. 2015. *Qualität des tagesaktuellen Informationsangebots in den österreichischen Medien. Eine crossmediale Untersuchung*. Wien: RTR.

Sparks, Colin. 2000. "The panic over tabloid news." In *Tabloid Tales*, edited by Colin Sparks and John Tulloch, 1–40. Lanham, Maryland: Rowman & Littlefield.

Stark, Birgit and Melanie Magin. 2019. " Neuer Strukturwandel der Öffentlichkeit durch Informationsintermediäre: Wie Facebook, Google & Co. die Medien und den Journalismus verändern." In *Öffentlichkeit in der Krise. Gedenkschrift für Kurt Imhof*, edited by Mark Eisenegger, Patrik Ettinger, and Mario Schranz, 393–422. Frankfurt: Campus.

Steiner, Miriam. 2016. "Boulevardisierung goes Facebook? Ein inhaltsanalytischer Vergleich politischer Nachrichten von tagesschau, heute, RTL Aktuell und Sat.1 Nachrichten im Fernsehen und auf Facebook. " In *Politische Kommunikation – neue Phänomene, neue Perspektiven, neue Methoden*, edited by Laura Leißner, Halina Bause, and Lennart Hagemeyer, 27–46. Berlin: Frank & Timme.

Steiner, Miriam. 2019. "*Re-Evaluating the Concept of 'Softening the News' in the Platform Society*." Paper presented at The Interim Conference of ECREA's Political Communication Section, Poznan, September 12–13.

Steiner, Miriam, Melanie Magin, and Birgit Stark. 2019. "Uneasy Bedfellows: Comparing the diversity of German public service news on television and on Facebook." *Digital Journalism* 7 (1), 100–123.

Steiner, Miriam, Melanie Magin, Birgit Stark, and Pascal Jürgens. (2019). "Aus Versehen informiert? Facebooks Bedeutung für die Nachrichtennutzung nebenbei – eine Mehrmethoden-Analyse." In *Meinungsbildung in der Netzöffentlichkeit. Aktuelle Studien zu Nachrichtennutzung, Meinungsaustausch und Meinungsbeeinflussung in Social Media*, edited by Patrick Weber, Frank Mangold, Matthias Hofer, and Thomas Koch, 19–36. Baden-Baden: Nomos.

van Dijck, José and Thomas Poell. 2015. "Making Public Television Social? Public Service Broadcasting and the Challenges of Social Media." *Television & New Media* 16 (2), 148–164.

Vraga, Emily, Leticia Bode, and Sonya Troller-Renfree. 2016. "Beyond Self-Reports: Using Eye Tracking to Measure Topic and Style Differences in Attention to Social Media Content." *Communication Methods and Measures* 10 (2-3), 149–164.

Welbers, Kasper and Michaël Opgenhaffen. 2019. "Presenting News on Social Media: Media logic in the communication style of newspapers on Facebook." *Digital Journalism* 7 (1), 45–62.

5 Tabloids in Zimbabwe

A moral-ethical research agenda

Khulekani Ndlovu

Introduction

This chapter reflects extant scholarship about tabloids in Zimbabwe, detailing the economic, political, and cultural conditions in which Zimbabwean tabloids emerged, are consumed, and the cultural work they perform in the everyday lives of their readers. Specifically, the chapter adds to existing scholarship by suggesting that the moral-ethical turn in media studies might yield much needed insight into tabloid mediations of mundane and proximal suffering in the Global South. This would expand research on tabloid media to include the hitherto neglected question of "what people *actually do* when confronted with mediations of suffering" (Kyriakidou, 2011, 13). Impetus for this research agenda derives from the recognition that "no other spectacle can raise the ethical question of what to do so compellingly as suffering" (Chouliaraki, 2008, 832). Using the *B-Metro*'s mediation and reception of child abuse as a case study, the chapter illuminates how the mediated visibility of suffering is "performative … enacts paradigmatic forms of agency toward suffering" and "moralises audiences by habituation" (ibid.).

Thus far, the tabloid phenomenon in Zimbabwe has been largely confined to print media, though there is evidence of the emergence of online tabloids. While acknowledging that tabloidization of the mainstream press feeds into tabloid culture, the ensuing discussion is limited to the tabloid press.

The socio-political context of tabloids in Zimbabwe

The Zimbabwean print tabloid sector is dominated by Zimpapers publications (the government owns 51 per cent of Zimpapers shares). These are the *B-Metro* (English), *H-Metro* (English) *Umthunywa* (Ndebele), and *Kwaedza* (Shona). This ownership trend departs from the regional trend, where tabloid media are privately owned enterprises (Mabweazara and Strelitz, 2009). Generally, the emergence and the resurgence of tabloid newspapers in Zimbabwe have coincided with periods of heightened political indeterminacy. Tabloid newspapers in Zimbabwe emerged in the first decade of independence as indigenous language papers. *Umthunywa* was established in 1985 with the express intent of catering for the Ndebele linguistic community (Mabweazara and Strelitz, 2009, 116). Similarly, *Kwaedza* was launched in 1986 to service the Shona speaking media market (Hove 2017, 165). The emergence of these tabloids has to be understood as a manifestation of the colonially inspired identity politics of ethnocentric regionalism (Moyo, 2003). Just like the colonial African press which "sought to inoculate the African black elite from political engagement", the original imagined role of these indigenous language tabloids was that of depoliticization (ibid., 5). Such a function has been criticized as being inimical to the democratic purpose of media and critical citizenship because of its dumbing down effect (Connell, 1998; Örnebring and Jönsson, 2004; Johansson, 2007; Rowe, 2010; Steenveld and Strelitz, 2010). The imagined and actual roles of these tabloids cannot be severed from the socio-political and economic context of their emergence and consumption. In addition to giving the Ndebele language a newspaper presence, the introduction of *Umthunywa* was "a well-calculated political gesture in the face of the post-independence political tension that engulfed Matabeleland" (Mabweazara, 2009, 455). Thus, from its inception, *Umthunywa* was "enmeshed in circumstances that mirrored material deprivation and the political marginalization of Bulawayo by the 'power bloc' over the years" (ibid.).

In the absence of a corresponding historicization of the emergence of *Kwaedza,* the above account concerning *Umthunywa* can also be related to *Kwaedza.* This is due to the newspapers being launched one year apart from each other, and that both papers are published by the Zimpapers group, whose editorial policy has been shown to be uniform across all its publications. The period in question is historically known as the Gukurahundi, otherwise called the 'Matabeleland disturbances'. This was a time of ethno-political conflict in which the Zimbabwe National African Union Patriotic Front (ZANU-PF), which governed the post-colonial state, went on a violent rampage in the Matabeleland and Midlands provinces of Zimbabwe, targeting members of Joshua Nkomo's Zimbabwe African People's Union (PF ZAPU) (Ndlovu-Gatsheni and Willems, 2010, 196–196). The official rationalization by the state was that it was targeting rogue members of ZAPU's military wing, the Zimbabwe People's Revolutionary Army (ZIPRA). In the process 20,000 people lost their lives in what Robert Mugabe would later describe as a moment of madness (Catholic Commission for Justice and Peace, 1997). This violent episode was concluded by the signing of the Unity Accord in 1987 between PF-ZAPU and ZANU-PF.

Coincidentally, 1987 marked the beginning of the gradual decline of *Umthunywa.* The 12-page tabloid was reduced to 4 pages, became an insert in *Kwaedza,* and was subsequently discontinued in 1993 (Mabweazara and Strelitz 2009, 116). Reasons for the initial demise of *Umthunywa* included viability challenges, political meddling, and a supressed regional economy. *Umthunywa* was eventually relaunched in 2004 after a decade-long hiatus. A revamped editorial team applying market-oriented tabloid tactics established *Umthunywa* as "the prototypical representation of 'tabloid' journalism in Zimbabwe"

(Mabweazara and Strelitz 2009, 117). Despite the lapse of time between its initial and second launch, when *Umthunywa* re-remerged, political and media repression was still rife in Zimbabwe. Additionally, post-2000 Zimbabwe has been characterised by entrenched political and media polarization. When considered from the perspective of the media consumer, tabloid media offered "opportune respite from the predictable and heavily polarized mainstream media" (Mabweazara 2009, 450). As such, the resurgence of tabloid journalism cannot be divorced from government-induced politics of diversion (see Ndlovu 2015; Chuma 2005). From a media-centric perspective, tabloidization offered a strategic escape from overt political censorship of the media owing to the apolitical nature of its populist and human-interest narratives. It should be noted that the cultural studies rebuttal is that tabloids cover different politics; the politics of the everyday (Bird 2009).

It is against this backdrop that the relaunched *Umthunywa* achieved commercial success at a time when mainstream papers' circulation figures plummeted as a result of public apathy and propaganda fatigue. Evidence suggests that tabloid media made significant inroads in terms of market share. Such a view finds added support from statistics quoted by Mabweazara (2009, 449) that demonstrate that the vernacular tabloid *Umthunywa* outsold the *Sunday News* as it achieved peak circulation figures of 30,000 copies. The *Sunday News* is a quality weekly that shares the same publisher with *Umthunywa* and also circulates in Bulawayo. It can be inferred that the introduction of English tabloids by Zimpapers (B-*Metro* in Bulawayo and *H-Metro* in Harare) was strategic and motivated by the need to replicate the success of the vernacular tabloids. Recent statistics indicate that the *B-Metro* and *H-Metro* tabloids are popular among media consumers. Hove (2017, 164) has documented that

> *H-Metro's* readership as of 2015 was 864,116, making it the third largest selling daily paper after the major national papers, *The Herald* and *Daily News* … *B-Metro* is the second most widely read newspaper after the weekly *Sunday Mail*. It has a readership of 504,583 according to the 2015 ZAMPS report.

Zimpapers' introduction of the *B-Metro* and *H-Metro* tabloids also has to be understood as a response to the need to mitigate the economic threats emanating from the multifaceted Zimbabwean crisis. This crisis is an amalgam of interlocking historical and contemporary political, economic, and cultural problems that continue to bedevil the Zimbabwean nation-state (Mhiripiri and Ureke 2018, 89). The varied and contested causes of the Zimbabwean crisis include *inter alia* violent "confrontations over land and property rights" (Chiumbu and Musemwa 2012, ix), a "lethargic nation building project" (Santos and Ndlovu 2015, 147), and "post-colonial state sponsored genocide and repression" (Santos 2018, 4). This permanent state of crisis that has characterised Zimbabwe's recent history prompted the United Nations to declare Zimbabwe a "rogue state" (Mhiripiri and Ureke 2018, 89). Major indicators of the crisis include the Gukurahundi genocide which claimed 20,000 civilians, the 2008 cholera crisis which claimed 5,000 lives, the crash of the Zimbabwean dollar amidst the highest inflation outside a war zone, and the 2008 violent election runoff (see Chiumbu and Musemwa 2012).

From the perspective of the Zimbabwean crisis, it is plausible to read Zimpapers' introduction of English tabloids as part of an economic survival strategy. From a media economics perspective, English is the language of the advertising dollar, since it is the de facto *lingua franca* in post-colonial Anglophone Africa. Thus, the English tabloids would appeal to a bigger market compared to the vernacular tabloids, which only appealed to a linguistic niche market.

Theorisations and empirical findings about tabloid media in Zimbabwe

To date, work on tabloids in Zimbabwe has theorized tabloid media as an alternative public sphere (Mabweazara and Strelitz, 2009; Mare, 2016). Within this view, Zimbabwean tabloid newspapers constitute a counter-hegemonic discursive arena for the ethnically, regionally, and politically marginalized. This does not discount the oft-cited rationalization that tabloids are popular by virtue of their predilection for sensationalism, scandal, and melodrama. Rather it foregrounds the contextual nuances that are peculiar to the Zimbabwean socio-historical and political context alluded to above. The popularity of these tabloids hinges on their resonance with the interests and aspirations of disenchanted publics.

Mabweazara's (2009) seminal study found that this function was more pronounced for Ndebele readers of *Umthunywa* as captured in their declaration that "it's our paper". Such identification has to be understood as expressive of "a sense of alienation from 'the mainstream' and represents the failure of other societal institutions (among them the more prestigious news organizations and traditional political organizations) to address adequately issues of vital concern to members of the public" (Mabweazara 2009, 458–460).

It should be noted that rather than depoliticizing its Ndebele readers, as is usually assumed of tabloids, *Umthunywa* has had the opposite effect of heightening the ethno-political consciousness of its readership. Reading *Umthunywa* translates to an ethnic and regional solidarity that is animated by the collective trauma of Gukurahundi and continued economic and political marginalisation of the Matabeleland region (ibid.). The Ndebele language in which *Umthunywa* is published is a marker of identity and the locus of regional protest against the Zimbabwean power bloc.

Mare's (2016) study of the *H-Metro* lends added credence to the view that tabloids in Zimbabwe function as an alternative publish sphere for the politically disenchanted. The notable difference with Mabweazara's study is that in place of an ethnic dynamic as in the case of *Umthunywa,* there's a pronounced political dynamic behind the *H-Metro's* popularity. Mare's findings indicate that consumption of the *H-Metro* is an act of protest against toxic party politics and mainstream media's complicity in the same. Such a development was exacerbated by the polarized media context, "which has turned newspapers into surrogates for contesting political parties" (103). The foregoing conditions explain the surge in the popularity of tabloid media in Zimbabwe.

Similarly, a study of the *B-Metro* tabloid found that its popularity derives from its focus on the politics of the everyday, rather than the polarizing and predictable party politics discussed above (Ndlovu 2019). Respondents took issue with the fact that mainstream media's obsession with elite politics leaves minimal room for the papers to articulate readers' concerns and validate their lived experiences. It is against this backdrop that the *B-Metro* readers hailed the paper for publishing content that speaks to their Africanity, youthfulness, and their status as 'ordinary persons'. Thus, the *B-Metro*'s appeal derives from its accommodation of racial, cultural, demographic, and class identities of those who feel their sense of being is negated by mainstream media. Such a posture validates the view that tabloids act as "a locus of contestation" (Wasserman 2010, 123), where reading the *B-Metro* is an act of protest against the exclusionary elitism and political partisanship of the mainstream media. The remark by one respondent that it would take a miracle to see an ordinary person in the mainstream media, speaks to the "'common people's' yearning for their social existence to find a discursive existence in the symbolic world of media" (Wasserman, 2011, 3). The *B-Metro*'s allure emanates from its capacity to satisfy this yearning among its readers.

Such assessments notwithstanding, Hove (2017) has questioned the emancipatory potential of tabloid media for female readers. Her study focused on how the *B-Metro* and *H-Metro* textually encode a patriarchal gender order. Her analysis revealed that the tabloids' reportage works according to a sexist regime of representation. Within this representational schema, tabloids emphasise women who transgress socially constructed norms of respectability. The familiar stereotypical tropes that emerge from her analysis are those of the "witch", "cheating wife", and "sexually deviant woman". The sexism of the tabloids is epitomized by the page 3 *B-Metro* 'babe' who is meant to voyeuristically pleasure the imagined male audience. The *B-Metro* babe who is typically young (less than 30 years of age) and slim reflects dominant imaginations of the ideal feminine body. Thus, the tabloid reproduces the sexual objectification of women that is characteristic of the patriarchal gender order. Hove also concludes that the tabloids' recurrent motif of "wife-bashing men" uncritically emphasises violent masculinities without a corresponding emphasis on solutions to the toxic violence (ibid., 174). The next section empirically demonstrates how the moral-ethical turn can broaden understandings about the work performed by tabloids in mediating suffering.

On the moral-ethical work of tabloid media in Zimbabwe: A research agenda

This section argues that though tabloids are often maligned in media scholarship and public discourse, they nevertheless perform an often overlooked function of highlighting social injustices. Using the *B-Metro*'s mediation of child abuse and its reception as a case study, this section illuminates how the mediated visibility of suffering is "performative … enacts paradigmatic forms of agency toward suffering" and "moralises audiences by habituation" (Chouliaraki 2008, 832). In this study, child abuse is taken to be a form of suffering, an existential threat and risk that is inimical to the welfare of children in contemporary society. Suffering denotes the "assemblage of human problems that have their origins and consequences in the devastating injuries that social force can inflict on human experience" (Kleinman et al. 1996, xi). Child abuse is one of the socially induced problems confronting modern day Zimbabwe. Within this work, suffering denotes the "lived experience" of abused children who are "inhabiting social structures of oppression" (Frost and Hogget 2008, 441).

Ong (2015) records that the mediation of suffering has recently gained prominence within media scholarship, spawning a philosophical and research agenda that has come to be distinctively called the 'moral-ethical turn' in media studies. Different lexical variants are used within the literature to signify the moral-ethical turn. Some notable common variants include "ethics of media", "moral spectatorship", and "morality of media" (Chouliaraki 2006, 23; Couldry et al. 2013, 1; Dahlgren 2016, 382) The concept of a moral-ethical turn has not gone uncontested, owing to the illusion of "newness" (Couldry et al. 2013, 2) that it creates. The main rebuttal to the assumed novelty of the moral-ethical paradigm has been that ethics have been a permanent feature of media scholarship from its inception. However, the notion of moral-ethical turn is relevant for signposting a theoretical and empirical shift towards the domain of ethics that concerns the "mediated relationship with the other" (Silverstone 2007, 10. Central to this shift is a different conception of the moral or the ethical as it relates to media. The question of ethics has for the most part been confined to journalistic codes of conduct (their observance and non-observance), whereas that "is only one part of the domain of ethical questions raised by the media" (Couldry et al, 2013, 2). There is an implicit justification of the moral-ethical turn in Couldry and colleagues' sentiments, given that they extend the discourse to a previously marginalized domain of ethics. Furthermore, the moral-ethical turn makes sense within the context of Silverstone's distinction between ethics and the ethical/moral. According to Silverstone (2007, 11) "ethics relates to practice and procedure; to the ways in which journalists go, don't go and should go about their business", whereas the moral speaks to "first principles; to judgement and elucidation of thought and action oriented towards the other". Thus, the moral-ethical turn points to a focus on the latter rather than the former. More recently, South African communication theorist Pieter J. Fourie (2017, 110), has made the case for the need for new normative theory "that takes *ethical communication* instead of *media ethics* as a point of departure" (italics original). He posits that

> *ethical communication* is more human/person oriented, whereas *media ethics* is more career and profession oriented; *ethical communication* asks questions about the ethical sustainability of human communication (and thus media

> as human communication), whereas *media ethics* asks questions about the ethical sustainability of a media practice and performance (ibid., 110–111).

Mediated morality is therefore an empirical category as opposed to a normative one. The notion of a moral-ethical turn captures the fact that "the idea of moral responsibility for mediated distant others" has become "a specific intellectual motif" and speaks to the ascendance of "moral spectatorship onto the research agenda of media studies" (Dahlgren, 2016, 382). In sum, the moral-ethical turn can be expressed as the question of "how do we respond ethically to the pain of others" (Wasserman 2015, 218), "others who only appear to us within the media" (Silverstone, 2002, 762).

This study addresses the paucity of African research that investigates the mediation of suffering by media in the Global South, as most empirical studies on the subject have focused on how global Western media report the distant suffering of non-Western others. The contribution of non-Western, local media in mediating suffering to local audiences remains for the most part unexplored (Ong 2015). Chouliaraki (2006) focused on the mediation of September 11th and other catastrophes by European television broadcasters, and Joye (2010) conducted a textual study of the coverage of the 2003 SARS outbreak by two Belgian television stations. Furthermore, Wright (2011) conducted a reception study of the mediation of the Democratic Republic of Congo civil war by the BBC's Radio 4.

Tait (2011) researched the representation of the Darfur crisis by *New York Times* columnist Nicholas Kristof between 2004 and 2009. More recently, Kyriakidou (2015) investigated how Greek audiences received the mediation of the 2004 Asian tsunami, Hurricane Katrina in 2005, and the 2005 Kashmir earthquake. The unintended consequence of the Eurocentric nature of existing research is that it creates what Szorenyi (2009, 94) has termed a "privileged audience" of "white spectatorship". This Eurocentric research bias is the product of a "racialized history" of viewing which

> might be summarised as: we can take for granted that our life does not include certain kinds of suffering; we are at a distance from those who do suffer; the visible suffering of others is available to us as a means to reflect on our own lives and subjectivities.
>
> (ibid.)

The empirical works cited above also exhibit an exclusionary focus on 'distant' suffering, which tends to obscure the empirical fact that suffering is an immediate, 'proximal', everyday reality. Kyriakidou (2011, 13) notes that "the assumption is that regarding suffering there is a clear distinction between zones of safety and danger, with the Western world occupying the former". More recently, there have also been calls to broaden the research agenda to include proximal suffering and overcome the stereotypical confines of the existing research canon. Ong (2015, 607–608) has highlighted that "the mediation of suffering is not only a distant but also a proximal phenomenon and even everyday condition", yet "we know little about ordinary people in the developing world acting upon images and stories of suffering – their own and those of others". Similarly, Orgeret (2016, 3–4) notes that the mediation of suffering has for the most part been investigated within a "single, cross-cultural mediapolis" and thus ignores the role of non-Western media in mediating "suffering at home". Thus, using the concept of proximal suffering, this chapter transposes the conceptual and methodological logic of the moral-ethical turn from the global to the local by investigating the representations of suffering children by the *B-Metro* tabloid in Bulawayo, Zimbabwe. The restriction of suffering to cataclysmic events, chosen using the newsworthiness criteria of Western transnational media, constitutes a global hierarchy of suffering that privileges certain kinds of suffering, while inevitably trivialising others (Morse, 2016, 2). Within this global hierarchy, the suffering of children has for the most part been neglected, given "the mundane and undramatic nature of most child abuse cases" (Wilczynski & Sinclair, 1999, 268).

Furthermore, tabloid mediations of suffering have received relatively little scholarly attention within the field of media studies. Hanusch (2010, 500) is one of the few scholars who has investigated how tabloids mediate suffering and categorically asserts that "tabloidization … is important when discussing graphic images of suffering in the press". Though commendable, the study fails to go beyond the focus on the sensationalist nature of the representations, nor does it consider how the newspaper audience responds to the images of suffering others which the logic of the moral-ethical paradigm enables. Similarly, Bird (2002, 144) focused on "the distinct role of tabloids in the coverage of September 11" via a case study of the American tabloid the *National Enquirer*. Both Hanusch's and Bird's studies focus on the extent of sensationalism in covering both forms of human suffering and do so with the intent of empirically validating the tabloid-quality press binary. Of note, few studies have systematically explored how the "embodied vulnerability" (Durham, 2016, 116) of children to abuse is represented by media in the Global South, let alone by tabloid media. In the exceptional instances where research has focused on tabloid representations of abuse (see Wilczynski & Sinclair, 1999), the focus has been on content and not the reception of that content (Weathered, 2015). Furthermore, within the context of the moral-ethical paradigm there is a need for research that probes the extent to which these representations cultivate an "ethic of care for children" who are "physically, mentally … developmentally unequipped to protect themselves from adult depredation and exploitation" (Durham 2016, 116).

B-Metro readers' sentimentality and judgement as the exercise of moral agency

Following Kyriakidou (2015), the following sections present a typology of witnessing that captures readers' moral reactions to *the B-Metro*'s mediations of child abuse. Interest in the *B-Metro* was sparked by its sustained coverage of child abuse.

The study used a multi-method design comprising of a study of the context of production, textual analysis, and reception analysis. This section presents reception analysis data gathered using focus group data. Six focus groups were convened between July 2018 and November 2018 in Bulawayo. Participants were recruited using a combination of convenience, purposive, and snow ball sampling. Fourteen men and 16 women between the ages of 21 and 49 years participated in the focus groups. Participants were provided with prompts of *B-Metro* stories published between January 2016 and August 2018.

The succeeding sections capture respondents' reactions which are read as "action at a distance" (Thompson, 1995, 100). Action at distance consists of emotion, judgement and behaviour directed towards the suffering of others.

Sentimental witnessing

Readers exhibited varied emotional and moral stances vis-a-vis the abuse of children, vacillating between compassion and indignation. Regarding compassion, respondents confessed to feeling bad, touched, traumatised, and hurt by representations of child abuse.

> [You] feel so bad because you live in a community full of perverts who don't care about the rights of other human beings. People who do such things, their conscience would be dead. It touches you.
>
> (FG1, Respondent 1)

The following account by a female respondent epitomizes readers' compassionate reactions to mediations of child maltreatment.

> [T]here's a *B-Metro* story about social media audio circulating of a woman beating a four-year-old child. I was traumatized when I listened to the audio, I would literally cry because I would picture my child and ask myself would I do that to my child.
>
> (FG3, Respondent 1)

Empathy, crying, and the reference to trauma bear testimony to a heightened sense of emotional investment in the welfare of children. Readers' sentimentality was also expressed as indignation. The references to being angry and appalled illustrate an indignant reading of the child abuse stories.

> Such stories make me angry, usually its parents that abuse their children or people that can be trusted. Like this story of this woman who kidnaps her neighbour's kid for her husband to rape her and infect her with HIV. That's unacceptable because these kids are under our care for us to nurture them. When it's now us who harm the children, it's very bad.
>
> (FG3, Respondent 3)

> The form one (in first year of high school) girl married off to aunt's hubby story … I thought this was a cultural practice that no longer existed in 2018. I was astonished by the fact that the family actually sat down and agreed to marry off the girl without her consent … I'm appalled to think that in this day and age that there are people that abuse children in this manner.
>
> (FG6, Respondent 3)

Denunciative witnessing

Respondents also acted as moral agents when they passed judgement regarding child abuse. Denunciation was the typical moral stance taken by most respondents. It should be noted that sentimentality and denunciation are not mutually exclusive but are mutually constitutive. The distinction that is made between the two is analytical but not empirical. A nuanced reading of the responses that reflect sentimental witnessing also reveals that they contain denunciative elements. References to "perverts who do not care about other people", "monsters", and "people with a dead conscience" are all judgments about the immoral nature of child abusers. What sets the responses detailed in this section apart from those cited in the foregoing section is their explicitly denunciative character.

> I think what these stories are showing us is that people are enjoying being abusive; we are a society of paedophiles … I'm looking at this stepmother who's inserting sticks into the privates of her stepchildren. Poverty has got nothing to do with this. She's just being inhumane; she's just being evil; maybe she's expressing her own sexual needs and feels she cannot experiment elsewhere except with these children. This is a sick society that needs to be cured of this sickness.
>
> (FG6, Respondent 3)

The reference to a "society of paedophiles", "a sick mind", "being inhumane", and the conclusion that "this is a sick society that needs to be cured of this sickness" cumulatively denounce child abuse as being an immoral, unjustifiable, and undesirable social pathology. Denunciative witnessing also manifested as the identification and condemnation of a perpetrator responsible for the abuse, as well as the attribution of blame (Ashuri and Pinchevski, 2009, 146). The following response to "Prophet 'rapes', impregnates two teens story" (*B-Metro* 26 May–1 June 2017) illustrates the above.

> It's unfortunate that this prophet died, he should have faced his sentence. He didn't only take their virginity, he destroyed them. He was sick and we all know what sickness it was (AIDS) and both of them were pregnant. They were not only left with the burden of a sickness but a sick child as well.

The above response is denunciative, since the remark that the abusive prophet "should have faced his sentence" connotes that his actions were criminal. The abuse is denounced for its devastating effects that include disease, subsequent stigmatisation of the rape victims, and the loss of their innocence. Denunciation also figures as the decrying of the parents' failure to rescue the girls when the media revealed their whereabouts. Their inaction is interpreted as making them complicit in the abuse of their children. Denunciation in this instance, becomes verbal "violence at a distance" (Boltanski, 1999, 57) that is directed at a perceived persecutor.

Anxious witnessing

In this mode of witnessing, respondents exhibited fear and dismay regarding the mediated and social reality of child abuse. This type of response shares affinity with the view that "children at risk" discourses engender moral panic in those who encounter them (MacDonald, 2003, 109). Respondents stated that stories of child abuse make them insecure, as they can no longer trust that their children are safe with their maids or husbands, as those entrusted with children sometimes turn out to be abusers. The following response demonstrates the above.

> I once read a story in the *B-Metro* and it really haunted me. A couple had a 5-year-old child and the mother would wake up in the morning to go and sweep the yard and the father would rape the infant. It pained me because my child was also 5 years old at the time. You feel so helpless because when I leave my children with their father, I'll be assuming that they are safe.
>
> (FG3, Respondent 3)

Concerns about the betrayal of trust, assertions of the inevitability of child abuse, and apprehension about father danger illustrate the anxious mode of witnessing.

Gendered witnessing

Reception analysis data points to a gendered perception of child abuse. Respondents discussions of children's vulnerability to abuse exclusively focused on the girl child and made no mention of boys' vulnerability to abuse. The following conversation about the "Prophet rapes teens story" is a case in point.

> Actually, the girl child is a target for these spiritual people, self-styled prophets, nangas and so forth. There's the social belief that if you sleep with a young girl you get power. I can imagine how many prophets believe if you sleep with a young girl you get power … cause if they wanted sex why don't they look for an adult woman.
>
> (FG2, Respondent 1)

The above response might be faulted for promoting the stereotypical view that women are more impressionable than men. It is worth noting that female respondents also expressed the view that girls were more susceptible to manipulation and abuse in religious groups.

> You find that a woman will be having problems with her husband, she'll seek advice from her pastor, community leader, doctor, from anyone who can offer advice about what to do. If you look at churches, they're full of women. That's why they take advantage of us because they know were looking for help.
>
> (FG2, Respondent 2)

A gendered view of abuse is also evident in the anxiety about father danger that was discussed in the previous section about anxious witnessing. The assumption that child abuse is a masculine immorality finds support in the observation that respondents' definitions of child abuse were gender neutral, whereas the discussion of these stories emphasised the *vulnerability* of the girl child to the *neglect* of the boy child. These observations emphasize the prevalence of a heteronormative social imaginary.

Critical witnessing

In this mode of witnessing, respondents demonstrated "reflective scepticism" (Lai, 2011, 6) about the validity of the explanations of child abuse contained within the *B-Metro*'s articles.

This critical posturing is manifested in respondents' disagreement about where the blame for child abuse lies and the adequacy of interventions meant to eradicate it. The following excerpt about the "Business man acquitted for raping girl (13)" (*B-Metro* June 24–30, 2016) illustrates the above.

> [T]ake this story of this man who says he didn't know and never bothered to ask her age and slept with the girl because of the size of her body. He thought she was of legal age yet she was 13. I find it odd that a court of law could buy that.
>
> (FG3, Respondent 4)

> I have a relative who was in a similar case, charged with sleeping with a minor. He asked the magistrate if someone who is 20 years old wouldn't be allowed into a bar and the magistrate said there would be no reason not to. The accused then said I met her in a bar and she told me she was 20 and look at the size of her body … he was acquitted.
>
> (FG3, Respondent 2)

> If you meet someone at a bar, a bar is a no-under-18 area, and she said she was 20 would you query it? As ladies we say that men abuse us but we are accomplices in our own abuse, we lie about our age.
>
> (FG3, respondent 3)

> There's a lady that I know who was also in a similar situation. She lied to her boyfriend, told him she was 21, yet she was underage. She was going out with someone who was 40 and she was 15. They had a baby but the case was never reported.
>
> (FG3, Respondent 6)

The respondents' problematisation of the presumed innocence of children and their objection to the assumption that abused children lack agency is evidence of a critical witnessing posture. The discussion demonstrates that children demonstrate agency when they lie about their age and choose to be in age restricted adult environments and willingly engage in sexual activity. The acknowledgment of children's agency disrupts the commonsensical view that children's victimhood is an inevitable outcome of their innocence. Scholars have highlighted that "this discourse of innocence is extremely resistant to challenges, whether logical, experiential, evidential or otherwise" (Meyer, 2007, 89). Within this view, "childhood has become a moral rhetoric that can legitimize anything without actually having to explain it" (ibid.). Respondents search for a more convincing explanation of why the businessman was (or shouldn't have been) acquitted, as well as the debate about whether the rape should be attributed to the child's own conscious decisions, qualifies the above as critical witnessing. Its criticality emanates from its refusal to accept the simplistic view that "because it is children" (ibid., 99) no other explanation is needed. In sum, the disposition to "look for the story behind the story" captures the essence of critical witnessing.

Ethical witnessing

In this mode of witnessing the *B-Metro*'s readership expressly emphasised the need to care and act about the suffering of children. I have chosen the label 'ethical witnessing' to denote this type of witnessing, since the essence of mediation, the moral work of media, is to discursively engender an ethic of care. Ethical witnessing manifested in respondents' reference to the "discourse of common humanity" (Chouliaraki & Orgad 2011, 343).

> We need to care about other human beings, being able to feel sorry for someone. Love someone you don't know, just consider them human and you are human, you're my brother, you're my sister, so I should practice being human with the people around me.
>
> (FG4, Respondent 1)

The discourse of common humanity is synonymous with the African indigenous ethic of *ubuntu*. *Ubuntu* is a communitarian ethic whose essence is captured by the maxim *umuntu ngumuntu ngabantu,* meaning "I am because we are and since we are, I am" (Fourie, 2008, 63). At the core of *ubuntu* is the moral conviction that an individual's humanity is inextricably linked to that of other members of the human family. The collective consciousness that characterises *ubuntu* predisposes one to be hospitable, caring, and humane. Within such a moral view, child maltreatment is symptomatic of the loss of *ubuntu*. The loss of *ubuntu* manifests as being indifferent regarding the care of children and a general disregard for the sanctity of human life. It is against this backdrop that respondents identified the reinvigoration of the ethic of *ubuntu* as a necessary antidote to the endemic nature of child abuse.

> I think the other thing concerns the values of the society. We no longer have *ubuntu*, e.g., if you look this "bed your daughter" story … because his cattle were dying, he consults a sangoma [traditional healer in Southern Africa] who says he must sleep with his daughter. Would you be in your right mind and still have *ubuntu* and a conscience when you do that?
>
> (FG3, Respondent 2)

> I think we need to go back to our values; we've lost *ubuntu*, when the woman next door would be my mother. We now live in a society that is too individualistic that *ubuntu* is now gone. We need a miracle for *ubuntu* to come back, that's the only solution.
>
> (FG3, Respondent 1)

Respondents also exhibited ethical witnessing when they acknowledged that it was their responsibility to eradicate the suffering of children. Such a stance is ethical since mediated morality is essentially "grounded on the enquiry into the status of, care for and responsibility for the Other" (Silverstone, 1999, 136).

> It's our duty to protect his children. Some of these things are happening around us, we've read stories about children being raped and you kept quiet; it's time to speak out. As an individual pick up the responsibility to make a change.
>
> (FG3, Respondent 2)

> It's up to us like those neighbours that intervened in the case of the epileptic child, though they should have acted earlier, the man was supposed to rot in jail.
>
> (FG3, Respondent 4)

Ethical witnessing was also manifested in respondents' desire for corrective action that would remedy the problem of the abuse. Respondents were thus heeding the "moral call to action" (Chouliaraki 2006) embedded in the *B-Metro*'s child abuse reportage.

> They tell us about these child abuse stories; young girls being married off. Are they telling Childline or the Girl Child Network?
>
> (FG5, Respondent 5)

> I'd be interested to know what happened to the prophet, was he jailed? Maybe it's asking too much of the *B-Metro* but I would want to know what happened to the kids, was there any intervention, was there any child protection organization that took the children, or is there a way people can contribute towards helping these girls?
>
> (FG2, Respondent 1)

Diagnostic witnessing

A defining characteristic of this type of witnessing was respondents' inclination to offer causal explanations for the behaviour captured in the *B-Metro*'s mediations of abuse. Most respondents cited family disintegration, religious deviance, regressive cultural practices, and the compromised mental and emotional health of society as probable causes. Respondents attributed family disintegration to the distressed economy that has forced many parents to be migrant labourers in the more affluent South African economy.

> Maybe it's a child headed family, they are many of these days because of HIV and migration. A lot of people going to South Africa leaving the kids alone. In Nkulumane where I stay you find children as young as grade seven living alone.
>
> (FG3, Respondent 6)

Most respondents espoused the view that religious deviance has also increased the vulnerability of children to abuse.

> Such stories like this one that I see here that a pastor is testing virginity, such churches should be closed … church leaders are supposed to be respectable people. Those who behave in such an abusive manner should be punished by the law. No pastor is certified to test virginity.
>
> (FG5, Respondent 2)

> [T]he government must intervene in religion; there's too much freedom. The government must screen and register all religious organizations and rescue our minors from religious sects.
>
> (FG6, Respondent 6)

Regressive cultural practices were also cited as being responsible for the continued abuse of children.

> I think as a society we need to review some of our cultures and consider the rights that have been given to children. Some of our cultures are outdated,

> especially this practice of marrying a minor to an adult. The government must intervene, especially regarding some of these cultural practices that infringe on the rights of minors.
>
> (FG6, Respondent 6)

Other respondents advanced the view that the emotional and mental health of society (and abusers in particular) cannot be ignored when accounting for the abuse of children.

> I think people have problems. You'll find that for a person to abuse a child like this, they have unaddressed emotional problems and the question of *ubuntu* as well. In earlier times the extended family would counsel you, that would help you vent out any emotional problems.
>
> (FG3, Respondent 3)

Conclusion

This chapter has reviewed extant research about tabloid media in Zimbabwe. The discussion has highlighted that within the context of the Zimbabwean socio-political setting, tabloids are the locus of ethnic, regional, and political contestations between dominant and marginalised identity groups. Furthermore, the review of the empirical literature has shown that tabloids espouse a patriarchal gender order that manifests in the sexual objectification of women and discursive policing of female sexuality and behaviour. Contrary to the normative assumptions that tabloids depoliticize their readership, however, analysis reveals that tabloid consumption in Zimbabwe is an expression of a counter hegemonic political consciousness. Using the *B-Metro* mediations of child abuse, the chapter has advanced the view that the moral-ethical approach can expand scholarship about the work performed by tabloids in Zimbabwe. Responses to the representations of child abuse show that *a priori* predictions about readers' compassion fatigue are not always reconcilable with empirical data, which shows that tabloid mediations can create the necessary proper distance necessary for audiences to care about "at risk children" (MacDonald, 2003, 114). Research into the moral work performed by tabloids mediations of suffering can temper the stereotypical denigration of tabloid media in academic and popular discourse.

References

Ashuri, Tamar and Amit Pinchevski. 2009. 'Witnessing as a Field'. In *Media Witnessing: Testimony in the Age of Mass Communication*, edited by Paul Frosh and Amit Pinchevski, 133–157. London: Palgrave Macmillan UK.

Bird, S. Elizabeth. 2009. Tabloidization: What is it, and does it really matter? In *The Changing Faces of Journalism: Tabloidization, Technology and Truthiness*, edited by Barbie Zelizer. London: Routledge.

Boltanski, Luc. 1999. *Distant Suffering: Morality, Media and Politics*. Cambridge: Cambridge University Press.

Catholic Commission for Justice and Peace in Zimbabwe. 1997. *Report on the 1980s disturbances in Matabeleland and the Midlands*. Harare: The Legal Resources Foundation.

Chiumbu Sarah and Muchaparara Musemwa. 2012. 'Perspectives of the Zimbabwean Crises'. In *Crisis! What Crisis?: The Multiple Dimensions of the Zimbabwean Crisis*, edited by Sarah Chiumbu and Muchaparara Musemwa. Cape Town: Human Sciences Research Council Press.

Chouliaraki, Lilie. 2006. *The Spectatorship of Suffering*. London: Sage.

Chouliariki, Lilie. 2008 'The media as moral education: Mediation and action'. *Media, Culture & Society* 30 (6): 831–852.

Chouliaraki, Lilie and Shani Orgad. 2011. 'Proper Distance: Mediation, Ethics, Otherness'. *International Journal of Cultural Studies* 14 (4): 341–345.

Chuma, Wallace. 2005. 'Zimbabwe: The Media, Market Failure and Political Turbulence'. *Ecquid Novi: African Journalism Studies* 26 (1): 46–62..

Conboy, Martin. 2006. *Tabloid Britain: Constructing a Community through Language*. New York: Routledge.

Connell, Ian. 1998. 'Mistaken Identities: Tabloid and Broadsheet News Discourse'. *Javnost - The Public* 5 (3): 11–31.

Couldry, Nick, Amit Pinchevski, and Mirca Madianou, eds. 2013. *Ethics of Media*. New York: Palgrave Macmillan.

Couldry, Nick, Sonia Livingstone, and Tim Markham. 2007. *Media Consumption and Public Engagement: Beyond the Presumption of Attention*. New York: Palgrave Macmillan.

Dahlgren, Peter. 2016. 'Moral Spectatorship and Its Discourses: The "Mediapolis" in the Swedish Refugee Crisis'. *Javnost - The Public* 23 (4): 382–397.

Durham, Meenakshi Gigi. 2016. 'Children, the Media, and the Epistemic Imperative of Embodied Vulnerability'. *Journal of Children and Media* 10 (1): 115–122.

Fourie, Pieter J. 2008. 'Ubuntuism as a Framework for South African Media Practice and Performance: Can It Work?' *Communicatio* 34 (1): 53–79.

Fourie, Pieter J. 2017. 'Normative Media Theory in the Digital Media Landscape: From Media Ethics to Ethical Communication'. *Communicatio* 43 (2): 109–127.

Frost, Liz and Paul Hoggett. 2008. 'Human Agency and Social Suffering'. *Critical Social Policy* 28 (4): 438–460.

Hanusch, Folker. 2010. *Representing Death in the News*. London: Palgrave Macmillan.

Joye, Stijn. 2013. 'Research on Mediated Suffering within Social Sciences: Expert Views on Identifying a Disciplinary Home and Research Agenda'. *Interdisciplinary Science Reviews* 38 (2): 106–121.

Kyriakidou, Maria. 2011. 'Watching the Pain of Others: Audience Discourses of Distant Suffering in Greece'. PhD diss., The London School of Economics and Political Science.

Kyriakidou, Maria. 2015. 'Media Witnessing: Exploring the Audience of Distant Suffering'. *Media, Culture & Society* 37 (2): 215–231.

Lai, Emily R. 2011. Critical thinking: A literature review. *Pearson's Research Reports* 6: 40–41.

Mabweazara, Hayes Mawindi. 2009. 'Regional Identity and the Politics of Belonging in the Consumption of Zimbabwe's Vernacular Tabloid Newspaper, uMthunywa in Bulawayo'. *Journal of African Media Studies* 1 (3): 449–467.

Mabweazara, Hayes Mawindi and Larry Nathan Strelitz. 2009. 'Investigating the Popularity of the Zimbabwean Tabloid Newspaper *uMthunywa*: A Reception Study of Bulawayo Readers'. *Ecquid Novi: African Journalism Studies* 30 (2): 113–133.

Macdonald, Myra. 2003. *Exploring Media Discourse.* London: Arnold.
Mare, Admire. 2016. '"Our Own WikiLeaks": Popularity, Moral Panic and Tabloid Journalism in Zimbabwe'. In *Everyday Media Culture in Africa: Audiences and Users,* edited by Wendy Willems and Winston Mano, 93–112. New York: Routledge.
Meyer, Anneke. 2007. 'The Moral Rhetoric of Childhood'. *Childhood* 14 (1): 85–104.
Mhiripiri, Nhamo A. and Oswelled Ureke. 2018. 'Theoretical Paradoxes of Representation and the Problems of Media Representations of Zimbabwe in Crisis'. *Critical Arts* 32 (5-6): 87–103.
Morse, Tal. 2016. 'The Construction of Grievable Death: Toward an Analytical Framework for the Study of Mediatized Death'. *European Journal of Cultural Studies* 21 (2): 242–258.
Moyo, Last. 2003. 'Status of Media in Zimbabwe'. In *Encyclopedia of International Media and Communications,* edited by Donald H. Johnston, 667–681. San Diego, CA: Academic Press.
Ndlovu, Everette. 2015. 'Three Waves of Media Repression in Zimbabwe'. *African Journalism Studies* 36 (2): 25–44.
Ndlovu, Khulekani. 2019. 'Mediated visibility, morality and children in tabloid discourse'. PhD diss., University of Cape Town.
Ndlovu-Gatsheni, Sabelo and Wendy Willems. 2010. 'Reinvoking the Past in the Present: Changing Identities and Appropriations of Joshua Nkomo in Post-Colonial Zimbabwe'. *African Identities* 8 (3): 191–208.
Ong, Jonathan Corpus. 2015. 'Witnessing Distant and Proximal Suffering within a Zone of Danger: Lay Moralities of Media Audiences in the Philippines'. *International Communication Gazette* 77 (7): 607–621.
Örnebring, Henrik and Anna Maria Jönsson. 2004. 'Tabloid Journalism and the Public Sphere: A Historical Perspective on Tabloid Journalism'. *Journalism Studies* 5 (3): 283–295.
Santos, Phillip. 2018. 'Agonistic Dysfunction on Facebook in Zimbabwe: A Discourse Ethics Perspective'. *African Journalism Studies* 39 (4): 3–21.
Santos Phillip and Khulekani Ndlovu. 2015. '"Democratic Unfreedom" on Facebook in Zimbabwe'. *African Journalism Studies* 36 (4): 145–163.
Silverstone, Roger. 1999. *Why Study the Media?*London: Sage
Silverstone, Roger. 2002. 'Complicity and Collusion in the Mediation of Everyday Life'. *New Literary History* 33 (4): 761–780.
Silverstone, Roger. 2007. *Media and morality: On the rise of the mediapolis.* Cambridge: Polity Press.
Steenveld, Lynette and Larry Strelitz. 2010. 'Trash or Popular Journalism? The Case of South Africa's Daily Sun'. *Journalism* 11 (5): 531–547.
Szorenyi, Anna. 2009. 'Distanced Suffering: Photographed Suffering and the Construction of White in/Vulnerability'. *Social Semiotics* 19 (2): 93–109.
Tait, Sue. 2011 'Bearing Witness, Journalism and Moral Responsibility'. *Media, Culture & Society* 33 (8): 1220–1235.
Thompson, John B. 1995. *The Media and Modernity: A Social Theory of the Media.* California: Stanford University Press.
Wasserman, Herman. 2010. *Tabloid Journalism in South Africa: True Story! African Expressive Cultures.* Bloomington: Indiana University Press.
Wasserman, Herman. 2015. 'Listening Past Difference: Towards a Compassionate Ethics of Communication'. *Stellenbosch Theological Journal* 1 (2): 217–234.
Wasserman, Herman, ed. 2011. *Popular Media, Democracy and Development in Africa.* New York: Routledge.

6 Trivializing entertainment news in India

Elements of tabloidization in the news coverage of Bollywood celebrities

Sreedevi Purayannur

Introduction

A loss of traditional values in journalism, denoted by shifts from public-service oriented news content to entertainment news, propelled by commercialism and market-driven policies at the news organization level, has been a point of discussion among Indian journalists and scholars of Indian journalism alike (Thussu 1999, 2007b; Rao and Johal 2006; Mehta 2010; Chadha 2017; Ram 2007, 2011; Ninan 2012). Most accounts of structural and market-level changes of Indian news media record the changes in content away from what is traditionally considered serious journalism and towards entertainment news. Successive chairmen of the Press Council of India (PCI), an independent institution that aims to uphold press freedom as well as improve journalism standards, have remarked on the dangers of such a trend (Katju 2011; Ray 2006). For instance, Justice G.N. Ray (PCI chairman, 2005–2011), speaking at a conference in 2006, argued that trends in tabloidization, and what he called the 'Page 3' syndrome in Indian news media, result in increased coverage of entertainment and celebrity news, with "important issues such as health care education and issues relating socio-political reforms which require to be addressed with seriousness have been given the back seat" (Ray 2006, 2).

These accounts point to a tabloidization of news content in the way Sparks (2000) characterized the term. His deliberations on what 'tabloid' means for journalism in the 21st century reveal a conscious news content prioritization of sports, scandals, and celebrity news over politics, economics, and society. However, it is a term that is seldom found outside academic discussions of Indian journalism, and there has been no definitive study of Indian journalism through the lens of tabloidization.

This chapter will examine the tabloidization of entertainment news in legacy media and their digital news platforms in India. The first section contains a brief history of the Indian press, focusing on the impact of the liberalization of Indian economy on Indian news media markets, both regionally and nationally. This historical account is then used to situate the advent and evolution of tabloidization in the Indian context. While Indian newspapers resist easy classification into 'tabloid' and a 'quality' genres, as in the British context, the same cannot be said of television and online news. This chapter will develop such a classification of Indian television content, and then concludes showing a vast and diverse network of television channels and newspapers in India contribute to an externally pluralistic media landscape (Hallin and Mancini 2004), providing a balance to forces of commercialism and tabloidization.

This chapter presents two case studies of the tabloidization of entertainment news, one in digital-print media and the other in television. The first case examines how *The Times of India* used the social media platform Twitter to bring attention to a certain Bollywood actress' body in 2014. *The Times of India* was a pioneer in adopting market-oriented policies that, according to many scholars and journalists, treated newspapers like soft-drink products (Mahalingam 1998; Prasad 2008). The case is an interesting one not only for the outraged criticism it generated but also for the newspaper's unusual defensive editorial stance. The second study explores the coverage of the unnatural death of popular actress Sridevi, coverage which included re-enactments of her drowning in a bathtub on prime-time television. This case illustrates tabloidization in Indian television broadcasting.

Contexts of Indian journalism

The origin of journalism in India is commonly traced to its first newspaper, the *Bengal Gazette*, first published in 1780 (Raghavan 1994; Thussu 2007b). The Indian press has since flourished, being a key player in the public sphere throughout the nineteenth- and twentieth-century colonial period, the early twentieth-century independence movements, and the country's history since 1947 as an independent nation. Scholars and journalists (Raghavan 1994; Saptarishi 2005; Sainath, in Loo 2009) have argued that, despite its birth in the eighteenth century, today's Indian press is also perhaps largely a product of the nationalist movement.

Since colonial times the Indian news media have forged a tradition of speaking truth to power; indeed, the investigative and analytical skills of journalists, as well as their determination to inform their readership of politically important events, played a significant role in India's struggle for independence in the early twentieth century. However, news media's choice and treatment of content have changed since the economic liberalization of the 1990s. Liberalization ushered in intensive competition and opened up the market to international investment, first in television and then with digital media. Subsequently, certain sections of the Indian media have faced criticism for the growing sensationalism and tabloidization of their coverage of local and national news, as well as an increased focus on soft news (Thussu 2007a; Sonwalkar 2002).

Reflecting the observation that news media systems in modern nation states are influenced by their political systems (Siebert, Peterson, and Schramm 1956; Hallin and Mancini 2004), the Indian news media system can be characterized as diverse and pluralistic, like the country itself. It has also been coloured by the political upheavals of pre-independence India, the nation-building of the

Nehruvian years, and the fiercely competitive, technologically advanced post-liberalization era. However, there has been a gradual change in the nature of Indian journalism from the missionary zeal of the pre-independence era to the idea of journalism as a vocation during the Nehru years, to today's commercial enterprises seeking to sell products to consumers (Kohli-Khandekar 2010; Raghavan 1994; Saptrishi 2005).

The proliferation of news outlets accompanying the technological advances and market reforms of 1991 led to intense competition and a shift towards profit-oriented journalism. Today, India has more than 100,000 newspapers and close to 1,000 television channels, and is projected to become one of the top ten media and entertainment markets in the world (Pricewaterhousecooper 2017). Globally and in India, commercialization brings about not only a rise in the number of outlets but also a shift in the tone of coverage (Picard 2004, Hampton 2010, McManus 2006, Demers 1999). Hampton (2010, 6) defines commercialization as the "gradual shift away from financial dependence on political parties to dependence on circulation and advertising revenues". Some historians argue that, to attract advertisers, Indian news media embraced commercialisation by tailoring their content to make it more appealing to the wealthier social classes who will buy their products (Saptrishi 2005; Kohli-Khandelkar 2010; McManus 1992). It is a practice which Curran et al. (2009, 6) warn may "impede the exercise of informed citizenship".

Emergence of free-market values

Journalism in India has faced many challenges in the rapidly changing social, political, and media landscape since the changes in economic policy of the 1990s (Ram 2011). Several scholars have argued that liberalization has created a new, affluent middle class in India, which provides today's news media with an audience which is potentially lucrative but imposes its own demands on what is covered, and how (Seneviratne 2008; Prasad 2008). The market-oriented strategies adopted by most newspapers led journalists to cover, as routine, subjects like electronics, cars, fashion, and lifestyle that appeal to the purchasing power of this social group.

Indian news media's tendency to cater to the tastes of an affluent readership, as required by the advertisers on whose money they rely, has attracted criticism. Sparks (2000) points out that when 'serious' media adopt tabloid news values, they sacrifice fact-checking and sourcing in favour of attention-seeking content bordering on the lurid. In 2011, Justice Markandeya Katju, former chairperson of the Press Council of India, directly criticized the amount of time and space news media devoted to covering entertainment and promoting superstition, by having sections and programmes devoted to astrology, and their insensitive and discriminatory coverage of terrorist attacks. As an example, he described how they diverted audience attention to trivial issues like Lady Gaga's visit to India and Kareena Kapoor's visit to Madame Tussaud's in London, even as 80 per cent of the country's population was at the time living in poverty and coping with unemployment and poor healthcare. Katju (2011) also called for a regulatory body for the broadcast media, following the model of the Press Council of India.

Moreover, and perhaps more ominously, liberalization also brought about the contentious, potentially damaging development of private agreements between news outlets and corporate organizations. As Prasad (2008) argues, when newspaper owners are conglomerates with diversified business interests, like the Hindustan Times Media group, they not only give coverage to their sister concerns, they also fail to investigate the business practices of big corporations. Such partnerships also include cross-promotion of the group's own business interests, such as carrying front page 'news' on a wellness centre owned by the Times Group, without revealing ownership (Sukumar 2012). Or entering into private agreements with other companies under which the Bennett, Coleman and Co., Ltd (BCCL), which owned the Times Group, received shares in return for advertisements and publicity campaigns (D'Rozario 2008).

A shift towards the 'tabloid'

As part of this development, scholars have also noted a gradual move towards the tabloidization of news content in both legacy media and digital news outlets, edging the press as a whole nearer to the British model. The consequences of this may be lower journalistic standards in hard news, including politics and economics, and a corresponding increase in soft news such as scandal, entertainment, and a focus on the private lives of citizens and public figures, as well as a change in what the media define as information required for self-governance (Esser 1999; Uribe and Gunter 2004).

Pallugummi Sainath, then rural affairs editor of the prominent newspaper *The Hindu*, was one of the first journalists to remark on the growing commercial orientation of content in the Indian news media. In an interview with Loo (2009) for the latter's book *Best Practices of Journalism in Asia*, he remarked that commercialization and corporatization can result in the trivialization of content, contrasting the enormous coverage given to the Lakme Fashion Week in Mumbai in April 2006 with the lack of attention given to the suicide of four hundred farmers in the same state during the very same month.

> This April [2006] in India, the number of farmers committing suicide in just one region, Vidarbha, crossed 400. This was very poorly covered. Very few national media groups sent their reporters to this region. But they sent well over 500 journalists to cover the Lakme Fashion Week.
>
> (Sainath, in Loo 2009, p. 44)

The shift towards tabloidization and trivialization has been attributed to the market-oriented policies of profit-seeking news owners and the intense competition within and between newspapers, radio, and television since liberalization. With over ten billion rupees of foreign direct investment by 2008 alone, print media barons had to come up with new strategies to survive in a suddenly competitive market (Kohli-Khandekar 2010). Expanding news media empires launched more editions in more cities, using aggressive marketing to protect their territories while bringing in the expertise of young entrepreneurs from other business areas. As Vipul Mudgal, the editor (research) of the *Hindustan Times*, said, with many marketing executives in media coming from soft drink companies, they treat newspapers as products with the shelf-life of a day, during which they must be distributed over the largest area possible (Rodrigues 2009).

Tabloidization is also reflected in the way news outlets differentiate themselves from competitors, with some marketing themselves on the presence of their tabloid-like content and others marketing themselves on its absence. One of the most public examples was seen in advertisement campaigns run by *The Hindu* and *The Times of India* in 2012. Television advertisements showed *The Times of India* ridiculing *The Hindu*'s serious approach to news with a "Wake-up" call, to which *The Hindu* retaliated by asking readers to "stay ahead of the times" and move away from film and celebrity news. These campaigns carried over into print advertisements, with *The Hindu* stressing its focus on political, economic, and international news, and claiming to subject stories to serious treatment, while *The Times of India* focused on its coverage of celebrity news and more personalized take on hard news. Our readers, claimed *The Times of India* in an advertisement on February 12, 2012, "know the name of the Comptroller Auditor General of India, and yet love to see Bollywood actors Deepika Padukone walk and Shah Rukh Khan talk". In an advertisement that same week, *The Hindu* responded to *The Times of India* with the words "Government malfunctions are more important than wardrobe malfunctions".

Tabloidization of Indian newspapers

Sparks (2000) defines a tabloid as a form that turns attention away from economic and political content and towards entertainment news, marked by a shift towards coverage of the private lives of celebrities and ordinary people in order to attract audiences. Scholars have measured tabloidization in several ways. Rooney (1998, 95) found that between 1968 and 1992, the content of two British tabloids, the *Daily Mirror* and *The Sun*, moved from matters concerning the public sphere to news that "encouraged acts of consumption". Rooney studied competition between these two newspapers and the subsequent effect on content and reporting practices as a way to measure tabloidization. He found advertising content reflected the consumption patterns of readers during the same period. His content analysis showed a sharp decline in public affairs reporting in both newspapers, with 'sports and showbiz' content dominating their pages (Rooney 1998). McLachlan and Golding (2000) operationalized tabloidization through four indicators: range, form, mode of address, and market structure. Range is the volume and prominence of coverage for various areas, and form is the content format of the newspapers. Mode of address refers to the tone and style of writing used in tabloids, while market structure refers to the changes connected to the market as papers move toward tabloidization (McLachlan and Golding 2000). What these and other measurements have in common is an agreement that an increase over time or a predominance of celebrity-oriented content is a sure sign of tabloidization.

The Times of India offers an example. Although not formally a tabloid, *The Times of India* differentiates itself within the market with a soft news focus and advertisements oriented to a certain type of consumer. Either despite or because of its differential claim to entertainment-oriented content, it is the largest circulating English-language daily in the country and the only one to figure in the top 10 publications in the Indian Readership Survey. It is the flagship publication of the Times Group. The Group was under British ownership from 1838 to 1948, when it was bought by its current owner, the Sahu Jain Group, after which it underwent many changes in ownership structure, the most prominent being the replacement of the post of editor by that of executive editor (Mahalingam 1998; Prasad 2008). The executive editor reports directly to the managing director of the Jain Group and has the authority to override editorial decisions made by journalists.

The Times of India *vs Deepika Padukone*

Uribe and Gunter (2004) have argued that tabloidization is not a 'static' concept and *The Times of India's* 2014 coverage of Bollywood actress Deepika Padukone offers an example of a lurch along the tabloidization spectrum. Padukone is an accomplished woman: a national-level badminton player, a model, an award-winning Bollywood actress, and a film producer. Apart from her professional accomplishments, she is most noted for talking about her struggles with mental health, a move which has been credited with spreading awareness of depression (Jain, Pandey, and Roy 2017).

On September 14, 2014, *The Times of India*'s official Twitter account put out a 2013 video clip that zoomed in on Padukone's chest, tweeting "OMG: Deepika Padukone's cleavage show". The tweet has since been deleted. The outrage at this headline was instantaneous, including responses from journalists, other newspapers, fans, and the actress herself. She called out the newspaper giant for trivializing 'news' and mixing up her cinematic and real-life personas. In a style typical of the platform and which at least one scholar has called "a radical approach" (Biju 2017, 38), Padukone tweeted "YES! I have breasts AND a cleavage! You got a problem!?" An intense debate followed about the role of the news media and the boundaries of entertainment news (Banerji 2018), with the hashtag #IStandwithDeepika soon trending on Twitter.

The Times of India responded by tweeting that its intentions had been good: "@deepikapadukone, It's a compliment! You look so great that we want to make sure that everyone knew!:)" When this response fuelled further outrage, the paper published an article asserting the actress had shown hypocrisy by "flaunting her body off-screen" and then being offended by the newspaper's tweet (Gupta 2014). This prompted Padukone to write on her Facebook page: "Digging out an old article and headlining it "'OMG: Deepika's Cleavage Show!' to attract readers is using the power of influence to proliferate recessive thought". Similar sentiments came from the industry; one condemnatory article in the UK's *Guardian* said the original tweet was an example of trivial content that served no purpose other than titillating clickbait to drive traffic to *The Times of India* website or sell more copies of its newspaper.

This incident serves not only as an example of tabloidization of a serious news media outlet, but also of how the trend towards tabloid coverage has been compounded by the technological advancements which underlie the spread of digital outlets (Ram 2007). Indeed, it appears that Indian print and digital news media are on a path to convergence, if the number of online editions of television channels and newspapers are anything to go by. The website *onlinenewspapers.com* lists 394 online newspapers in India, including, among others, online editions of popular dailies like the *Daily News and Analysis (DNA), Deccan Chronicle, The Hindu, The Indian Express*, and the *Hindustan Times*. Almost all of India's television stations also have interactive websites featuring up-to-date news through articles, photographs, and videos. Although official statistics are not available, online journalism is clearly growing in India. However, the important sector of web-only English language news outlets in India such as *The News Minute* and *First Post* remains relatively small.

Television news in India – quality vs tabloid TV

Television was launched in India in September 1959 by the Government of India, which remained in control until market liberalization in 1991. During television's first three decades, the public service broadcaster Doordarshan (DD) remained the only player in the market and served as a publicity machine for central and state governments. Its content ranged from informational to educational, addressing such matters as agricultural advice for farmers and supplemental education for schools. State-run television was also extensively used to propagate messages concerning family planning and disease eradication.

The FDI policies of the 1990s, however, brought about what Manchanda has termed an "invasion from the skies" (1998, 136), India's satellite television boom. International channels started beaming directly into Indian homes via satellite, and Indians could watch channels like the BBC and CNN. India's first foray into 24-hour service came when STAR (Satellite Television for the Asian Region) started broadcasting through the first geo-stationary satellite over the Indian Ocean. With ZEE TV's launch a few months later, India was fully initiated into the 24-hour entertainment culture, with many Western programmes 'Indianized' and proving to be huge successes.

Market-penetration and proliferation of network television

India's first satellite news channel was Star News, launched in 1998 as part of Rupert Murdoch's STAR TV network (Thussu 2007a). The industry has grown dramatically since then, in both size and complexity (Thussu 2007b), with at least half of India's nearly 900 stations being 24-hour news channels (BBC 2019). Moreover, the burgeoning news and entertainment sectors have tapped into the country's rich multilingual culture, with dozens of news and entertainment channels now broadcast in a wide range of languages, including Hindi, Marathi, Punjabi, Malayalam, Telugu, and Tamil.

Factors contributing to the vastness and diversity of the network of television channels are language, ownership, and content. India has twenty nine states and seven union territories. With state borders drawn along geo-linguistic lines, language is the primary definer of audiences and advertising. For instance, English news channels operate on a national level but target urban and affluent audiences with near-native English proficiency. While proportionally, English is the second most spoken language in the country, being spoken by more than ten per cent of India's 1.3 billion population (Office of the Registrar General & Census Commissioner 2020), English language television does not figure in the top ten news channels by market share (Thussu 2007b). Since Indian states are linguistic as well as geographical divisions, regional channels automatically become stratified according to language; the sole exception to this is Hindi, which is spoken in more than one state. So, in contrast to English channels, each state language is represented by a number of television channels. Although more recent official statistics are not available, in 2016 the Broadcast Audience Research Council India reported a marked shift in focus towards regional content for national networks (Broadcast Audience Research Council 2019).

The secondary differentiator for Indian broadcasting is ownership. Television channels are owned by international and national networks, political parties, or private individuals, or have political or business affiliations, all of which contribute to a highly polarized, yet externally pluralistic news media landscape in India (Hallin and Mancini, 2004). Ownership patterns can be discerned at both regional and national levels. As one example, the ZEE network runs multiple channels across content genres and languages. Examples of political parties owning stakes in television can be seen with the English-language news channels Republic TV and NDTV: the former is partly owned by a member of the ruling Bharatiya Janata Party (BJP), while the owners of the latter have family ties to top officials in the Communist Party of India.

The quality–tabloid divide

Moving to the third factor, the television news industry has faced criticism of its content transformation, and the shift from a democracy-driven focus to a commercially oriented one. Thussu describes the shift as a

> noticeable change in style and content away from a considered, professional approach to a flashier and visually more dynamic presentation; the emphasis

> seems to be not on the journalistic skills of news anchors and reporters but on how they look on camera, with style taking precedence over substance.
> (Thussu 2007b, 103)

Based on content, the quality-tabloid dichotomy is more evident, although it leans towards a spectrum rather than a binary division. Thussu's observations point to a trend towards tabloidization in form and content among even the more 'serious' news channels, which are devoting more time to "cinema, crime and cricket", the three Cs of India's infotainment (2007b, 104), as well as the shift in reporting practices to include dubious and unverified sources like cell phone photographs and hidden cameras. Other scholars have remarked on the range or extent of tabloid culture in Western media systems, frequently using quality of content as a metric of tabloidization (Gripsrud 2000; Merrill 1968; Paletz 1998). Merrill (1968) classified international newspapers according to a broad spectrum with hard-news-oriented newspapers at one end and entertainment-focused newspapers at the other.

Paletz's (1998) work also divides news media into categories of elite, prestige, popular, and tabloid, using criteria of content priority on the hard news–soft news spectrum, but it is Gripsrud's (2000) tiering of the 'tabloid' itself that is most closely related to the Indian context. On Tier 1 are news outlets that rely heavily on entertainment, but observe a similar journalistic rigour to that of 'quality' media. Gripsrud's example for this tier includes BBC's *Nationwide*, a current affairs programme that aired from 1969 to 1983 and focused on news, sports, and entertainment. On Tier 2 is television content that focuses on the personal and private lives of celebrities, but does so with dignity, such as *The Oprah Winfrey Show*. What Gripsrud classifies as 'trash' is Tier 3, comparing this to the gladiatorial spectacles of the Roman Empire, which provides content whose aim is to "shake the audience, provide kicks, laughs, and whatever may increase adrenaline levels" (2000, 291). He gives the example of *The Jerry Springer Show*, which was distributed by NBC and aired for 27 years between 1991 and 2018. That show regularly encouraged fights between guests and often involved "merciless exploitation of participants" (2000, 291).

Most television news content in India falls into one or the other of Gripsrud's (2000) tiers, depending on the issue being covered, though many English-language news channels and regional channels have managed to stay clear of the Tier 3 category. Even so, approaches to and presentation of news can differ widely between these channels. Most news channels host debates around current affairs, but the tone can range from a staid discussion to a frenzied shouting match. For example, coverage of the November 2008 Mumbai terror attacks by even some of the most prominent news channels was severely criticized by many journalists as well as the general public, who wondered, for example, why attacks on the five-star Taj Mahal and Oberoi Trident hotels in 2008 were given greater prominence than the attack on the Chhatrapati Shivaji Terminus (CST) railway station in 2006. As A. K Bhattacharya pointed out:

> The seven bombs that exploded at seven locations in local trains in Mumbai in July 2006 killed almost as many people as last week's terrorist attacks. But the coverage of those blasts was quite muted compared with what happened now.
>
> (Bhattacharya 2008)

Some India scholars, however, have also demonstrated the political and democratic power of Indian television. Mehta (2010) showed the democratic impact that regional-language programming could have at the grassroots level by chronicling the access to and behaviour of elected representatives. He observed that politicians increasingly used networks from their own regions to speak to their constituencies and voter bases, used instances of investigative reporting that provoked anger from local politicians worried about upcoming elections to illustrate the impact of regional television, and argued that at the local (as opposed to national) level, it made perfect economic sense for channels to prioritize social issues as these increased ratings and advertisements.

With Gripsrud's (2000) classification as a starting point, but paying due recognition to the unique characteristics of Indian media, television content can be classified along two continuums (Figure 6.1), tone and content, as shown in the figure below. Content in the first quadrant include English-language news channels like the NDTV or the CNBC TV-18, while Republic TV falls in the second, and the regional Telugu-language channel TV Nine, which frequently dramatizes crime coverage, belongs in the fourth. However, as concerns their coverage of breaking news like the 2008 attacks, almost all news channels would fall into the third quadrant (Mitra 2009).

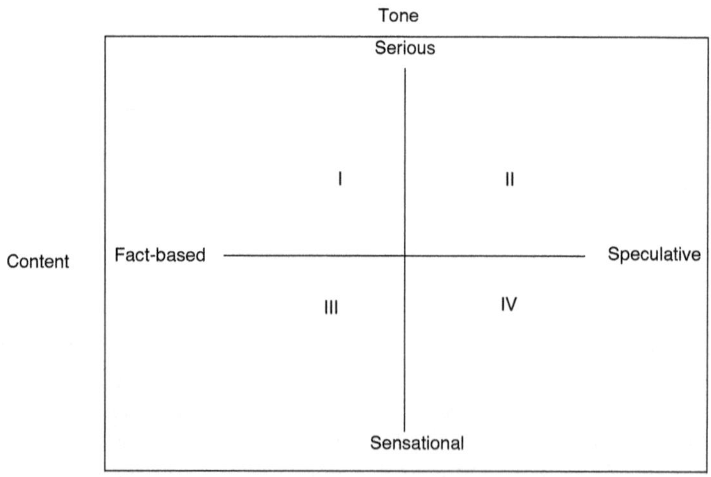

Figure 6.1 Classification of Indian television channels by approach to content and tone

Coverage of the death of Sridevi

In February 2018, Sridevi, a popular Bollywood actress from the 1990s, drowned in a bathtub in a hotel in Dubai, where she was attending a family wedding. Sridevi was a glamorous icon, having appeared in more than 300 films across five languages, and won numerous awards, including the *Padma Shri*, India's highest civilian honour. She would also appear in the *In Memoriam* section of the 90th Academy Awards in 2018. It is no surprise, then, that her death generated extensive media attention and became the focus of prime-time news for many days, especially given the increasing focus on Bollywood news (Thussu 2007b). What was unexpected was the lengths to which certain television channels went in dramatizing her death and speculating about the causes.

Enactments, speculation, and drama

Immediately after her death, while the Dubai authorities were still investigating the cause, which was ultimately ruled to be accidental drowning, theories ranged from suicide to murder. Such speculation offered a wide playing field for television anchors to air their opinions. Hindi news channel ABP News re-enacted "the last 15 minutes of life" on February 25, 2018, using look-alike actors, going so far as to promote this episode using a poster with the backdrop of a bathtub, a half-full glass of wine, and a portrait of the actress herself photoshopped in. A Telugu-language news channel, TV 9, had a reporter jump into a bathtub to debate the practical aspects of drowning (TV9 Telugu 2018). According to The News Minute, this channel also had a "morphed visual of Sridevi lying dead in a bathtub", while her husband looked on (The News Minute, 2018). English-language news channels were not far behind: both Times Now and CNN TV-18 had graphics and visuals that ostensibly covered different factual aspects of a bathtub drowning, but included obscure and irrelevant details and conspiracy theories in an apparent attempt to increase viewership and ratings at the height of interest in a tragic incident. Coverage also involved intense speculation on the actress's character and the private lives of her family. Her relationships, her drinking habits, and the role of the husband in the death were all given significant airtime.

Gripsrud's (2000) categorization of tabloids offers a useful lens through which to examine the treatment of Sridevi's death. He argued that not all entertainment news is tabloid in nature, and offered the example of a well-crafted interview with a celebrity which details the individual's professional activities to demonstrate what constitutes 'good' entertainment news. Moreover, he suggests that in newspapers, 'good' entertainment news should appear in clearly demarcated sections or supplements, while broadcasters should devote specific segments to such content, while still following journalistic accuracy and sourcing standards. In Indian television, however, entertainment news is seen as a driver of audience numbers and a means of survival for news businesses. In this context, the coverage of both Padukone and, in particular, the death of Sridevi, border on what Gripsrud (2000) classifies as 'trash', with many television programmes prioritizing spectacle and speculation over fact-based reporting.

The nature and content of coverage in this case are not only trivial, but change the informational function of journalism. Arguably, this trend of catering to the lowest common denominator (Thussu 2007b; Mehta 2008) while increasing viewership serves no democratic purpose. This conclusion holds true not only in the Indian context, but globally (Esser 1999).

Conclusion: external pluralism, balancing tabloidization

Drawing from Hallin and Mancini's study (2004) on media systems, which categorized Western media models using descriptive indicators of the press such as history, the extent of political-news media affiliations, professionalism in journalism, and journalistic independence from the state, the Indian system can be characterized by elements of external pluralism, commercial orientation, and by professional ideologies of journalists.

External pluralism in the Indian context is made possible by the sheer number of news outlets in the country, which ensures a diverse set of views are available. However, there are distinct markers of political parallelism and internal polarization at the institutional level. For example, *The Hindu* newspaper is often perceived to be left-oriented, while the television channel *Republic* is considered right-leaning, Political affiliation in privately-owned news outlets is also characterized by a dependence on private and government advertising for a large part of newspaper revenues, and symbiotic relationships between newspaper management and political parties at the national and regional levels (e.g. *Hindustan Times* editor Shobhana Bhartia being nominated to the upper house of the parliament by the Indian National Congress). However, the number of players in the market, irrespective of the political and ideological orientation of individual news outlets, contributes to different viewpoints in the public sphere. Complementing this pluralism is a community of journalists whose professional ideologies are based on values of loyalty to readers, accuracy, autonomy, and objectivity (Purayannur 2018).

In the coverage of both Padukone and Sridevi, the quality–tabloid divide can be seen in the nature of the debates in the Indian public sphere. In the days that followed *The Times of India*'s 'offensive' tweet about Padukone, the newly-formed digital publication *The News Minute* published several critical articles, with editor Dhanya Rajendran even writing a piece on the perceived irrelevance of the mainstream news media when celebrities could reach out to their fans through social media. Several international publications picked up the news, with the UK newspaper the *Guardian* making comparative references to British tabloid the *Sun*'s 'Page 3' model of objectifying women's bodies and Lucy-Anne Holmes' 2013 campaign against the practice.

In coverage of Sridevi's death, it was the legacy media and some digital news outlets that carried the debate forward, calling for restraint and sobriety rather than a frenzy of dramatization (TV 18, The News Minute). Members of the film fraternity also joined the debate and, relying heavily on social media, spoke of the need for more fact-based journalism and less speculation. *News 18* published a particularly well-argued piece by Simantini Dey, a senior journalist, about the pitfalls of near-voyeuristic journalism:

> while certain media outlets feed off of the viewers' voyeuristic instincts to know the intimate secrets of actors' or actresses' lives (and deaths), the viewers, in turn, derive some sort of sadistic pleasure in knowing that all was not perfect, after all, in the lives of their almost perfect favourite stars.
>
> (Dey 2018)

Despite the growing emphasis on what Thussu calls "global infotainment", a priority on stories about "celebrities, crime, corruption and violence" presented in the form of a spectacle (2007, 8), the Indian news media follow a tradition of external pluralism. This dates to colonial times, and continues to offer multiple voices against and for issues, creating a vibrant public element in India's democratic fabric. The trend of trivialization and personalization of content is simultaneously balanced by not only different forms of entertainment journalism (Gripsrud 2000) but also criticism of the less rigorous forms of journalistic practice.

References

Aggarwal, Vir Bala, and V.S. Gupta. 2001. *Handbook of Journalism and Mass Communication*. New Delhi: Concept Publishing House.

Aikat, Debashis. 2009. *An Inexorable Watchdog: The Evolution of India's News Media in Reshaping Democratic Traditions*. Chicago: International Communication Association.

Banerji, Ranjona. 2018. "The Talking Point." In *A Handbook of Journalism: Media in the Information Age*, edited by Eshwar V. Anand and Krishnamachary Jayanthi. London: SAGE Publications.

BBC. 2019. "India profile - Media." 29 April. Accessed December 12, 2019. https://www.bbc.com/news/world-south-asia-12557390.

Bhattacharya, Pramit. 2008. "Elite media for elite India". *Business Standard* [online]. Accessed August 19, 2020. https://www.business-standard.com/article/opinion/a-k-bhattacharya-elite-media-for-elite-india-108120301087_1.html.

Biju, P.R. 2017. *Political Internet: State and Politics in the Age of Social Media*. Oxon & New York: Routledge.

Broadcast Audience Research Council. 2019. "Policy for Genre Classification of Television Channels (Amended)." September. Accessed January 12, 2020. https://www.barcindia.co.in/policy-updates/policy-for-genre-classification-of-tv-channels-amended-september-2019.pdf.

Chadha, Kalyani. 2012. "Twitter as media watch-dog? Lessons from India's Radia tapes scandal." *Global Media and Communication* 8 (2): 171–176.

Chagas, Viktor. 2016. "Political Economy of Popular Journalism in Comparative Perspective: an analysis on tabloidization in Brazil, India and South Africa." *Brazilian Journalism Research* 12 (1): 58–77.

Cochrane, Kira. 2013. "No More Page 3 campaigner Lucy-Anne Holmes on her battle with the Sun." 10 March. Accessed October 23, 2019. https://www.theguardian.com/media/2013/mar/10/anti-page-3-the-sun-campaigner.

Curran, James, Shanto Iyengar, Anker Brink Lund, and Inka Salovaara-Moring. 2009. "Media System, Public Knowledge and Democracy: A Comparative Study." *European Journal of Communication* 24 (1): 5–26.

Datta-Ray, Sunanda K. 1996. "Press Freedom and Professional Standards in Asia." In *Walking the Tightrope: Press Freedom and Professional Standards in Asia*, edited by Asad Latif, 25–30. Singapore: AMIC Publications.

Demers, David. 1999. "Corporate Newspaper Bashing: Is it Justified?" *Newspaper Research Journal* 20 (1): 83–97.

Dey, Simantini. 2018. "Media's Voyeuristic Instincts and Viewers' Sadistic Pleasures Create Circus Around Sridevi's Death." February 27. Accessed January 5, 2020. https://www.news18.com/news/opinion/medias-voyeuristic-instincts-and-viewers-sadistic-pleasures-create-circus-around-sridevis-death-1674135.html.

D'Rozario, Clifton. 2008. "How private treaties influence reporting." June 17. Accessed April 25, 2017. http://www.thehoot.org/media-watch/media-business/how-private-treaties-influence-reporting-3174.

Esser, Frank. 1999. "Tabloidization of news: A comparative analysis of Anglo-American and German press journalism." *European journal of communication* 14 (3): 291–324.

Gripsrud, Jostein. 2000. "Tabloidization, Popular Journalism, and Democracy." In *Tabloid Tales: Global Debates over Media Standards*, edited by Colin Sparks and John Tulloch, 285–300. Maryland & Oxford: Rowman & Littlefield Publishers, Inc.

Gupta, Priya. 2014. "Dear Deepika, our point of view…" September 23. Accessed October 23, 2019. https://timesofindia.indiatimes.com/entertainment/hindi/bollywood/news/Dear-Deepika-our-point-of-view-/articleshow/43084705.cms.

Hallin, Daniel C., and Paolo Mancini. 2004. *Comparing Media Systems: Three Models of Media and Politics*. Cambridge: Cambridge University Press.

Hampton, Mark. 2010. "The Fourth Estate Ideal in Journalism History." In *The Routledge Companion to News and Journalism*, edited by Stuart Allan, 3–12. New York: Routledge.

Jain, Parul, Uma Shankar Pandey, and Enakshi Roy. 2017. "Perceived Efficacy and Intentions Regarding Seeking Mental Healthcare: Impact of Deepika Padukone, A Bollywood Celebrity's Public Announcement of Struggle with Depression." *Journal of Health Communication: International Perspectives* 22 (8): 713–720.

Katju, Markandey. 2011. "The Role the Media should be playing in India." November 5. Accessed August 23, 2012. http://www.thehindu.com/news/justice-markandey-katju-on-the-role-of-media-in-india/article13473879.ece.

Khaleeli, Homa. 2014. "Boobs aren't news, but try telling that to the Times of India."-September 20. Accessed October 31, 2019. https://www.theguardian.com/lifeandstyle/womens-blog/2014/sep/24/times-india-bollywood-deepika-padukone-cleavage.

Kohli-Khandekar, Vanita. 2010. *The Indian Media Business*. New Delhi: Response Books.

Loo, Eric. 2009. *Best Practices of Journalism in Asia*. Singapore: Konrad Adenauer Stiftung.

Mahalingam, Sudha. 1998. "A newspaper scandal: Editorial changes in The Times of India raise disturbing questions." June 6. Accessed May 2, 2012. https://frontline.thehindu.com/other/article30247601.ece.

Manchanda, Usha. 1998. "Invasion from the skies: the impact of foreign television on India." *Australian Studies in Journalism* (7): 136–163.

McLachlan, Shelley, and Peter Golding. 2000. "Tabloidization in the British Press: A Quantitative Investigation into Changes in British Newspapers, 1952–1997." In *Tabloid Tales: global debate over media standards*, edited by Colin Sparks and John Tulloch, 75–90. Maryland & Oxford: Rowman & Littlefield Publishers, Inc.

McManus, John H. 1992. "What kind of Commodity is News?" *Communication Research* 19 (6): 787–805.

Mehta, Nalin. 2010. "India Live: Satellite, Politics and India's TV News Revolution." In *The Rise of 24-Hour News Television: Global Perspectives*, edited by Stephen Cushion and Justin Lewis, 319–336. New York: Peter Lang Publishing, Inc.

Mehta, Nalin. 2008. *India on Television: How satellite TV has changed the way we think and act*. New Delhi: Harper Collins.

Merrill, John C. 1968. *The Elite Press: Great Newspapers of the World*. New York: Pitman Publishing Corporation.

Mitra, Antara. 2009. "All for brownie points!: reappraising the new commercial media and media–terrorism nexus in the context of the Mumbai attacks of 26/11." *Asia Europe Journal* 7: 433–447.

Natarajan, J. 1955. *A History of Indian Journalism*. Delhi: Government of India Press.

Ninan, Sevanti. 2012. *Headlines from the Heartland: reinventing the Hindi public sphere*. New Delhi: SAGE.

Office of the Registrar General & Census Commissioner, India. 2020. "C-17 POPULATION BY BILINGUALISM AND TRILINGUALISM." January 9. Accessed January 12, 2020. http://www.censusindia.gov.in/2011census/C-17.html.

Paletz, David L. 1998. *The Media in American Politics*. New York: Longman.

Picard, Robert G. 2004. "Commercialism and Newspaper Quality." *Newspaper Research Journal* 25 (1): 54–65.

Prasad, Kiran. 2008. "The False Promise of Media Liberalisation in India." In *Free Markets, Free Media? Reflections on the political economy of the press in Asia*, edited by Cherian George, 59–71. Singapore: Asian Media Information and Communication Centre, Nanyang Technological University.

PricewaterhouseCoopers India. 2017. "Global Entertainment and Media Outlook 2017–2021." Accessed December 29, 2017. https://www.pwc.in/industries/entertainment-and-media/global-entertainment-and-media-outlook-2017-2021.html.

Purayannur, Sreedevi. 2018. "Quality in Journalism: Perceptions and Practice in an Indian Context." Unpublished PhD thesis, University of Sheffield.

PwC India. 2017. "Global Entertainment and Media Outlook 2017–2021." Accessed December 29, 2017. https://www.pwc.in/industries/entertainment-and-media/global-entertainment-and-media-outlook-2017-2021.html.

Raghavan, G. 1994. *The Press in India: A New History*. New Delhi: Gyan Publications.

Ram, Narasimhan. 2011. "Sectional President's Address: The Changing Role of the News Media in Contemporary India." December 10–13. *Proceedings of the Indian History Congress* 72. Punjabi University, Patiala: Indian History Congress. 1289–1310.

Ram, Narasimhan. 2007. "Newspaper Futures: India and the World." August 15. Accessed March 8, 2011. www.hinduonnent.com/af/india60/stories/2007081550100300.htm.

Rao, Shakuntala, and Navjit Singh Johal. 2006. "Ethics and News Making in the Changing Indian Mediascape." *Journal of Mass Media Ethics* 21 (4): 286–303.

Ray, Ganendra Narayan. 2006. "Tabloidization of the Media: The Page Three Syndrome." Kolkata: Public Relations Society of India and Mass Media Center, Government of West Bengal, 1–6.

Rodrigues, Usha M. 2009. November 30–December 2. "*Bucking the Trend: Indian Print Media.*" JEA 2009: Journalism education in the digital age: sharing strategies and experiences. Proceedings of the 2009 Journalism Education Association (Australia) Conference. Perth: Journalism Education Association (Australia), 1–14.

Rooney, Dick. 1998. "Dynamics of the British tabloid press." *Javnost – The Public* 5 (3): 95–107.

Saptrishi, Aruna. 2005. *History of Journalism.* Delhi: Saujanya Books.

Seneviratne, Kalinga. 2008. "Journalism by Whom, For Whom?" In *Free Markets, Free Media? Reflections on the political economy of the press in Asia*, edited by Cherian George, 20–47. Singapore: Asian Media Information and Communication Centre, Nanyang Technological University.

Siebert, Fred, Theodore Peterson, and Wilbur Schramm. 1956. *Four Theories of the Press.* Urbana and Chicago: University of Illinois Press.

Sonwalkar, Prasun. 2002. "'Murdochization' of the Indian press: from by-line to bottom-line." *Media, Culture & Society* 24 (6): 821–834.

Sonwalkar, Prasun. 2001. "Opposition to the Entry of Foreign Press in India, 1991–1995: The Hidden Agenda." *Modern Asian Studies* 35 (3): 743–763.

Sparks, Colin. 2000. "Introduction: The Panic over Tabloid News." In *Tabloid Tales: global debates over media standards*, edited by Colin Sparks and John Tulloch, 1–40. Maryland and Oxford: Rowman & Littlefield Publishers, Inc.

Sukumar, R. 2012. "Ed Space: Staying Ahead of Times." Livemint.com. January 27. Accessed February 21, 2012. http://www.livemint.com/2012/01/27190104/Ed-Space–Staying-ahead-of-times.

The News Minute. 2014. "Cutting out the middleman: How Deepika Padukone's fight with Times Of India is a lesson in media management." September 20. Accessed October 12, 2019. https://www.thenewsminute.com/article/cutting-out-middleman-how-deepika-padukones-fight-times-india-lesson-media-management-20357.

The News Minute. 2014. "Times of India saw her cleavage, Deepika Padukone shows them she has a spine too." September 22. Accessed November 23, 2019.

The News Minute. 2018. "Sridevi death and the circus on TV: A reporter even jumped into a bathtub." 2018 February. Accessed November 23, 2019. https://www.thenewsminute.com/article/sridevi-death-and-circus-tv-reporter-even-jumped-bath-tub-77103.

https://www.thenewsminute.com/article/times-india-saw-her-cleavage-deepika-padukone-shows-them-she-has-spine-too-20319.

Thussu, Daya K. (1999). "Privatizing the Airwaves: The Impact of Globalization on Broadcasting in India." *Media, Culture & Society* 21: 121–131.

Thussu, Daya Kishan. 2007a. "The 'Murdochization' of news? The case of Star TV in India." *Media, Culture & Society* 29 (4): 593–611.

Thussu, Daya Kishan. 2007b. *News as Entertainment: The Rise of Global Infotainment.* London: SAGE Publications.

TV9 Telugu. 2018. "Sridevi Death Mystery: Is it possible to drown and died in Bathtub? - TV9 Special Report." February 27. Accessed January 5, 2020. https://www.youtube.com/watch?v=UOuAtf9MDoE.

Uribe, Rodrigo, and Barrie Gunther. 2004. "Research note: The tabloidization of British tabloids." *European Journal of Communication* 19 (3): 387–402.

Wu, Huizhong. 2018. "Indian media condemned for 'ghoulish' coverage of Sridevi death." 28 February. Accessed January 05, 2020. https://www.cnn.com/2018/02/28/asia/sridevi-death-media-coverage-intl/index.html.

Zelizer, Barbie. 2004. *Taking Journalism Seriously: News and the Academy*. London: Sage.

7 Tabloid and populist sensitivities in Denmark

Henrik Bødker

Introduction

The 1973 general election in Denmark is generally known as the "landslide election" as it severely reshuffled parliament and sent a new populist party, the Progress Party, bursting into parliament as the second-biggest party after the Social Democrats. The party, whose main policies were lower taxes and less red tape, was led by Mogens Glistrup (1926–2008), a lawyer whose "flamboyant style and references to the 'ordinary Dane' … resonated with ordinary people, and he used the tabloid press as his channel" (Klages 2003: 404).[1] It is this presumed affinity between tabloids and populism that this chapter seeks to investigate by taking a closer look at how the Danish tabloid *Ekstra Bladet* related to, respectively, the 1973 election and another landslide election in 2015 when the Progress Party's de facto successor, the Danish People's Party (formed in 1995), became the second-biggest party after the Social Democrats. This election and its links to what was to be claimed to be uncontrolled inflow of refugees in the same year, prompted significant activity on the debate section, somewhat aptly called "nationen", translated as "The Nation", on the website of *Ekstra Bladet,* which by then had become one of the most visited news sites in Denmark.

By looking at these two instances 42 years apart, this chapter aims, on the one hand, to present insights into the role and developments of tabloids within the political landscape of Denmark and, on the other, to contribute to a broader discussion about how tabloids, broadsheets, and populism co-exist and develop through complex relations where communicative boundaries and transgressions are constantly negotiated. The main aim is not to determine whether tabloids are populist as such but rather to get a sense of how tabloids, in both analogue and digital times, have been related to populist politicians and sentiments. It addresses a gap Bächler and Hopmann (2017: 29) identify within research on "populist political communication in relation to the media", which has been less "extensive" in Denmark.

For more than a century the Danish tabloid scene has been dominated by *Ekstra Bladet* (1905) and *BT* (1916), both of which were launched as supplementary titles to the two main Copenhagen (and national) broadsheet papers, *Politiken* (1884) and *Berlingske Tidende* (1749). The subsidiary and supplementary roles were signalled by the titles of the two tabloids: *Ekstra Bladet*, literally 'the extra paper', and *BT*, the initials of its "mother" title. These two supplementary outlets largely aligned themselves politically with the titles they supplemented, which meant, very broadly, that *Ekstra Bladet* was left of centre and *BT* right of centre. Both, however, differentiated themselves from their "mother" papers in both form and content by applying what have become trademarks of tabloids: short stories focused on sensation, a large amount of illustrations and later photos, celebrity and human-interest stories, and increasingly dominant headlines. While the label of "tabloid" is sometimes also used in Denmark, the Danish papers have generally been referred to as "sensationspressen" (the sensational press), "formiddagspressen" (the morning press, as opposed to broadsheet, which used to come out in the afternoon), and "smudspressen" (the filthy press). Seemingly in this spirit, the slogan for *Ekstra Bladet*, "tør hvor andre tier", translates to 'dares where others stay silent'. Catering mainly to working and middle classes, this conveys that the tabloid will tell you "truths" that broadsheets will not and, just as importantly, in a language and form that differs from the mainstream papers.

While all print newspapers in Denmark have been affected by the shifts in news consumption and related financial woes, the print tabloids have been harder hit than the print broadsheets: "in the last 25 years *BT* and *Ekstra Bladet* have lost 77% and 80% of their circulation, nearly twice as much as the [broadsheet] nationals" (Wedenborg 2015, n.p.). Online, however, the story differs, and both tabloids were, according to the Danish Ministry of Culture, among the four most-visited news sites in 2015, joined by the two public broadcasters' sites.[2] The following section will delineate the main theoretical strands linking populism, journalism, and tabloids.

Tabloids and populism

The notions of tabloids and populism are slippery on their own and putting them together does not help. The following is, nevertheless, an attempt to give some conceptual clarity to this complex relationship, which arguably, in more or less explicit and more or less conceptually clear ways, underpins many discussions about tabloids as, for instance, when Conboy (2006: 9), in his study of British tabloids, talks about how "[n]ationalism and a populist vision of contemporary Britain are embedded in the language of these papers on a daily basis". Beyond this more general usage of the adjective "populist", there are a few studies that address such linkages more systematically, such as Akkerman (2011). It is also worth noting that the discussion of media and populism has intensified within political communication, media, and journalism scholarship with the recent rise of populist politicians and parties. Much of this attention has, however, been focused on social media, which constitute, according to Gerbaudo (2018), an "elective affinity" with populism. The diversification of the news landscape accompanying the digital age has also been linked to populism; in relation to this, Krämer (2014) offers a conceptual approach, distinguishing between somewhat overlapping discussions of how news media (should) relate to populist politicians and parties, i.e. media *and* populism, and "media populism", by which he refers to populist tendencies within news media themselves, irrespective of the focus of the coverage. This, he broadly exemplifies by discussing overall features of talk radio and tabloids.

While Moffitt (2014) defines populism wholly as a specific style of communication, Krämer (2014: 46) makes the case that "[s]tylistic and ideological populism tend to converge" and argues for seeing populism as "favouring the perspective and interests of a [supposedly] majority ingroup that is nonetheless construed as subaltern", "anti-institutionalism", "claims to communicate and respond directly to the political basis bypassing the devalued elites and institutions" in an "emotional and moralist style, plainspoken, sometimes aggressive, but appealing to common sense" (Krämer 2014: 46). This aligns with Moffitt's (2014) notion of the performance of political crisis, and "the demand to act decisively and immediately" (391). It is this notion of immediacy, linked to broader issues of temporality (see Bødker and Anderson 2019), that bridges populism's urgency with the affinities of tabloid journalism, which often takes a stand on behalf of and speaks for a suffering "people" against bureaucratic institutions, governing structures, and elites, presented in plain moralistic language that demands immediate change. Drawing these conceptual threads together, one can argue both populism and tabloids: claim to articulate views, demands, and feelings not otherwise articulated; combine issues in ways that do not necessarily align with established hierarchies in and/or ideologies in journalism and/or politics; offer short-term "contracts" in relation to specific issues rather than a long-term relationship through subscription or party membership; and, hold related positions that are complementary to and somewhat in opposition to perceived centres of power and standards such as conventional journalism and traditional party politics. Along with the broad stylistic and ideological affinities pointed out above, this overview underpins the analysis of the two populist instances of *Ekstra Bladet.*

Lastly, and before turning our attention to the landslide election of 1973, it is important to add a few thoughts on how populism relates normatively to studies of popular culture. Such thoughts are necessary in a context with a growing prominence of populist politicians, something which has forced some tabloids to reconsider their role, as we will see in the discussion of *Ekstra Bladet.* Addressing tabloids, Gripsrud (2000: 286) talks about an academic "populist enthusiasm", which he here links to John Fiske, who sees entertaining tabloids as representing "failures of that from which they [the disadvantaged] are excluded" and their consumption as "antiestablishment pleasures". Gripsrud, however, dismisses Fiske's argument by pointing out that tabloids indeed are as enmeshed in "the ideological common sense" as they are in "questioning [its] boundaries". This view partly echoes McGuigan's earlier criticism in *Cultural Populism* (1992: 39), where he warned that the enthusiasm of "students of popular culture may lead to 'uncritical populism'".

Neither Gripsrud nor McGuigan link the notion of populism to tabloids themselves, and theirs is a critique of those academic approaches to tabloids which uncritically embrace the popular. Johansson takes this a bit further, noting that "scholarly defences for tabloid media generally focus on the more 'benign' and playful formats … whereas it is harder to see the democratic capabilities in an arguably more reactionary form of populism such as the *Sun*" (2007: 85). Here populism is not understood as an enthusiasm for the popular but rather a demarcation of the less benign and more reactionary parts of the tabloid landscape. While such a distinction is highly normative it is an improvement from evaluating tabloids as a whole. As a parallel thought exercise, consider how odd it would be to have broad discussions of whether quality newspapers as a monolithic genre are good for democracy. The tendency to evaluate tabloids as a whole is a reminder that tabloids are regularly seen as the 'other' side of proper journalism. This view has been challenged by broader reorientations to "the popular", which have been (in turn) criticized for uncritical valorisations of the form, such as McGuigan's notion of "cultural populism". This surfaces parallel issues for journalism and journalism studies, namely: how should one balance understanding (and reporting) of what may be legitimately felt political sentiments? For journalists, this includes the question of how best to represent these within commercially-driven and/or ideologically-driven media organisations. While it seems clear one should not succumb to "cultural populism", one should, on the other hand, also not quickly latch on to the notion that tabloids merely cater to the unthinking, uninformed, duped, and reactionary who deeply resent governing structures and elites.

This brief discussion underlines that the relationships between, on the one hand, media, cultural, and journalism studies and those between tabloids and populism, on the other, are complex and shifting. This relates to issues of representation, and the extent to which tabloids either give voice to a preformed "ordinary", or rather the extent to which they construct such a thing based on their own ideological and commercial incentives. Both the cases of *Esktra Bladet* discussed below raise precisely such issues of representation. In examining these we can ask to what extent (tabloid) journalism acts as a seemingly unmediated channel for popular/populist sentiments. Doing so also allows us to see to what extent politicians used the tabloid press, as it was argued about Mogens Glistrup.

This discussion should be considered within a wider set of debates, as well. At issue is how journalism (and not only tabloids) should engage with the rise of populism. This has increasingly gained attention as populism has become more prominent in Western democracies. Hafez (2014) describes a "complicated relationship" that has resulted, arguing that, not surprisingly, "right-wing populism might be an ideal candidate for functionalist media theory, but it is also the complete antidote to rational deliberation theory" (2014: 5). As such, he concludes that media risk legitimizing populist discourses, adding "there is as much reason for the mass media to cover as there is to systematically ignore and boycott populism" (2014: 6). While Hafez (2014) does not distinguish between mainstream and tabloid media, Mazzoleni finds the "classical distinction" continues to be useful, arguing tabloid "media give passionate attention to what happens in the usually animated precincts of populist movements" (2007: 51–52). Attention to populism is one thing, another is the form such coverage takes. It is this latter aspect which

Akkerman (2011) addresses. Based on a study of British and Dutch tabloids, she concludes

> there is no ground for the idea that popular newspapers are more sympathetic towards populist parties than quality newspapers. Theories that predict a favourable bias of popular newspapers towards these parties do not hold for the two cases analyzed here.
>
> (942)

However, Akkerman does see a link between popular newspapers and right-wing populist parties in the form of "the platform that popular newspapers provide to the vox populi" (942). The analysis below of *Ekstra Bladet* partly affirms this view in the Danish context.

Ekstra Bladet and two populist interventions

The landscape of print news media in Denmark has traditionally been characterised by a high degree of political parallelism through which the major newspapers originally were tied to the main parties in parliament; this was known as the party press system. While over the course of the twentieth century the main newspapers shed any formal connections to political parties, they remained loosely linked to major ideological positions largely founded upon traditional socio-economic and political-ideological differences (conservative, liberal, and leftist progressive). However, the two 'landslides' outlined above shook this up.

The first shake-up came in 1973, when the newly formed Progress Party stormed into Parliament, winning 28 of 179 seats and breaking the existing structure. Running counter to 'normal' politics in both content and style, the Progress Party's success forced newspapers to decide either to stick to or recalibrate their positions from the existing political parallelism towards a new one. The question of media/political recalibration emerged again in 2015, when The Danish People's Party became the second biggest party in parliament, winning 37 of 179 seats – the Social Democrats got 47. Formed in 1995 on an anti-EU and anti-immigration platform, the DPP is the de facto successor to the Progress Party. While the shock of the DPP's rise was dampened as it was the second such landslide, it was nevertheless a significant and somewhat surprising result that, in its aftermath, illustrated how social media and participation pushed the boundaries of political discourse and further disrupted the political-press relationship.

With these two moments in mind, looking at the left-of-centre *Ekstra Bladet* allows us to investigate how tabloid and populist sensitivities were negotiated in relation to political allegiances and how this may have shifted over time from a pre-digital news landscape. The two linkages between populism and tabloids singled out in this chapter both relate to spectacular election results in the history of Danish politics and as such give us an insight into how one of the major tabloids was related to and/or in implicated in these processes. While the 1973 landslide and resulting political dynamic is mainly one concerned with economic issues and the state and/or elite, in 2015 the prevailing issues are anti-immigration and nationalism. For the first discussion, analysis is based on a reading of the coverage of Mongens Glistrup and/or The Progress Party in the pages of *Ekstra Bladet* from 27 November to 11 December, 1973, incorporating coverage from one week leading up to the election and coverage for one week following.

The second analysis is based on a leading article in the aftermath of the 2015 election (29 August, 2015) in which *Ekstra Bladet* editor Poul Madsen declares that he disagrees with the sentiments of "the nation", the newspaper's online forum. The analysis also includes the approximately 450 reader comments to Madsen's leading article. What follows is consequently not a systematic and longitudinal investigation of how *Ekstra Bladet* has been related to and implicated in populism in a broader sense, but rather a preliminary probe into two key instances meant to illustrate, and raise questions and theoretical discussions of the relationship between tabloids and populism.

Setting the stage: The Progress Party and a new political landscape (1973)

Mogens Glistrup (1926–2008) founded the Progress Party in 1972 and in the run-up to the general election on 4 December 1973 he was frequently featured in *Ekstra Bladet.* Glistrup was a tax lawyer, and one of the main polemic proposals of the new party was to abolish income tax. He was a member of the Danish Parliament from 1973 to 1983 and again from 1987 to 1990; between 1983 and 1985 he served time in prison for tax fraud. He did, in a sense, ask for the attention of the authorities, as he was well known for equating tax cheats with Danish saboteurs during the German occupation (1940–45) and, in a 1971 TV appearance, for showing his official tax slip showing 0% tax paid while he was running a successful business and living a comfortable life. In *Ekstra Bladet* and elsewhere, in fact, he was often depicted on the swing above his indoor swimming pool. It was widely known that he was already being investigated for tax fraud before the election in 1973, but no charges had been issued when the election took place.

Based on the sampling outlined above, 57 articles were found relating to Glistrup and the Progress Party. Despite using 'and/or' search strings for coverage of either Glistrup or the party, no articles mention the Progress Party without also mentioning Glistrup. In a sense, he *was* the party and on more than one occasion is referred to as party "owner" rather than leader. It is also notable that his newcomer status and the changed political landscape were addressed in leading articles on a number of occasions where it becomes clear that *Ekstra Bladet* largely saw Glistrup as a dangerous charlatan. This finding partly surfaces in the consistent attention paid, both pre- and post-election, to the criminal case against Glistrup for tax fraud. *Bladet*'s coverage raises questions of if or when Glistrup would be formally charged and, after the election, asks how these charges would relate to the issue of the immunity members of parliament enjoy, and which can only be relinquished by parliament.

The front page from Saturday, 1 December, three days before the election, broadly reflects how *Ekstra Bladet* approached Glistrup. The main headline, based on "the election analysis" made by *Ekstra Bladet*, claims Glistrup as one of the big winners of the coming election. However, the headline immediately below states that "Glistrup is fighting for his life against the police" and the last headline refers to Glistrup's "dark fate", which is not based on news analysis but is the result of horoscopes commissioned by *Ekstra Bladet* for all the party leaders. The overall page offers a fairly standard mix of tabloid features, including sex, politics, crimes, and horoscopes. The left-hand side of the front page feature the girl(s) of the week in *Ekstra Bladet*, a story headlined: "Killed when she denied having sex with a boy", and a headline about the "oil crisis" and the laying off of workers. However, the mixing of politics and astrology is a one-off, and the coverage of Glistrup is, as will become evident, more substantially wrapped within a fairly thorough engagement with broader political debates.

In terms of Glistrup's tax case, the coverage is relatively neutral, though it utilizes terms such as "tax-circus", "tax-juggler", "marzipan-eating" (on account of Glistrup's self-proclaimed love of this sweet) and describes him as "the zero-lawyer", referring to his previous stunt with his tax slip on TV. He repeated this stunt in the televised closing debate among party leaders just prior to the election, and in turn *Ekstra Bladet* published a photo of him doing so. *Bladet* opposes the political message Glistrup is making with his tax-slip stunts, and in a leading article (Nov. 30) cautions voters against falling for "cheap promises of tax reductions". These are, the article continues, unfeasible at a time of rising oil prices and unemployment. Using belittling adjectives, the coverage largely paints Glistrup as not a "real" politician like those from the "old" parties. This old–new distinction becomes a running feature in coverage and is partly visible in a dedicated *Ekstra Bladet* section called "Election 73: it is about us", featuring *vox populi* reports from voters. The first of these features a collection of comments from workers at a sugar factory in Nykøbing Falster, headlined "Anker J [the sitting Prime Minister] must govern if we become unemployed: workers at the sugar factory … do not wish for a new government" (Dec. 1). The headline reflects a number of comments from workers seeking stability amid the rising unemployment of the time. In a similar 'vox pop' under the headline "Wish for no political experiments", on Dec. 3, the day before the election, a majority of workers at Varde Steelworks praise the sitting government.

By making public these insights from workers at very traditional and unionized industries, *Ekstra Bladet* is clearly positioning itself in relation to traditional political fault lines, inscribing itself into an established political and journalistic parallel structure. *Ekstra Bladet* does indeed afford a lot of space to leaders from the old parties, mainly the Social Democrats, who were the big losers in the election. While *Ekstra Bladet* describes the party as "for decades having been the main stabilizing element in Danish politics" by taking "responsibility and honour for the social progress", they are also castigated for their "leadership's doubtful stubbornness in their ivory tower" (leading article, Dec. 5). The election indeed prompted a process of reckoning, asking: why had this happened and what did the new political landscape entail?

The election resulted in a somewhat muddy parliamentary situation and it took until Dec. 19 for a new government to be formed, headed by the liberal-right party. The coverage in the week after the election was very much focused on possible constellations of a new government but, paralleling *vox populi* from factories mentioned above, *Ekstra Bladet* features on the day after the election a collection of voter voices, under the headline: "The voters envision a quick re-election: Shocked over Glistrup as head of the country's second-biggest party" (5 December). Yet, on the same day, a leading article headlined "Clarity" writes: "Yesterday we got the really right-wing radicals gathered in the Progress Party … We now have them assembled under one umbrella … and thus know where they can be found, and where they can be fought". One day later, on December 6, the front page features a big photo of Glistrup under the headline: "I want to become Prime Minister"; yet the subheading does not really take this claim from the "tax-juggler" seriously. At the same time, *Bladet*'s coverage ironically calls some of the other 27 newly elected representatives for the Progress Party "fine specimens", which here refers to people with questionable morals; the day before, the paper carries a large article headlined "Politician on election night: Glistrup is a reactionary thug", and this article also addresses who is to blame for him being elected. A member of parliament says, under the subheading "Criticism of the Press":

> I fully acknowledge the responsibility of politicians for this situation. But I want to stress that a significant part of the press — especially the morning press [e.g. the tabloids] — which for a number of years with its somewhat grubby anti-parliamentarism has nourished the ground that has allowed a reactionary such as Glistrup to emerge (5 December).

Similar arguments had also been aired in the broadsheet papers, e.g. in *Demokraten*, which already in January 1973 quoted a politician criticising Glistrup's "cynical pop-political exploitation of the superficiality of the media and their willingness to sell themselves for a joke". It is interesting to note, however, that in a leading article on December 6 headlined "The Guilty", *Ekstra Bladet* fully blames the previous Social Democratic prime minister for stepping down early and, in effect, creating the conditions for the Progress Party and Glistrup to succeed. The press is not mentioned among "the Guilty", so one must assume that *Ekstra Bladet* itself does not take any responsibility. In a leading article the day after, however, it is made clear that "our old reactionary friend *Jyllands-Posten*" is among those at fault, as they support the formation of a government relying on the support of Glistrup. The leading article later argued that the election also had made clear the position of "another of our leading reactionary outlets", *BT*, "where it has always belonged". Notably, the political distinctions drawn between journalistic outlets, i.e. the centre-left papers as opposed to right-wing and reactionary ones, is in focus rather than a distinction between tabloids and broadsheet, a distinction which, as we shall see below, becomes sharper as populist politics became more prominent and anti-immigration.

What is clear from this short probe into how *Ekstra Bladet* approached the first major populist party and politician in Denmark is that the historical political parallelism of parties and newspapers remained in place in the mid-1970s, as opposed to later when a people-elite distinction became more pronounced in tabloid coverage. While some coverage of Glistrup certainly features key tabloid characteristics such as personalisation, sensation, and crime, this was largely within a framework that fully recognised the existing structures of politics and, within that, a leaning towards the left. While the "people" in *Ekstra Bladet* are "ordinary", they are also largely a working-class constituency, and the elite in opposition is largely an economic elite.

The political climate in Denmark in the post-war period had been dominated by the Social Democrats, who governed during a period of a fairly stable growth in living standards. This era came to an end with the "oil crisis" and the "landslide" election of 1973. In this context, the populist intervention of Glistrup largely focused on economics and getting more money to individual citizens and away from bureaucrats. Given the circumstances, this was relatively easy to address within the existing political parallelism of politics and newspapers, and *Ekstra Bladet* was able to maintain its position within these structures while remaining on the side of "the people". As we will see below, however, this balance becomes increasingly difficult to maintain as populism in Denmark shifted from attention to issues such as economics to hot-button issues such as immigration. This, in a sense, realigned political allegiances and recast the people–elite distinction within a very different landscape.

Letting the nation speak: The Danish People's Party's pinnacle of power (2015)

By 2015, *Ekstra Bladet* had become a prominent online player in the Danish news landscape. A significant factor in its rise was the online forum 'nationen', or "the nation". Launched in 2007, 'nationen' quickly grew to become the largest and most active forum among Danish newspapers. In *Ekstra Bladet*'s own description, 'nationen' is a place where "you can comment and discuss all the articles on ekstrabladet.dk – and you can define your own issues and air any opinion, provoke, and debate as much as you like – obviously within the limits of the law".[3] To comment, you have to register and its conditions stipulate that "offending and threatening language is not allowed and will be deleted according to the policy on commentary".[4] Moderation is, however, largely dependent on participants flagging something as offending, resulting in rather different standards of 'offensive' content. As a result, by 2015 "the nation" had become known for its harsh, direct, and often hurtful tone. By establishing this forum and naming it 'nationen', *Ekstra Bladet* was seemingly aligning itself with some kind of "normality" or "ordinariness" within the national community. In contrast to 1973 where it played a role of mediating how a populist leader embodied public sentiments, online it allowed the direct uttering of a variety of public and populist sentiments.

This analysis is from late August 2015, when 'nationen' was teeming with comments following what in Denmark was known as the "refugee crisis". It also follows the Danish general election of June 18, in which the Danish People's Party got 21.1% of the votes (second to the Social Democrats' 26.3%). This situation seemingly created a climate in which extremely harsh anti-immigration positions could be aired publicly. On Aug. 29, however, the paper ran a leading article by chief editor Poul Madsen headlined "I do not agree with the nation!".[5] In the article, Madsen declares that he does not agree with "many of my own readers", which, he continues, "can be interpreted as a rather unwise move fostered in a moment of passing madness or as a complete lack of business acumen". Madsen disagrees with the overall sentiment expressed on 'nationen' that Denmark can opt out of the refugee situation by closing its borders. But, he writes, "[R]efugees will continue to come", and he names specific users from 'nationen' challenging them to come up with solutions, arguing "abusive language, coarse generalizations and platitudes about Muslims will not solve anything". He is not, however, asking for "a better tone" and continues: "We surely cannot solve the refugee problem by polishing the tone. That is why I gladly accommodate 'the nation' and its rough debate". 'Nationen' offers something different, contrasting the elitist language of the metropolitan "café-latte segment" and the newspapers reflecting their views, often described as "naïve" on questions of immigration. However, in distancing himself and *Ekstra Bladet* from such naïveté, Madsen writes that "even the café-latte drinkers' chief editor Bo Lidegaard", from the liberal-left broadsheet *Politiken*, has come to realise "that we simply cannot welcome all refugees".

This short article elicited around 450 comments, the majority of which opposed Madsen's proposed solution of allowing Syrian refugees to work as soon as they come. Many comments accuse the editor of being naïve, "elitist", "politically correct", and out of touch with the problems of real (lower-income) people. From there, comments get increasingly extreme, calling for "civil war" and the "annihilation" of immigrants.

Among these 450 comments, there are also those that support Madsen's push to move beyond "usual quick fixes characterising the nation: 'lock them up', 'lock them out', 'punish them', 'build a wall', 'sink the ships' 'shoot them', 'deport them' and what the creative otherwise can come up with". A lot of the debate referred to here is easily characterizable as populist in the sense that it refers to a clear people-elite split Krämer (2014) describes, invoking a deep crisis and calling for quick solutions in language that is both plain and rude. Both beyond and within the comments there is a related discussion of the role of *Ekstra Bladet* and its place in covering those issues deemed important by self-defined ordinary people.

"I have subscribed to your newspaper for many years", one commenter writes, "and you say (or advertise) that you are a mouthpiece of those lowest in our society" but "now you have shown your real face" and "I will therefore no longer subscribe to your paper". In a similar vein, somebody else asks the editor "to buzz off back to metroXpress. You tramp". While Madsen was never at *metroXpress*, and rather worked at another (now defunct) commuter newspaper, the meaning here is clear: As the editor of a tabloid you are expected to side with "the people" and not with those in power, whether these are politicians passively watching "our country getting raped" or people in the "immigration industry", who profit from the status quo.

There are also commentators who call out Madsen for his hypocrisy, as *Ekstra Bladet* "has been the biggest and most cross-country mouthpiece for xenophobia for almost twenty years and your remorse, Poul Madsen, cannot change that. You have brought people's latent hatred to the surface, so howl with them!". "You have", writes the commentator, "been the proponent of a tough rhetoric towards 'the foreigners' ever since they [*Ekstra Bladet*] ran a campaign by that name in the 90s". In this campaign, which ran from March 31 to June 8 in 1997, *Ekstra Bladet* offered, according to Hervik (2011: 56), "a clear right-wing populist platform, with an immoderate belief that 'ordinary people,' despite their common sense, moral superiority, and innate wisdom, have been denied the opportunity to make themselves heard". In an effort "to let 'ordinary' people speak, *Ekstra Bladet*'s reporters tracked down the authors of letters to the editor in order to interview them" (Hervik 2011: 46). It, in fact, gave the "letter writers" the opportunity to voice their "indiscreet, gut-level opinions" in "full blown articles" (Hervik 2011: 63). This practice of incorporating readers' perspectives was later changed, writes Hervik (2011), and online, when joining "the nation" it is made clear that this did not allow you to "become a journalist with a right to decide on the content of *Ekstra Bladet* or ekstrabladet.dk – that right we do not relinquish so easily even if many surely would hope so!".[6]

In making his disagreement with "the nation" clear, Madsen seems to be reasserting the "ownership" of the tabloid's main content. However, when looking at his leading article alongside comments and reactions to it, what also emerges is the challenge tabloids face when trying to continuously balance between the/a people and the political establishment, and in particular how this is inflamed when it comes to issues such as immigration, which have been clearly affiliated with both tabloids and populism. This is not unique to the Danish case. As Conboy (2006: 9) writes of British tabloids, "[n]ationalism and a populist vision of contemporary Britain are embedded in the language of [tabloid] papers on a daily basis", and "a propensity to sense and exploit issues likely to stir nationalist feelings within the readership". From *Ekstra Bladet*'s campaign in 1997 forward, in drawing attention to nationalist sentiments, the tabloid brought itself into this balancing act; and as reactions to Madsen's article show, with anti-immigration sentiments growing, it was unable to wrest itself easily from this position. As a result, "the Danish People's Party was quick to seize upon this unique opportunity to publicize its nationalist program and contestation of foreign presence" (Hervik 2011: 62). Just as *Ekstra Bladet* in 1973 had given access and attention to Mogens Glistrup, the paper now gave "easy access" to the leader of the Danish People's Party, a platform on which she could "express populist, anti-immigration sentiments" (Hervik 2011: 63).

The difficult balancing act for a tabloid between considering public sentiments, commercial priorities, journalistic values, and an adherence to some level of 'establishment' values have to a certain degree been exacerbated in a digital climate where a tabloid editor is expected to embrace the views of an online forum, "the nation", as a mouth-piece of the "real". In October 2015, Poul Madsen was invited to discuss his reasons for disagreeing with the nation on a weekly radio magazine focused on media-related issues on the Danish public service station DR.[7] Given that *Ekstra Bladet* had a history developing a very critical and harsh anti-immigration rhetoric from the 1990s, Madsen was asked: "What has changed?" He pinpoints two things: the rise of Facebook as a platform where people can seemingly say anything without opposition; and the 2015 general election and the "landslide victory" (Madsen's words) of the Danish People's Party, which to Madsen reflects a widespread fear that *Ekstra Bladet* can help to dissipate. *Ekstra Bladet* is, as Madsen argues, in contact with a constituency of Danes that is not reached by other news media. We will, he says,

> accommodate this debate, which functions as a kind of 'safety valve' where people can utter things not normally heard in public debate and often is different from the debate pages on *Politiken* but that does not mean that we have to agree with the main argument of the debate.

Madsen is here distancing himself from both quality newspapers and their unwillingness to feature such a debate, and social media where this debate is unfiltered and unopposed. In the current media landscape, *Ekstra Bladet* must reposition itself in relation to the unfiltered voices of the 'normal' people.

The possibility of participation offered by a forum like "the nation", however, opens up a possible rift that was glossed over in a print era when a tabloid was expected to represent, by mediating, anti-establishment voices. Such voices are now much more vocal on the tabloid's digital platforms. As the 2015 case shows, this heightens some of the inbuilt tensions reflected in tabloid cultures, including their role in possibly instigating populist sentiments. In 1973, populism emanated from Mogens Glistrup, sentiments that secured coverage in *Ekstra Bladet*. In 1997, *Ekstra Bladet* acted upon a public anti-immigrant sentiment, which arguably helped the fairly new Danish People's Party. In 2015, the populists were thriving on *Ekstra Bladet*'s online platform to such an extent the chief editor felt it necessary to distance himself, or risk the newspaper's editorial content being mistaken for the circulation of populist sentiments online.

Conclusion

Overall, the two cases discussed here make clear that tabloids, populism, and the various relationships between them are both highly contextual and highly relational. The analysis shows these links are co-constituted by broader political structures, allegiances, the issues at stake, and both the broader news landscape and prevailing media technologies. As such, this chapter reinforces Zelizer's argument that tabloid journalism more generally constitutes "a continuum of practices, that exist in degrees which must be judged against their immediate context" (2000: x). As *Ekstra Bladet* had no immediate experience dealing with populist politics in the 1970s, it largely dealt with populism within the structures that had governed Danish politics in the post-war era. It largely treated the populist intervention of Glistrup as a passing fad, similar to Krämer's broader argument that "tabloid journalism depends heavily on the political establishment, so it often constructs a populist perspective on politics that is nevertheless in line with the interests of the established political actors" (2014: 51).

While this was clear in 1973, it was also visible in Madsen's negotiation of "the nation" in 2015, which revealed *Ekstra Bladet*'s difficult balancing of public sentiments, commercial considerations, establishment politics, and journalistic values. A key new element here was the participation allowed by digital media. The tabloid–populist relationship is increasingly related to what goes on in online fora, either on tabloid news sites or elsewhere. This certainly complicates the position of tabloid newspapers in the media landscape.

One should, however, at least based on the analysis here, be careful when equating the affinities between tabloids and populism as necessarily entailing an ideological affinity. While style and ideology can never be fully separated there is no one-to-one relationship either. As seen in the 1973 case, while the coverage in *Ekstra Bladet* in certain ways could be called populist, it was also framed within an established and oppositional political ideology.

In this case, and perhaps also in a more general sense, it can be argued that a tabloid newspaper partly defines itself through its relations to what is perceived as populism, and that populism partly defines its style in relation to what is perceived as a mediated centre understood as "the social construction of centralised media ('the media' in common parlance) as our central access-point to the 'central realities' of the social world" (Couldry 2005: 177). When *Esktra Bladet* covered Glistrup, it clearly made the "event intelligible" by basing its coverage on an existing understanding of society, its structures, and how things worked (Hall, Critcher, Jefferson, Clarke, and Roberts 1978: 55).

Yet, such a discursive policing of populism invites its own transgressions as what is perceived as acceptable is continuously negotiated. Glistrup was in fact, in a break during a TV show, dared by the journalists to show his tax return on live TV (Lykkeberg 2008, n.p.), which he did and which became a recurring element in the news coverage. Fully understanding the mediated formation of the populist interventions discussed here, therefore, requires a more thorough examination of the broader news landscape, i.e. how both TV and newspapers, including the competing tabloid *BT*, engaged with populism in the same circumstances. Going forward, in order to understand how both mainstream and tabloid journalism and populism co-constitute each other, how this sits within a complex triangular relationship, and how this is framed within different historical and cultural contexts, we need more studies and particularly studies beyond the nations where tabloids are more well-known. This chapter is a small step in that direction.

Acknowledgements

I wish to thank the editors of this volume for a close reading as well as for insightful and constructive comments.

Author's note

The articles from *Ekstra Bladet* in the period 27 November to 11 December 1973 have been obtained from the archive at ekstrabladet.dk. Normally, there would be access through the Danish Royal Library but due to restrictions because of COVID 19 there was no access to the reading room.

Notes

1 All citations from material in Danish have been translated by the author.
2 https://mediernesudvikling.slks.dk/2015/webtrafik/
3 About 'nationen' at https://ekstrabladet.dk/nationen/article4075877.ece
4 Conditions for 'nationen' at https://ekstrabladet.dk/betingelser/nationen.jsp
5 The radio programme can be accessed here: http://hdl.handle.net/109.3.1/uuid:cd40fb12-4253-4363-84c9-a6144ab7ec8e
6 About "the nation" at https://ekstrabladet.dk/nationen/article4075877.ece
7 The programme "Mennesker og Medier" (People and Media) aired on 16 October 2015; obtained from http://hdl.handle.net/109.3.1/uuid:cd40fb12-4253-4363-84c9-a6144ab7ec8e

References

Akkerman, Tjitske. 2011. "Friend or foe? Right-wing populism and the popular press in Britain and the Netherlands." *Journalism* 12 (8): 931–945.

Bächler, Christian and Hopmann, David N. 2017. "Denmark: The Rise of the Danish People's Party." In *Populist Political Communication in Europe* edited by Toril Aalberg, Claes de Vreese, Jesper Strömbäck, Frank Esser, & Carston Reinemann, 29–41. London: Routledge.

Bødker, Henrik and Anderson, Chris. 2019. "Populist Time." *International Journal of Communication* 13: 5948–5966.

Conboy, Martin. 2006. *Tabloid Britain: Constructing a Nation through Language.* Milton Park: Routledge.

Couldry, Nick. 2005. "Transvaluing media studies: or, beyond the myth of the mediated centre." In *Media and cultural theory* edited by James Curran and David Morley, 177–194. Abingdon: Routledge.

Gerbaudo, Paulo 2018 "Social media and populism: an elective affinity?" *Media, Culture & Society* 40 (5): 745–753.

Gripsrud, Jostein. 2000. "Popular Journalism, and Democracy." In *Tabloid Tales: global debates of media standards* edited by Colin Sparks and John Tulloch, 285–300. Lanham, Maryland: Rowman and Littlefield.

Hafez, Kai. 2014. *Islam in "liberal" Europe: Freedom, Equality, And Intolerance.* Translated by Alex Skinner. Lanham, Maryland: Rowman & Littlefield.

Hafez, Kai. 2017. "A Complicated Relationship: Right-Wing Populism, Media Representation and Journalism Theory." *Global Media Journal*, German edition 7 (2).

Hall, Stuart, Critcher, Chas, Jefferson, Tony, Clarke, John, & Roberts, Brian. 1978. *Policing the Crisis: Mugging, The State, and Law and Order.* London: The Macmillan Press Ltd.

Heft, Annett, Mayerhöffer, Eva, Reinhardt, Susanne, and Knüpfer, Curd. 2019. "Beyond Breitbart: Comparing Right Wing Digital News Infrastructures in Six Western Democracies." *Policy and Internet* 12 (1): 20–45.

Hervik, Peter. 2011. *The Annoying Difference: The Emergence of Danish Neonationalism, Neoracism, and Populism in the Post-1989 World.* New York: Berghahn Books, Incorporated.

Johansson, Sofia. (2007) "'They Must make Sense': Tabloid Newspapers as an Alternative Public Sphere." In *Media and Public Spheres* edited by Richard Butsch, 83–95. Basingstoke: Palgrave MacMillan.

Klages, Elizabeth P. 2003. "Populisme eller hvad? Fremskridtspartiet og Dansk Folkeparti som reaktioner på politics as usual" ["Populism or what? The Progress Party and Danish People's Party as reactions to politics as usual."] *Politica* 24 (4): 402–412.

Krämer, Benjamin. 2014. "Media Populism: A Conceptual Clarification and Some Theses on its Effects." *Communication Theory* 24: 42–60.

Lykkeberg, Runne. 2008. "Og dansk politik blev aldrig det same" ["And Danish politics was never the same."] *Information*, July 3. Retrieved from https://www.information.dk/indland/2008/07/dansk-politik-aldrig-samme.

Mazzoleni, Gianpietro. 2007. "Populism and the Media". In *Twenty-first century populism: The spectre of western European democracy* edited by Daniele Albertazzi and Duncan McDonnell, 49–69. London: Palgrave Macmillan.

McGuigan, Jim. 1992. *Cultural Populism*, London: Taylor and Francis Group.

Moffitt, Benjamin. 2014. "Rethinking populism: Politics, mediatisation and political style." *Political Studies*, 62: 381–397.

Wedenborg, Freja. 2015. ""Oplagskrisen er gået værst ud over tabloidaviserne." ["The circulation crisis has hit the tabloid newspapers the hardest."] *Journalisten*. Retrieved from https://journalisten.dk/oplagskrisen-er-gaaet-vaerst-ud-over-tabloidaviserne on 6 February 2019.

Whannel, Garry. 2020. "Is it 'the economy, stupid'? Economic relations and cultural studies: Some reflections on Jim McGuigan's Cultural Populism." *European Journal of Cultural Studies.*

Zelitzer, Barbie. 2000. Foreword. In *Tabloid Tales: global debates of media standards* edited by Colin Sparks and John Tulloch, ix–xi. Lanham, Maryland: Rowman & Littlefield Publishers, Inc.

8 Recent shifts in the Australian tabloid landscape

Fissures and new formations

Stephen Harrington

Introduction

In the mid-1990s, Hirst et al. (1995: 79) declared that "tabloid television is here to stay". Based on their analysis of trends in Australian television, such a declaration was probably received by most observers at the time to be almost obvious, and entirely uncontroversial. Tabloid TV had become a staple of the television news in Australia, and appeared to be a permanent fixture of the landscape; it was a ratings winner. The movement in the Australian news media seemed to be in one direction only: towards a more sensationalist, lurid, and shocking news agenda, with a "demand for drama and entertainment" (Hirst et al., 1995: 82) and for that news to be presented by media personalities interested only in ratings and profit, rather than information and public service.

Fast forward 25 years, however, and the tabloid landscape in this country has changed markedly. Like many advanced Western democracies, the Australian media have transformed, as audience consumption patterns and new technologies have changed when and how news can be accessed, pushed back the competitive horizons for news outlets to a global level, and massively altered the business structures that sit behind them. The latter, the economics of news content production, is, not surprisingly, one of the biggest changes of all that the industry has had to face over the last 25 years. In this chapter, I will argue that the two main 'tabloid' media forms, television and newspapers, have responded to that economic pressure in very different ways. On the one hand, major newspapers in Australia, dominated by Rupert Murdoch's News Corporation, have mostly doubled-down on tabloidization, in both form and content, as a survival strategy. On the other hand, we have seen a precipitous decline of tabloid television in Australia, where once-dominant 'current affairs' formats have been essentially replaced by more thoughtful, critical news/entertainment hybrid formats.

The Australian and "The American"

One cannot discuss the political and cultural impact of tabloid news in Australia without first explaining two interconnected characteristics: the traditionally high concentration of media ownership, and the sheer dominance of News Corporation Australia (formerly, until 2013, known as 'News Limited', now branded as News Corp), under the control of the Murdoch family. On the first of those two issues, Australia has been described as among the worst in "established democracies", with just two companies responsible for "90 per cent of daily metropolitan circulation" (Tiffen, 2014: 100). One review, in 2013, noted that News Corp alone accounted for approximately two thirds of the sales of daily newspapers in Australian state capitals (Flew, 2013). This is compared to the roughly one-third in the UK (see Media Reform Coalition, 2019), where concerns over the political influence of the same corporate entity have been, perhaps, equally loud. In some cases, there are literally no alternatives; Brisbane, a city of some two million people, for instance, has been served by just one daily newspaper, the Murdoch-owned *Courier Mail*, since *The Telegraph* ceased operations in 1988.

The Murdochs' influence has existed in Australian publishing since the early twentieth century, with the rise of Keith Murdoch, later *Sir* Keith, who began as a junior reporter for Melbourne's *The Age* newspaper, quickly rose through the ranks of the Australian newspaper scene, after a stint working in the UK, and went on to become the chief editor of the *Melbourne Herald*. Sir Keith seemed to instinctively understand the political power that he had as a newspaper proprietor, and was rarely shy in leveraging it. This included a brief period in politics as the director general of information under Prime Minister Robert Menzies, a job carried out in such a strong-armed way, he provoked the ire of newspaper and radio editors who "were universally outraged at the 'totalitarian tyranny' of this Goebbels-type dictatorship" (Cannon, 2015, n.p.). Sir Keith's other major instinct was for growing a newspaper's readership, and for doing so through classic tabloid strategies: sensationalism, adopting fiercely populist positions (especially in relation to crime and justice), as well as the use of 'sex appeal' (Cannon, 2015). In 1949, seeking to cement a family legacy (Serle, 1986), he acquired a holding interest in the *Adelaide Times*, and in its publisher News Limited, which he then passed onto his son Rupert upon his death in 1952. In his biography *Before Rupert*, Tom Roberts summarised Keith Murdoch as someone who "built his career and accrued his power by navigating ruthlessly a network of connections and exploiting the hidden intersection of press and power. It was a trajectory already set by the time of Rupert's birth" (Roberts, 2015: x).

Robert Manne, in a 2011 *Quarterly Essay*, argued that Rupert Murdoch's "genius has been to discover different ways in which his two passions – a desire for money and a thirst for power – can be combined" (Manne, 2011: 4). He achieved the first of these this, as is now well-known, by turning his inheritance into a media empire that stretched across Australia, then taking over UK newspapers the *News of the World* and *The Sun* in the late 1960s and early 1970s and expanding his influence there, before turning his focus towards television and film holdings, for example BSkyB and Twentieth Century Fox in the UK and the US respectively. Rupert Murdoch's influence, and now his children's influence, are truly global. Indeed, although he is sometimes referred to by critics in Australia as "The

American", denoting his citizenship status since 1985, he retains a keen interest in the fortunes of his media outlets in Australia, even if they pale in significance, in economic terms, to some of the other major outlets he has control of, such as *Fox News* and the *Wall Street Journal.*

One of the more notable moments in the history of Rupert's pursuit of political power and control in Australia came in 1964, with the launch of *The Australian* which was, at the time, the country's only national daily newspaper, and to this day remains only one of two in that category (the other being *The Australian Financial Review*). From its inception, *The Australian* enjoyed a status as one of the country's most prestigious newspapers. Although generally conservative in its political leanings, it tended to steer away from the kind of overtly tabloid stories which were regular fodder for the city dailies. Instead, it catered to an affluent, well-educated, professional audience. Although some were broadsheet in form, those city dailies instead served a more working-class, suburban readership, and in doing so adopted a tabloid posture to their content, before converting entirely to tabloid formats in the mid-2000s. Now, however, and perhaps as a direct response to mounting financial pressures and declining circulation figures, it is quite difficult to tell the different newspapers apart in terms of their style of coverage, short of looking at their mastheads. For *The Australian,* although it remains a broadsheet paper, and is now one of only two broadsheet (in terms of format) national daily newspapers, and still very much clings to its past reputation, over the last decade or so it has undoubtedly begun following the path already well-trodden by its tabloid siblings, including engaging in far more overt partisan coverage.

News Corp publications in Australia, similar to Fox News in the US, have shown a particular fondness for 'culture wars' topics that are equally likely to stoke either anger or excitement among their increasingly older, conservative audiences. Unions and their leaders, 'leftist' academics, feminists, transgender rights activists, and Australia's national broadcaster, the ABC, are just some of the favourite punching bags of News Corp journalists, and for its columnists in particular. Manne, in describing the paper as both unique, and one of the country's most important, notes that it has, in recent years, evolved into

> an unusually ideological paper, committed to advancing the causes of neoliberalism in economics and neoconservatism in the sphere of foreign policy. Its style and tone are also unlike that of any other newspaper in the nation's history. *The Australian* is ruthless in pursuit of those who oppose its worldview … It exhibits distaste, even hatred, for what it terms 'the Left,' and in particular for the Greens. It is driven by contempt for its two natural rivals, the Fairfax press and the ABC, one of which it seems to wish to destroy altogether, the other of which it seeks to discredit for its supposed left-wing bias and to reshape.
>
> (Manne, 2011: p.5)

To that list of enemies, one might add people of colour, given the treatment that issues of race and immigration have received by the company. Particularly, cartoonists associated with the company have managed to stir up several major controversies on these topics in recent years. Notable examples of these include the *Herald Sun*'s Mark Knight, who drew an extremely outdated depiction of Serena Williams, following her controversial loss at the 2018 US Open final. In that case, Knight crudely accentuated Williams' physical appearance to such an extent that it reminded many of the racist depictions of African Americans in cartoons of the Jim Crow era, and was deservedly met by a global backlash. In 2016, Bill Leak's cartoon in *The Australian* played upon cruel, dehumanising stereotypes about Aboriginal parents and alcohol abuse in Australia's Indigenous communities.

It is hard to tell whether the stirring of controversy by cartoonists is accidental, or an offshoot of a broader attention strategy, where that backlash is used to further a political narrative about so-called 'political correctness' or, more recently, 'cancel culture'. The ambition of 'owning the libs', a US phrase used to describe conservatives' efforts to provoke outrage among their liberal counterparts, seems to have embedded itself into the corporate culture of News Corp, and now seems the *raison d'être* for the company as a whole. Indeed, a number of conservative commentators claimed that liberal's reaction to his aforementioned racist cartoon was a key cause of Bill Leak's sudden death in 2017. His eventual replacement at *The Australian* was none other than his son Johannes, who has followed the path set by his father and is, at the time of writing, being publicly denounced as a racist because of the language he has used in a cartoon depicting US Vice Presidential candidate Kamala Harris (see Meade, 2020a).

A tabloid agenda

The extent of Murdoch's influence on the editorial stance of News Corp newspapers is sometimes overstated. It is easy to forget that newsrooms are complex places, usually composed of a diverse group of mostly well-meaning journalists, and that a lot of political influence operates institutionally rather than directly. Censorship, in the words of veteran Australian journalist Chris Masters (2002: p. xi), "does not so much arrive as an assassin's bullet from the top floor; more like a thrust in the ribs by a colleague with a muffled whisper", and there have been numerous instances of Murdoch directly allowing news stories published in outlets he owns which were counterproductive to his business interests. A stunning example of this was when the CEO of Theranos, Elizabeth Holmes, directly approached Murdoch (who had invested around US $125 million into Theranos) in his New York office, asking him to quash a story by The *Wall Street Journal*'s John Carreyrou investigating her company. Murdoch declined, and that Carreyrou story, uncovering fraudulent and deceptive practices, sparked the eventual decline and collapse of Theranos, with the story later told in the book *Bad Blood* (Carreyrou, 2018). It has been reported that Murdoch eventually sold his entire tranche of Theranos stock for just $1 (Carson, 2017). However, it is also undeniable that the cabal of

Murdoch-owned newspapers in Australia has resulted in a significant concentration of power in Rupert Murdoch and his children, and that this power has consistently been leveraged for political purposes. It has become almost a ritual sight in Australian politics for prospective prime ministers, both Labor and Liberal, to travel to America ahead of the election to meet with Rupert Murdoch, and 'talk about political matters', and to also curry favour with or even garner official endorsements from News Corp back home. Opposition Leader Bill Shorten's refusal to do so in the run-up to the 2019 federal election which he lost, unexpectedly, made news at the time because it was such a notable departure from the norm (Tingle, 2019).

Although one should not ascribe blame for complex problems to simple causes, even a casual glance at the state of politics in the three countries where Rupert Murdoch has had the most influence, reveals three political systems in a state of functional decline to varying degrees. In the United States the proper functioning of government, and even of democracy itself, has all but ended thanks to ideological hyper-partisanship and inter-party enmity; fires that have been rabidly-stoked by Fox News, which has managed to create "a whole alternative knowledge system, with its own facts, its own history, its own laws of economics" (Frum, 2011). In the UK, voters are disillusioned after being told by right-wing, Murdoch-owned tabloids that leaving the EU would be both easy and a bold forward step for the country, only to later find out that Brexit would prove to be both incredibly complicated and come at a significant economic cost. Australia, meanwhile, has gone through a period of noticeable political dysfunction over the last 15 years, which has manifested itself most visibly in leadership instability at a federal level. In that time period, Australia has worked its way through six different prime ministers (one of them serving twice), with none of the PMs elected since Kevin Rudd in 2007 managing to stay in the role long enough to re-contest an election as the incumbent. In each case, their popularity dropped, and then were replaced within their party before seeing out a full term.

In 2018, Rudd, who was PM from 2007 to 2010 and then again for a brief stint in 2013, openly declared that he had been the victim of a News Corp plot, arguing that, ideologically, Rupert Murdoch is "deeply conservative, deeply protective of his corporation's commercial interests and, therefore, prosecutes a direct agenda through his newspapers which I've been on the receiving end [of]" (Rudd, in Karp, 2010). Similarly, Malcolm Turnbull, who both 'knifed' Tony Abbott (in 2015) to become Prime Minister, and who was then overthrown himself by Scott Morrison (in 2018), blamed "outside forces in the media" for the demise of his prime ministership (Davies, 2018). Of course, politicians always complain about their coverage in the news media. Donald Trump even made this a defining characteristic of his presidency. Unlike Trump, though, Rudd, has a fairly strong case to make. Along with Julia Gillard, both his successor and predecessor, who herself was hounded almost mercilessly at every turn by the press and by a rabid, Tony Abbott–led opposition, Rudd was a particular bogeyman of tabloid campaigns. Sydney-based News Corp tabloid *The Daily Telegraph*, perhaps most famously, announced in 2013 that a Federal election had been called by excitedly telling its readers that they now had a "chance to kick this mob [led by Rudd] out" (*Daily Telegraph*, 5 August 2013).

Gillard garnered similar attention. The Murdoch papers were among the most vociferous critics of the Gillard government, particularly in response to its introduction of taxes on both mining royalties and carbon emissions; both progressive policies that were overturned shortly after Abbott's ascent to power. Nevertheless, to declare its opposition to Rudd and support for Abbott so nakedly on day one of the campaign still caused some surprise and anger. Just a couple of days later, it doubled down. The *Daily Telegraph* drew ire again for more for crudely comparing, in a front-page attack, the leaders of the Australian Labor Party, Rudd and Anthony Albanese, to the Nazi camp commandants in *Hogan's Heroes*.

Journalists in the News Corp group now appear quite comfortable operating overtly in *simpatico* with conservative politicians. This has led to coverage being written to fit a political agenda, which then creates the illusion of an impetus for their own journalistic 'response', all of which is pre-planned. One such example of this operation was a concocted media panic about 'African gangs' in Victoria, ahead of the 2018 state election. This campaign ran in both the *Australian* and in Melbourne's *Herald Sun*, and seemed designed to provide the state opposition with an angle of attack against the Labor Premier Daniel Andrews, and help bolster the opposition's own 'law and order' credentials (see Budarick, 2018). The topic of African gangs dominated the front pages of both papers for weeks, even though commentators pointed out that crime statistics, and the lived experiences of Victorians, showed that the problem was a minor, if not entirely fictional, one. And, in a situation reminiscent of how the 'migrant caravan' from central America received so much attention in the lead-up to the 2018 midterm elections in the US, the whole issue was almost entirely forgotten after the election was held (Robin, 2019).

It is not entirely clear whether this increased level of partisanship from News Corp papers is a purely political strategy, a corporate strategy to shore up its readership, or both happening at the same time. Whatever the intent, adopting such an overtly ideological position in political coverage has almost entirely trashed the once-strong reputation of *The Australian*. Even if its more sensational approach may have slightly arrested the inevitable readership declines in the short term, the long-term damage that has come to the title is much more significant. Twitter users in Australia, for example, regularly share screenshots from News Corp sites, showing and mocking either its ludicrously one-sided analysis on the day's political stories, or to comment on columnists who seems to live in an alternative political universe and whose beliefs will turn on a dime if it will suit their political agenda, or to highlight how News Corp outlets are devoting a completely disproportionate amount of attention to the perceived missteps of its political enemies, however slight these may be. Perhaps the ultimate example of this at play was when Yassmin Abdel-

Magied, a young, outspoken Sudanese-born critic and writer, wrote "Lest. We. Forget. (Manus, Nauru, Syria, Palestine…)" on Facebook on ANZAC day in 2017, which caused so much outrage among conservative media and politicians (many of them supposed advocates of 'free speech'), that she had to leave the country and now resides in the UK (see Stephens, 2019). If political expediency and a more tabloid style were attempts to secure readership, notable declines in circulation figures would suggest this alone is not sufficient to shore up these titles, and a number of sizable cuts to the staff at these operations echoing that downturn. In 2020 alone, there were two separate rounds of forced redundancies, with hundreds of jobs lost in each of these (see Meade, 2020b). This reinforces the conclusion that *The Australian*'s tabloid turn has not saved the newspaper's operations in the way that senior management might have hoped. In many ways, this makes sense: taking an aggressively, visibly conservative editorial line risks immediately alienating half of your audience. Add to that the examples outlined here of semi-covert racism, and this shift in editorial approach has further limited the audience to a mostly white one. Finally, it has undermined trust in the overall journalistic mission of these newspapers, particularly as their own tacks change whenever the political winds shift. In short, they gambled their journalistic reputation for the sake of short-term sales and are now paying the price.

The reformation of 'tabloid' TV

Although tabloid news values have been around in Australian newspapers since at least Sir Keith Murdoch's time, tabloid TV didn't really gain much of a foothold until much later on. It wasn't until the 1980s, following Channel Nine's successful importing of the *60 Minutes* news magazine format from the US into Australia in 1979, when commercial TV operators realized that news and current affairs didn't have to be the economic 'loss leader' that they had been previously for the networks (Turner, 2005). Nevertheless, concerns over what was seen as 'infotainment' (see Brants, 1998) by those who saw the pure battle for ratings in that domain as a slippery slope of declining journalistic standards gathered more steam in the 1990s. This clustered most prominently around commercial current affairs (noting the quote that opened this chapter), particularly the nightly battle between *Today Tonight* (on channel Seven) and *A Current Affair* (on Nine), where observers felt that they had begun competing "through the provision of entertainment, rather than through their provision of news and information" (Turner, 2005: 49)

Today Tonight and *A Current Affair* almost defined the infotainment news genre in Australia, with their focus on classic, over-hyped tabloid stories: consumer outrage, neighbourhood disputes, celebrity gossip, diet pills, and similarly trivial topics. The genre and these shows became popular and despised in equal measure, popular among their regular viewers and equally despised by critics. From the latter perspective, it spawned the satirical ABC program *Frontline* (1994–1997) which offered a tongue-in-cheek 'behind the scenes' look at the production of a fictional current affairs show in the same mould. For a decade at least, *Today Tonight* and *A Current Affair* would consistently sit atop the daily ratings figures (See Turner, 2005: 1), and were seen by their respective networks as critical 'lead-in' programs for the rest of their nightly viewing schedules (Hirst et al, 1995).

Much of the debate around 'tabloidization' in Australia has split along quite clear positive or critical lines. Turner's (2005) critique of Australian current affairs television is a landmark here, and he noted in particular that the genre's trademark is and has been to adopt the rhetoric of strong, independent journalism. These programmes proclaimed themselves as fearlessly fighting on the side of the 'Aussie battler', but were often pointing fingers in the wrong direction, creating folk villains, or providing overly simplistic answers for complex problems; mere 'triviality' over substance. Scholars like Lumby (1997) have taken a different approach, and argued that tabloid news and current affairs could be viewed as a democratisation of the news agenda where the concerns and interests of 'ordinary' citizens are taken more seriously, while also noting that most news coverage had hitherto focussed on a narrow range of elite, male-oriented content. Turner (1999) questioned whether it was possible to work towards a middle ground, one that rejected the elitism that too often pervaded the critical view, but still recognised that much of what passes for news in commercial television tabloid press/TV has very little, if any, educative value.

Since commercial current affairs programmes reached their zenith in the mid-2000s (*Today Tonight* ceased production in most markets in 2014), there has been a substantial realignment in the types of popular news formats on offer for Australian viewers. This shift calls for a possible rethinking of how we think about the concept of 'tabloid news' in the first place. Rather than adopting the semiotic markers of 'serious' journalism in the pursuit of 'small fish' (to appropriate the name of an episode of *Frontline*), a new kind of hybrid television has emerged in its place; one which uses the aesthetics and attention strategies of entertainment to shine a spotlight on topics that were once only the purview of 'serious', broadsheet news. One of the most notable examples of this approach has been the Channel 10 program *The Project* (initially called *The 7PM Project*), which manages to find a balance between overt entertainment and serious, journalistic analysis. Hosted by political commentator Waleed Aly, who had previously worked as both a lawyer and an academic at Monash University, joined in a panel format by comedians, journalists, political figures, and other media personalities, the show has been praised for its ability to present serious analysis of news events in a way that is popular and accessible. It has been especially successful with young people, not just because it aired on a commercial TV station which has traditionally attracted younger viewers (Harrington, 2014: 178), but also because it covers topics which are more directly relevant to young people's lives, unlike current affairs programmes which so often would situate young people as the antagonists in a crafted tabloid narrative. The epitome of this was the case of the Paxton family children in the mid-1990s, when *A Current Affair* ran a story in which all three, who were unemployed at the time, were offered jobs on an island resort, albeit some 3,000 km away from where they lived in Melbourne. When they turned down those jobs, for obvious reasons, they were demonized in the media for days on end (See Turner, 2005: 62).

Another program that has eschewed outdated divisions between news and entertainment has been *The Weekly with Charlie Pickering*, which has aired on Australia's public broadcasting network, the ABC, since 2015. Borrowing heavily from the format of *The Daily Show*, Pickering, who was the host of *The Project* when it first began, is joined on the show by a small group of well-known Australian comedians, taking a humorous and critical look at the week's news events. Notably the show also borrows heavily from the genre pioneered by another US program, *Last Week Tonight with John Oliver*, and take 'deep dives' into critical issues which may not have particularly timely critical flashpoints, but which deserve attention and public awareness all the same.

These programmes, which are certainly not unique to Australia, but do have a particularly long history in this country (see Harrington, 2012), force us to fundamentally rethink the nature of tabloid media, and of broader cultural anxieties over the consequences of tabloidization. Whereas tabloidization has typically been framed as the incorporation of entertainment values into the news (for instance, Hirst et al, 1995), that interplay doesn't *have to* result in tabloid media as we have previous known it. Instead, we should think about tabloidization as a process that draws a popular audience by turning the traditional elements of journalism, both in terms of production and textuality, towards stories that are not within the traditional journalistic remit: celebrity gossip, small-time criminals, and the like. It is no surprise that even the most tabloid of television programmes, like *Hard Copy*, look like real news programmes, and the most tabloid of newspapers, like the *Daily Mail*, largely look and sound like the *New York Times* or the *Guardian*. Obviously such a move is made for commercial ends, because tabloid journalism seeks out a wide audience, and tends to be cheaper and easier to produce, because it can more easily rely on 'softball' interviews with celebrities, for example, and doesn't require investment of large resources for the sake of research. Journalism with lower standards is, put simply, cheaper to make. Therefore, entertainment should instead be seen as a kind of attention strategy, within a broader 'attention economy', that can instead be used to shine a brighter spotlight on topics and issues that were once only the purview of 'serious', broadsheet news.

This shift in the television landscape mirrors the approaches taken by some of the news outlets that have emerged online as well. While the Murdoch papers have steadfastly clung to an increasingly conservative, reactionary tabloid style, a small collection of platform-native, 'social news' outlets (see Hurcombe, Burgess, and Harrington, 2019) have sprung up to cater more directly to younger audiences. Although these news outlets, like *Pedestrian* and *Junkee* are hyper-commercial, and derive much of their traffic from carefully monitored social media click-throughs and native advertising (as more well-known global outlets like *Buzzfeed* and *Vice* do), they have adopted a radically different political and social outlook to Australian tabloids. Indeed, they might owe a great deal of their success to the fact that so many mainstream newspapers in Australia are now so conservative in their political views. By contrast, these publications are, for the most part, unashamedly progressive in their political stance. And, far from trying to disguise those viewpoints, they are celebrated and emphasized to engage audiences with a more 'authentic' journalistic voice. And, also in direct opposition to the largely white, suburban audience that tabloid newspapers have cultivated, these outlets appeal directly to a much more culturally and ethnically diverse audience, which is also reflected in their far more diverse staff profile. While serious questions remain about the long-term viability of these kinds of news and their ability to maintain a degree of audience trust in the long term, given they derive so much of their revenue from 'native advertising' which embeds advertising content in sponsored news articles, they perhaps represent a new frontier in tabloid news.

Conclusion: making news profitable

Like nearly every other media system in the world, Australian news has undergone a profound transformation at the hands of global social media platforms, and struggled to adapt to the changes wrought by these new massive players. In this chapter, I have argued that, in response to those challenges, Australian newspapers, dominated by News Corporation mastheads, have adopted an increasingly tabloid stance. Even *The Australian*, once the country's most respected broadsheet newspaper, has followed this path, perhaps for political reasons as much as for economic ones. Tabloid news and current affairs on television, however, have largely disappeared, and have been superseded by a new kind of hybrid television that has emerged in its place. Both trends, successful to quite different degrees, are effectively attempts to do the same thing: make the production of news profitable once again. Whether these strategies are enough to overcome the challenges associated with the major financial disruption to the news industry in the last two decades remains to be seen. What is clear, however, is that the Australian popular news media have effectively bifurcated into two different groups: one progressive, and one staking almost everything on the hope that tabloid values might save a failing empire. The extent to which the latter's political influence will continue to impact on Australia's political system remains to be seen.

References

Brants, Kees (1998). 'Who's afraid of infotainment?', *European Journal of communication*, 13(3), pp. 315–335.

Bruns, Axel, Graham, Tim, and Angus, Dan (2019). '*Trust Us, Again? Twitter Campaigning Strategies in the 2019 Australian Federal Election*', AoIR Conference, 2–5 October, Brisbane: Australia.

Budarick, John (2018). 'Why the media are to blame for racialising Melbourne's "African gang" problem?', *The Conversation*, 1 August, https://theconversation.com/why-the-media-are-to-blame-for-racialising-melbournes-african-gang-problem-100761.

Bye, Susan (2007). '*"Mothers Like Him": Graham Kennedy and the Great Divide*', Australia Media Traditions conference, 22–23 November, Charles Sturt University, Bathurst: Australia.

Cannon, Michael (2015). 'The Enigma of Keith Murdoch', *Inside Story*, 18 November, https://insidestory.org.au/the-enigma-of-keith-murdoch/.

Carreyrou, John (2018). *Bad Blood: Secrets and Lies in a Silicon Valley Startup*, New York: Alfred A. Knopf.

Carson, Biz (2017). 'Rupert Murdoch reportedly sold $125 million in Theranos stock for just $1', *Business Insider*, 24 March, https://www.businessinsider.com.au/rupert-murdoch-sells-theranos-stake-2017-3?r=US&IR=T.

Davies, Anne (2018). 'A very Australian coup: Murdoch, Turnbull and the power of News Corp', *The Guardian*, 19 September, https://www.theguardian.com/media/2018/sep/20/very-australian-coup-murdoch-turnbull-political-death-news-corps.

Flew, Terry (2013). 'FactCheck: does Murdoch own 70% of newspapers in Australia?', *The Conversation*, 8 August, https://theconversation.com/factcheck-does-murdoch-own-70-of-newspapers-in-australia-16812.

Frum, David (2011). 'When Did the GOP Lose Touch with Reality?', *New York Magazine*, 18 November, https://nymag.com/news/politics/conservatives-david-frum-2011-11/index4.html.

Harrington, Stephen (2012). 'From the "Little Aussie Bleeder" to Newstopia: (really) fake news in Australia', *Popular Communication*, 10 (1-2), pp. 27–39.

Harrington, Stephen (2014). 'Television' in, (eds.) Cunningham, Stuart and Turnbull, Sue, *The Media and Communications in Australia* (4th ed.), Sydney: Allen and Unwin, pp. 173–191.

Hirst, Martin, White, Tiffany, Chaplin, David, & Wilson, Justine (1995). 'When too much entertainment is barely enough: current affairs television in the 1990s', *Australian Journalism Review*, 17 (1), pp. 79–98.

Hurcombe, Edward, Burgess, Jean, and Harrington, Stephen. (2019). 'What's newsworthy about "social news"? Characteristics and potential of an emerging genre', *Journalism*, https://doi.org/10.1177/1464884918793933.

Karp, Paul (2018). 'Kevin Rudd says "power of the Murdoch media" to blame for Australia's coup culture', *The Guardian*, 23 October, https://www.theguardian.com/australia-news/2018/oct/23/kevin-rudd-says-power-of-the-murdoch-media-to-blame-for-australias-coup-culture.

Lumby, Catherine. (1997). *Bad Girls: The Media, Sex and Feminism in the 90s*. Sydney: Allen & Unwin.

Manne, Robert (2011). 'Bad News: Murdoch's Australian and the Shaping of the Nation', *Quarterly Essay*, 43.

Masters, Chris (2002). *Not For Publication*. Sydney: ABC Books.

Meade, Amanda (2020a). 'Johannes Leak cartoon of Joe Biden and Kamala Harris denounced as racist', *The Guardian*, 14 August, https://www.theguardian.com/media/2020/aug/14/johannes-leak-cartoon-of-joe-biden-and-kamala-harris-denounced-as-racist.

Meade, Amanda (2020b). 'News Corp cuts more jobs, this time at its metropolitan newspapers', *The Guardian*, 9 June, https://www.theguardian.com/media/2020/jun/09/news-corp-cuts-more-jobs-this-time-at-its-metropolitan-newspapers.

Media Reform Coalition (2019). 'Who Owns the Media?', 12 March, https://www.mediareform.org.uk/wp-content/uploads/2019/03/FINALonline2.pdf.

Roberts, Tom (2015). *Before Rupert: Keith Murdoch and the Birth of a Dynasty*, Brisbane: University of Queensland Press.

Robin, Myriam (2019). 'African gangs panic didn't outlast election', *Australian Financial Review*, 21 November, https://www.afr.com/rear-window/african-gangs-panic-didn-t-outlast-election-20191120-p53ce7.

Serle, Geoffrey (1986). 'Murdoch, Sir Keith Arthur (1885–1952)', *Australian Dictionary of Biography*, Melbourne: Melbourne University Press, http://adb.anu.edu.au/biography/murdoch-sir-keith-arthur-7693.

Stephens, David (2019). 'Lest We Forget Yassmin Abdel-Magied', *Independent Australia*, 26 April, https://independentaustralia.net/australia/australia-display/lest-we-forget-yassmin-abdel-magied,12615.

Tiffen, Rodney (2014). 'The Press' in, (eds.) Cunningham, Stuart and Turnbull, Sue, *The Media and Communications in Australia* (4th ed.), Sydney: Allen and Unwin, pp. 95–109.

Tingle, Laura (2019). 'Opposition Leader Bill Shorten rebuffs Rupert Murdoch on US meeting', *ABC News*, 28 January, https://www.abc.net.au/news/2019-01-28/bill-shorten-turns-down-meeting-with-rupert-murdoch/10755892.

Turner, Graeme. (1989). 'Transgressive TV: From in Melbourne Tonight to Perfect Match', in, (eds.) Tulloch, John and Turner, Graeme, *Australian Television: Programs, Pleasures and Politics*, Sydney: Allen & Unwin, pp. 25–38.

Turner, Graeme (1999). 'Tabloidization, journalism and the possibility of critique', *International Journal of Cultural Studies*, 2 (1), pp. 59–76.

Turner, Graeme (2005). *Ending the Affair: The Decline of Television Current Affairs in Australia*, Sydney: UNSW Press.

9 The post-communist "hybrid" tabloid

Between the serious and the "yellow"

Lada Trifonova Price

Introduction

24 Chassa, fondly referred to as "the people's favourite daily" and by the diminutive "*little Chasove*"[1] was hated by many but read by everyone as it became a powerful symbol of freedom of speech and the newly discovered power that the mass media could wield in Bulgaria's post-communist society. The small tabloid format pioneered by *24 Chassa* in the early 1990s became an overnight sensation, and was gradually adopted as the default model for a daily newspaper by the whole newspaper industry in Bulgaria (Štětka, 2011). Its language is alternatively described by scholars and media critics as an "abomination", "revolution", "speech heresy", "stammer", "uncontrolled avalanche", "anarchy", or "aggression against language" (Spassov, 2000). However, it was *24 Chassa*'s use of everyday spoken language that was seen as a means of revolt by the press against the official "wooden" rhetoric of the socialist period. Yet, this romantic vision of *24 Chassa* (24 hours) and its sister *168 Chassa* (168 hours) has also been tarnished by accounts that the two tabloids were products of a toxic political culture which rejected communism in favour of rampant capitalism, basing their products on "sensationalism, politically provocative articles, racy news with even racier imagery, nudity and misogyny as an indispensable strategy for success" (Ibroscheva, 2008, para. 11). With such highs and lows, these two newspapers warrant scholarly exploration.

Background and history

The media of the communist era operated under Marxist-Leninist principles of the press where the only acceptable and objective truth was the viewpoint of the party. It was the party that decided what facts should be selected and how they should be reported (Monova, 2012). In that sense, media did not practise journalism but propaganda. Following the end of totalitarian regimes throughout Eastern Europe in the late 1980s, a genre-spanning newspaper-publishing boom has been documented as one of the most significant phenomena on the road to democracy, with newspapers playing a central role in the making of peaceful revolutions that brought down communist regimes (Cheterian, 2009). In these early years of democracy, media in Bulgaria constructed and facilitated an "environment of change" by amplifying images of citizens' discontent, of self-mobilisation, of choosing new leaders, strikes, protests, and vital negotiations (Znepolski, 1997, 11). Liberated from the constraints of communist censorship, most journalists eagerly embraced their new right to freedom of speech and expression, established by Article 39 (1) of the new Constitution adopted in 1991. Censorship was officially abolished by Article 40, which declared the press should be free and not subjected to any form of overt interference (Bulgarian Constitution, 1991). The development of a free and independent press and the birth of post-communist tabloid newspapers in Bulgaria followed three main trends.

Firstly, the removal of ideological communist censorship and restrictions allowed for the rapid launch of hundreds of new titles and the establishment of the commercial press model. The press changed from being highly ideological to becoming highly commercial (Daskalova, 2010). In 1990, there were 540 newspapers with a total circulation of 1,098,632 (Tzankova, 2018), an extraordinary rise from the eight main daily newspapers published in the period between 1949 and 1990 (Vulkanova, 1995). By mid-June 1991, barely a year after the revolution, there were 850 new newspapers in print (Monova-Paneva, 1995), each fighting for space in the market. While far fewer survived that initial press boom, the explosion of titles in the early 1990s, coupled with the lack of strict regulation and the general ease in launching a media outlet, allowed the press to flourish. From that moment the press became a business enterprise but it only reached its full potential in a tabloid format (Spassov, 2000).

The introduction of private media ownership in the press, and later in broadcasting, started a process of commercialization of the media in Bulgaria, paving the way for the first privately owned newspapers. Newspaper entrepreneurs quickly grasped that two of the most forbidden topics during communism, politics and sex, would also bring them the most profits. However, the euphoria of the newspaper boom created the illusion that control of the press had been removed, which was hardly the case. Instead, private ownership introduced new types of control and growing economic dependency (Monova, 2012).

Secondly, in the early years of democracy media began to play a central role in establishing and representing the newly emerged power elites responsible for political and economic governance. News media rapidly became agents of public communication and the centres of power struggles where hostile and open wars between the elites were fought (Roudakova, 2008; Dyczok, 2009; Gaman-Golutvina, 2009; Voltmer, 2013). This is evident in the early rhetorical wars between the flagship newspapers of the socialist party and the democratic opposition, as illustrated in the next section. The idea of a free press was essentially enacted through the communist/anti-communist dichotomy on the pages of the party press.

Finally, while the media market was undergoing a rapid transformation, the lifting of all state restrictions on journalists' professional activities allowed scores of young journalists to enter the profession and embrace idealistic if naïve new norms of value-free objective reporting (Foley, 2006; Stewart, 2013). Learning by trial and error, they introduced and imposed a new model of writing, reporting, and professional practice that was a far cry from the essay-style, literary journalism of Bulgaria's past.

The party press: predecessors of the post-communist tabloid

This early period of democracy is marked by the rise and fall of the organs of the political parties in Bulgaria. The two major party daily newspapers, the Socialists' *Duma* (Word) and the Opposition's *Demokratsia* (Democracy), were highly politicized along partisan lines but both managed to attract huge readerships. *Demokratsia* was first published in February 1990 during the season it described as "the winter of our discontent", with the aim of giving a voice to all independent small dissident groups, unions, parties, and organisations that joined forces under the Opposition, the Union of Democratic Forces (UDF) (Naidenov, 1995, 38–39). Erratic spelling of headlines, abysmal print quality, and poor layout, among other faults, became part of the "romance" and appeal of this first democratic Opposition newspaper. Its rough appearance stood in stark contrast to the polished pages of the former communist newspapers, which only reinforced the belief that communism was well and truly over.

Demokratsia's nemesis, *Duma*, has a much longer history. It was born in 1892, renamed *Rabotnichesko Delo* (Workers Daily) in 1927, and from then on was the main communist party organ (Tzankova, 2018). Post communism, it faced an uphill struggle to transform itself from a newspaper where, as an old anecdote goes, the only true thing in it was the date, to a modern and progressive publication. The paper was reborn in April 1990, shortly after the Bulgarian Communist Party (BCP) was renamed as the Bulgarian Socialist Party (BSP), and rebranded as *Duma* with a new simple motto: "The Left Newspaper". In a drastic makeover, *Duma* shed its normative image, removed all communist symbols from its masthead in its aim to appear as a modern newspaper, while staking a claim as the voice of the Left. *Duma* and *Demokratsia* engaged in the first real and fierce polemic in Bulgarian journalism since the rise of communism. This enticed readers to buy and read the two papers in tandem, gripped by their heated daily exchange of unashamed insults (Naidenov, 1995), and rejoicing in political differences and open disagreements no longer being a reason to imprison people. *Duma* and *Demokratsia* remained among the three top-selling papers in the country until 1995 (Spassov, 2004) when, with the decline of the party press circulation, *Demokratsia* succumbed to a skyrocketing debt and closed down in 2002. *Duma* continues to be published as the organ of the Bulgarian Socialist Party despite its somewhat archaic format (Tzankova, 2018).

This period marks an important milestone in the development of Bulgaria's media system. For the first time in decades, language, both political and everyday, was not being measured, controlled, or checked. Newspapers actively encouraged pluralism of opinion and cherished opposing views. People and newspapers at that time exhibited symptoms of "word fever", a peculiar illness that was brought by years of forced silence (Znepolski, 1997, 4). However, readers tired of the fierce rhetoric and endless political clashes, and soon a major change in the media environment came with the birth of the first commercial newspapers in Bulgaria, *168 Chassa* and *24 Chassa*, and hundreds of newspapers that followed in their footsteps.

The *168* and *24 Chassa* revolution

The weekly *168 Chassa* was born in the spring of 1990, four months after the end of the communist regime, introducing Bulgarian audiences to a completely different newspaper design, style, and content from its party predecessors. Its first issue boldly declared: "Tomorrow starts with us!" (Monova, 2012, 105). It aimed to shock and challenge audiences with its uninhibited use of language and parody of the communist past, unapologetically dispensing with totalitarian jargon and taboos. Journalists, scholars, and readers alike perceive it as the newspaper that laid the foundation of modern Bulgarian post-communist journalism (Ianeva, 2018). Hundreds of newspapers were being published at the time, yet despite being the most expensive, *168 Chassa* instantly became a market leader. Readers were drawn to its investigations, analysis, and reporting on Bulgaria's complex new political and social landscape. The newspaper was established by a group of journalists[2] who had been colleagues in the communist *Otechestven Front* (National Front). Indeed, the publisher Press Group *168 Chassa* is known as an "enterprise, founded and managed by former Communists" (Hiebert, 1999, 97). Several of its founders were leading journalists during communism, and two of them were exposed as secret service informers in 2008 (Trifonova Price, 2015).

"I would not be surprised if 'mini-newspapers' become as fashionable as mini skirts", proclaimed one correspondent of *168 Chassa* when pondering all the exciting things that its daily sister-in-the making *24 Chassa* would offer its readers (Naidenov, 1995, 78). On its debut on 18 April 1991, *24 Chassa* stood out like a black sheep on the news kiosks in its "mini" tabloid format among its long-skirted rivals. The newest creation of the Press Group *24 Chassa*, radically transformed existing concepts of journalism and newspapers in post-communist Bulgaria, revolutionizing news. It was designed not as an elite newspaper, but a mass popular one. It proclaimed itself the "terminator of the press market" and the "newspaper of the new century" (Gotcheva, 2001, 78). Its motto, "a daily for the news as it is", reflected the paper's aspirations to become a "mirror" of the new post socialist reality (Spassov, 2000). As one of its former editors notes, life in the country was radically changing and *24 Chassa* wanted to reflect that change (Iankov, 2001).

Panaiot Denev (2009), a senior Bulgarian journalist and former editor-in-chief of *Demokratsia* claimed to have been in the room when the concept of the paper was dreamt up, with a simple idea that had already been implemented in other countries, such as Greece:

> This was the idea: you get on the bus in Mladost 4 (a suburb of the capital Sofia), let's say bus number 306, you have bought a newspaper, 6 to 8 pages, at the lowest possible price. You get off in the centre of town and you've read it, you throw it away and you know everything.

The intention was to make a newspaper that fitted the established criteria for modern journalism in the West and to become "an opposition to power" (Ianeva, 2018, 14). By then the idea of journalism as a watchdog for society had reached Eastern Europe and was starting to take root. Yet, the newspaper's goal seemed more fundamental than simply reporting the news as it happened and keeping an eye on the government. It was on the pages of this new tabloid where readers could receive a daily dose of reassurance. Reassurance, and comfort, that fundamental principles and rights such as freedom of speech and expression, the right to information, and pluralism had become a permanent feature of the post-communist public sphere.

The minimalist approach to text meant that an entire newspaper's content could fit perfectly into half the space (or less) than any of *24 Chassa's* competitors. With the high price of paper at the time, this meant *Chassa* was the cheapest on the market, costing two to three times less than its competitors. In practical terms, *24 Chassa* dispensed with the long-form journalism that other newspapers indulged in and insisted on clearly marked separation of fact and opinion, according to one of its founders and first editor-in-chief, Valeri Naidenov (2009). It managed to uphold the value of factualness of news reports throughout its development and has been classified as providing information, rather than conveying an interpretation of a given fact or statement, offering opinions, or evaluations (Wessler et al., 2008; see also Monova, 2012). However, this emphasis on facts is said to have drowned readers in text and minute details on the public and private lives of those in power. *24 Chassa* focuses on who, when, where, and how, but fails to ask the most important question of "why?" (Monova, 2012). In the decade since 2010 (when it was sold by its foreign owners) *24 Chassa* has been drawn to the frontline of media wars and questions such as why corrupt and incompetent officials in positions of power often remain outside the scope of its daily coverage.

The *24* and *168 Chassa* phenomenon

24 Chassa has been a dynamic and organic phenomenon not only in the history of the Bulgarian press but also in Bulgarian culture (Naidenov, 1995). While media critics have argued over key issues such as its news values and agenda, the reliability of its sources, and the potential for hidden opinion in its news stories, it is undisputed that *24 Chassa* was radically different from any other newspaper on the newsstand at that time. The key to its significance is rooted in three important developments in newspapers in Bulgaria in the early post-communist era.

Firstly, by early 1992, less than a year after its first edition, the small format enjoyed huge popularity, its success signalling the end of the era of dominance of the party press. Secondly, up to that point the press had not seen such determination to focus on news and only news, without commentary and pompous language. *24 Chassa* ensured the stories it published were value free. Thirdly, it aimed to stand above the political bickering of the parties and to be viewed as impartial, presenting all viewpoints equally, in contrast to the one-sided coverage of *Duma* or *Demokratsia* (Naidenov, 1995). As its first editor-in-chief Valeri Naidenov (2009) claims, "We managed to push aside the party press by offering readers exactly the opposite in content that was actually interesting and not concerned with those vying for power", adding, "Prior to 1989, all newspapers were impossible to read and reeked of decay but only five years later, they were completely transformed – every issue was interesting, lively and full of joy".

At first, the public trusted the newspaper wholeheartedly. In 1992–93, the levels of trust among its readership were unprecedented, with between 70 per cent and 80 per cent of active newspaper readers trusting the newspaper (Tomov, 2001). From 1992 to the present, *24 Chassa* has been among the top ten dailies in Bulgaria.

24 Chassa is regarded by media scholars as a "hybrid", leaning towards tabloid content. Bulgarian scholars have differentiated between two types of tabloid newspapers in the post-communist landscape: the "hybrid" and the "typical yellow" (Spassov, 2000, 53–54). Hybrid tabloids combine elements of both tabloid and quality newspapers, of serious and popular, even scandalous, reporting, but they tend to identify themselves as serious, quality newspapers (Spassov, 2004; Štětka, 2011). *24 Chassa* has also been characterized as a "broadloid", a term used for those newspapers that copy the style of tabloids while retaining some elements of broadsheets (Wessler et al, 2008). Hybrids contain serious analysis and features, often as full-page articles, written in accessible formats. They dedicate significant space to international news and opinion, and while the focus on sensational content is still there, its presentation is much softer than in "typical yellow" tabloids (Spassov, 2000). This combination could be explained by the lack of distinct social classes after the fall of communism, with the hybrid having to cater to all types of readers. This hybrid tabloid format holds a central place in the Bulgarian press system and is the format of the Bulgarian transition; one of its most important features is the ratio between information and analysis, containing an average of 70 per cent information and news and 30 per cent analysis, comments, and interviews (Monova, 2012). Hybrid newspapers such as *24* and *168 Chassa* continued to thrive at the expense of quality titles, which struggled in the 1990s and have had a very limited presence in the market since 2001 (Spassov, 2004), a prime example being the quality newspaper *Sega* (Now) ending its print edition in December 2019, moving online to keep costs down.

The features of the "typical yellow" tabloid are very much like its Western counterparts, with the following characteristics: more aggressive language, content dominated by sex and crime, less attention on politics and more on sensational news, little international news, and images and content that can be described as soft porn (Spassov, 2000). They tend to be weekly and mostly cover "unchecked gossip and scandal about celebrities and popular figures" (Štětka, 2011, 7).

Leading the pack

From four pages, the daily *24 Chassa* quickly jumped to eight, then 32, then 64, and then the profits rolled in. It became financially successful because advertisers were clamouring to get their messages into the pages of the daily and its weekly sister *168 Chassa* (Hiebert, 1999). This played a significant part in both newspapers' growth, as substantial profits allowed them to pay for good journalism. Its reporters quickly became famous for their critical questions and investigations, and the steady revenue from advertisers in these early years helped *24 Chassa* avoid having to accept payments and bribery from politicians: "we had more money than they did at the time", said Naidenov (2009). Journalists and scholars agree that *168 Chassa* also conducted some landmark investigations (Lozanov, Spassov, and Iankov, 2001). Its exposé, "Isle of Man – The golden chest" (1994) revealed the offshore accounts of Bulgaria's banking industry, specifically the missing funds from Biochim Bank. Its journalists exposed a well-used scheme to export East European capital to anonymous offshore companies: so-called "red" money obtained in dubious circumstances or privatization deals. The newspaper is also famous for its series of investigations into the shady privatization process of former state-owned resorts along the Black Sea, and has brought to light several banking scandals over the years. During such investigations, especially in the early years of democracy, many of the Press Group's national and regional reporters and correspondents were regularly harassed and beaten in the course of their work, either by crime figures or by local barons. Despite several complaints and attempts to get the authorities to intervene, nothing was done to protect them or find the perpetrators (Naidenov, 2009). Reporters often paid a price for their work.

24 Chassa was a pioneer in introducing Bulgarian readers to media campaigns, exemplified by its 2005–2006 "patriotic" national campaign for readers to nominate and vote for 24 "wonders of the motherland" (Vaglenov, 2007, 37). The campaign was developed in response to a Swiss initiative to select the Seven Wonders of the World in which 19 million people voted worldwide. Only two Bulgarian "wonders" were nominated but they did not make the final cut, so *24 Chassa* invited its audience to show their patriotic side by nominating and voting for places that "make readers proud to be Bulgarian", encouraging foreign visitors to see them. Readers responded with hundreds of nominations and a final list was compiled with help from historians, archaeologists, and on the basis of the highest number of nominations received (Vaglenov, 2007, 38).

Another campaign that *24 Chassa* participated in took a more sinister turn. In 2007, two academics, Martina Baleva and Ulf Brunnbauer, planned to speak to a conference in relation to the Batak massacre. Described as "one of the most horrendous acts in its history" (Rowlands, 2009), in 1876 the Turkish army killed 5,000 Bulgarians: men, women, and children. Once news of the talk trickled out, a large number of Bulgarian media outlets alleged the academics were denying the existence of the massacre and claiming the number of victims was exaggerated (Roth, 2010). Coverage of the conference talk sparked a wave of outrage and a media campaign against the researchers, spearheaded by *24 Chassa* and rival daily, *Trud*. The campaign included publishing strong views of prominent historians and public figures, the prime minister, and the president, condemning the event as anti-Bulgarian and as a sharp provocation to the dignity of national history (Roth, 2010). Following the openly hostile campaigns, the event was cancelled and the European Commission issued a stern warning to the Bulgarian authorities to take action against the people who sent the two researchers death threats. Eventually Bodo Hombach, the managing director of the WAZ Newspaper Group that owned the newspapers at the time, admitted that the campaigns led by *24 Chassa* and *Trud* were "a mistake" and that WAZ would learn from it (Rowlands, 2009).

Adversaries or allies to power?

With its rapid rise in popularity and influence, in the 1990s the new Bulgarian press came under government pressure and attempts to control its narratives. The press responded by becoming an open rival to all political parties. Hostility manifested in its scathing populist criticism towards those in power and in the language of its news. As an example, *24 Chassa*'s 1997 coverage of a protest outside the Bulgarian Parliament, which saw protesters break inside, was headlined: "Crowd breaks Parliament" with the subtitle "Crazed people attack the MPs' castle" (Znepolski, 1997,116). Through descriptions of violence and damage to the cars of MPs, the restaurant, and the National Assembly building, depicted as "castle", *24 Chassa* and *168 Chassa* presented a view of contempt towards those in power as having removed themselves from the rest of society including those attacking parliament. This is typical of the hybrid tabloid, which *24 Chassa* exemplifies by discursively promoting itself as a mouthpiece of the public while simultaneously positioning the public as being ignored by politicians (Spassov, 2004). In essence, *24 Chassa* embodies the successful uprising of the masses against the elite (Krastev, 2001). The use of manipulative textual mechanisms and phrasing that indicates the revolt of the masses, and their distrust in the authorities, aims to reinforce the public's trust in the paper's own version and description of the unfolding events.

This type of language also fostered a predominantly negative attitude and cynicism towards politics altogether, and *24 Chassa* adopted a narrative that depicted politicians as decidedly aggressive and macho (Lozanov, 2009). The slogan "they are all the same and they are all bad" became a common refrain for many newspapers, including *24* and *168 Chassa*. This included a pattern in headlines and articles alluding to male politicians as sexual predators, illustrating social tensions with highly charged innuendo (Znepolski, 1997). Poor people are often "ridden", "screwed", "victim of predators", with "naked behinds", while politicians' actions are presented as a sexual threat towards the public (Znepolski, 1997, 87). Such discourses allowed the newspapers to create a systematic, creative, and persistent illusion that they are intolerant of those in power while at the same time deeply concerned with the lives and suffering of ordinary people. In their desire to curry favour with the public, and demonstrate independence, they continuously criticized "corrupt" and "incompetent" authorities. This is a common trend in Eastern and Central Europe, where the "often vicious treatment" of governments contributed to perceived public disillusionment with politics and institutions (Jakubowicz, 2003, 239).

While the focus was on adversarial journalism in the mid 1990s, the newspaper was also not exempt from serious mistakes that cost it a significant amount of trust among its readership, and by the end of 1994 trust had plummeted, with only 26–27 per cent trusting the daily and 24–26 per cent distrusting it. This trend continued until 1997, when trust fell to 21 per cent and distrust jumped to 40 per cent (Tomov, 2001). It seemed that *24 Chassa* had taken its finger off the pulse of the nation and missed the rising wave of political discontent with the socialist government it had been tacitly supporting at the time. This loss of trust has been attributed to its unethical, openly partisan support of one of its own publishers, Ventsislav Yosifov, who had been nominated by the Bulgarian Socialist Party to be mayor of Sofia. For the first time since its launch, *24 Chassa* resembled a party organ, putting it in conflict with its more liberal or right-wing readers (Iankov, 2001). A turning point in the campaign to drum up support for Yosifov was the decision of the president of the *168 Chassa* Press Group, Petio Blaskov, to publish *kompromat* [3] on the opposition candidate the day before the mayoral election; in this case, a fake copy of his Communist Party membership record supplied by the Socialist campaign office. The fake record was presented to journalists at a press conference organized by supporters of Yosifov. However, most journalists present saw through the attempt to manipulate the election and agreed not to report on it. Only *24 Chassa* did, and the following day it was inundated with angry letters and phone calls from its readers, according to one of its former editors Rossen Yankov (2001). The newspaper's dominance in the market ended with the decision to publish the fake record (Nikolov, 2009).

However, there is general agreement that in its approach to power, *24 Chassa* largely served its readers' interests apart from a few "excruciating" moments (Lozanov, Spassov, and Iankov, 2001, 72). Both *24 Chassa* and *168 Chassa* have carried out watchdog reporting on state institutions and demonstrated an important role of practising nonpartisan journalism in times of political turmoil (Raycheva and Petev, 2003).

The "street" language controversy

The language of the new post-communist press, including language found in *24* and *168 Chassa*, has been the subject of much attention by Bulgarian scholars (e. g. Monova-Panova, 1995; Znepolski, 1997; Zambova, 2000; Spassov, 2000; Getsov, 2009; Monova, 2012). It has been described as direct, intentionally rude, negative, often marked by a nasty streak, full of barbaric, cynical words, the language of the nouveau riche simpletons, and the angry poor (Znepolski, 1997). The change from the formal, dry, boring language of communism was so significant that Bulgarians living abroad often could not understand the meaning of headlines on first reading (Balotova, 1996, cited in Spassov, 2000). After 1989 the way people talked to each other was transferred to the pages of the press and helped to establish a new journalistic language of the transition period (Spassov, 2000; 2010).

When *24 Chassa* entered the market in the spring of 1991, it broke language norms and grammatical conventions, especially in its headlines, and simultaneously attracted readers like a magnet while repulsing language experts. Academics bemoaned the state of the Bulgarian language being "torn apart" by the media (Panaiotov, 1995, 14), with foreign words said to be invading and drowning the "pure" Bulgarian language (Semov, 1995, 18). In its first issues, *24 Chassa* drew readers' attention through "a small language scandal manifesting itself in breaking habits and irritating good taste", which became a weapon in the fight against newspaper competitors (Znepolski, 1997, 80) and a clear statement against elitism.

However, the editor-in-chief of *168 Chassa*, Petio Blaskov (2009) disagrees with scholars' assessments:

> Our language was not the "language of the street", it was the language of the people. The people were longing to read in that language and we, as journalists, were longing to write in it … we wanted to write and read it because it was forbidden for over 40 years, it just did not exist.

Adopting everyday speech including common slang was another act of opposition to communist-type official media language, seen as too ideologically and politically charged. Newspapers of the early 1990s were proud of the fact that they had broken the language barriers and emulated the language of their readers (Lozanov, 2010). While it served to connect journalists with their audiences, it contributed to the establishment of two types of story narratives in *168, 24 Chassa,* and others: the "black" and the "yellow".

"Black" narratives include stories about the criminal elite, or *Mutri*, Bulgaria's former top wrestling champions, who found themselves out of work at the end of the regime and began organizing themselves into criminal gangs. Lozanov (2010) argues the press legitimized the new powerful criminal elite by providing just as much coverage of criminals as of legitimate public figures. This led to the permanent inclusion of the criminal elite as part of the powerful of the day. "Yellow" tabloid narratives focus on the hierarchy of money and lifestyle, in which criminals became very important and their crimes forgiven and accepted by the public as part of life (Lozanov, 2010; see also Daskalova, 2013). However, *24 Chassa*'s editor-in-chief Valeri Naidenov has argued that the readers did not want to read about official meetings, they wanted to read about Ivo Karamanski's[4] release from prison. "We are slaves of our readers", he claimed (cited in Getsov, 2009, 120).

Alongside serious coverage, *24* and *168 Chassa* indulged their readers in lengthy, vivid features about notorious and wealthy crime figures, turning the shady figures of the transition into urban legends. Readers of a certain age would still remember the life stories of Krokodila, Mechkata, Lisicata, Italianeca, Margina, and Madzo. This is a particular strength of the tabloid press, to create myths and legends that appeal to a mass audience (Monova, 2012). While by all accounts the reporting was often accurate and based on official police sources, the image of the underground world recreated by the newspapers through criminal slang was like a mafia movie about bad guys or "the big bosses" that had earned respect for their actions and power. Reporting on the latest crimes and arrests showed their evil as well as their human and weak sides. Their lives were mythologized in a constant narrative in which their families, descendants, mistresses, and enemies featured heavily (Daskalova, 2013). The lives of these figures were surrounded by mystery and gossip while their often untimely or dramatic murders further amplified coverage. Crime was presented as a game in which criminals, famous politicians, and legitimate business actors all participated, painting a colourful picture of a lawless society in the early days of the transition.

Today, *24 Chassa* continues to use everyday spoken language, slang, and words that breach the main ethical code for the press; for example, by stating the ethnic background of the people it reports on (Tzankova, 2018). Crime reporting of murders, attacks, theft, and so on remains the second biggest topic in its daily coverage, after current national and political events (Vulkov et. al., 2019). While Bulgarian journalists working for "hybrid" newspapers have often been accused of disregarding professional standards, it can be argued the early excesses of this genre, such as publishing explicit sexual images verging on pornography on front pages, crass language, and the obsession with mafia bosses and their lifestyles, served to test the limits of the newly acquired freedom of speech and expression. The territory where freedom could be fully demonstrated and achieved was at the level of language. Excessive and vulgar language was also lucrative since it generated maximum profit in minimal time while removing the need for journalistic effort and specialist training (Spassov, 2004).

Journalists

The staff of *24 Chassa*, fondly referred to "as our people", are an important part of the mythology of the newspaper (Naidenov, 1995). The revolution in language, for instance, was carried out mainly by those young journalists "with the linguistic experience of youth culture – subversive and undisciplined by definition"

(Spassov, 2004, 56). For those journalists who entered the profession in the early 1990s, the author of this chapter included, the environment and not the university was their best tutor. The policy of *24 Chassa* and most of the press to hire young and inexperienced people during this period had a twofold effect. On the one hand, young people learnt and reproduced "street" speech well, which helped the media sell more copies; they quickly learnt new skills on the go, and talked about issues freely and without inhibitions. On the other hand, first- and second-year journalism undergraduates did not have the necessary experience to analyze events in depth, nor were they able to evaluate them critically, a skill that is acquired after years of professional and life experience. The shortage of older and more experienced journalists required to write serious and quality content was felt acutely in the media environment throughout the transition (Daskalova, 2010). Scholars have also lamented the deficit in general knowledge in the majority of Bulgarian journalists and their "linguistic illiteracy" (Monova, 2012, 80).

Conclusion

If there is one thing that the newspapers *24* and *168 Chassa* can be described as without causing a controversy, that would surely be as an antipode of the old, state controlled press of the communist era. In many ways, and despite their numerous flaws, both have become a type of "drug", a "drug" that dulls the horror of readers' tacit knowledge of a complex and difficult reality that they have to navigate alone. *24 Chassa* offered entertainment and emotional authenticity as a way of dealing with the harsh reality of the transition. Readers became addicted to the "linguistic freedom" that *24 Chassa* offered, its uninhibited expression, reinforcing the illusion that the newspaper said things that otherwise could not be said (Spassov, 2001). The tabloid had a recipe for everything, and while it didn't give a reason or look for logic, it was always suspicious and knew whom to blame on behalf of its readers (Monova, 2012; Krastev, 2001).

The pages of the two newspapers allowed a multitude of voices to be heard, voices that shaped the new democratic political order, rhetoric and discourse. Since their debut and despite numerous setbacks, *24* and to some extent *168 Chassa* have dictated the main trends in the development of the press in Bulgaria. Whether they were branded as heroes or villains in public life, often accused of populism, undermining institutions, servitude to power, and other sins, they remain an important factor and institution in shaping public opinion in Bulgaria. They were pioneers in changing the post-communist press landscape, revolutionized news, and created the model of popular, accessible-to-all daily newspaper, in a form that Bulgarian readers liked and wanted to read at the end of the century. Despite the criticism, the two newspapers are an accurate historical record of the state of Bulgarian post-communist society, its soaring highs and dangerous lows.

Notes

1 The Bulgarian expression is "Malkite Chasove".
2 Petio Blaskov, Veleri Naidenov, Radostina Konstantinova, Dragomir Vassilev, Emil Dimitrov and Vladimir Raychev were the founders of the company that published the two newspapers (Vulkov et al., 2019).
3 *Kompromat* from Russian is short for compromising materials timed and published with the aim to destroy a political or business rival's reputation.
4 Notorious crime figure from the 1990s.

References

Blaskov, Petio. 2009. Former editor-in-chief of *168 Chassa*. Face to face interview conducted by the author in August, 2009.

Bulgarian National Assembly. 1991. "Constitution of the Republic of Bulgaria." Accessed 4 January 2020. https://www.parliament.bg/en/const/.

Cheterian, Vicken. 2009. "Colour Revolutions and the Media: Where is the Scoop?" In Dyczok, Martha, and Gaman-Golutvina, Oxana (eds.) *Media, Democracy and Freedom: The Post-Communist Experience*. Bern: Peter Lang: 205–230.

Daskalova, Nikoleta. 2010. Bulgarian media expert. Face to face interview conducted by the author in August, 2010.

Daskalova, Nikoleta. 2013. "Сериознити теми в жълтите медии: нюанси на таблоидната политика." ["Serious Issues in Tabloid Media: Nuances in Tabloid Approach."] In *Медии и Демокрация: Свобода, плурализъм и права*. [*Media and Democracy: Freedom, Pluralism and Rights*.] (Eds.) Rue, Juul, Spassov, Orlin, and Barch, Rudolph. Sofia: Foundation Media Democracy: 84–88.

Denev, Panaiot. 2009. Former editor of *Demokratsia*. Face to face interview conducted by the author in August, 2009.

Dyczok, Martha. 2009. "Introduction." In Dyczok, Martha and Gaman-Golutvina, Oksana. (Eds.) *Democracy and Freedom: The Post-communist Experience*. Bern: Peter Lang: 9–16.

Foley, Michael. 2006. Promoting Values as West Meets East. *The International Journal of Communication Ethics*, 3: 2/3. Accessed 17 January 2020. https://arrow.dit.ie/cgi/viewcontent.cgi?referer=&httpsredir=1&article=1042&context=aaschmedart.

Gaman-Golutvina, Oksana. 2009. "Conclusions. Media and Democracy in Transformation Design." In *Media, Democracy and Freedom: The Post-communist Experience*. In Dyczok, Martha and Gaman-Golutvina, Oksana (Eds.) Bern: Peter Lang: 231–242.

Getsov, Anton. 2009. *По следите на скрития смисъл*. [Looking for Hidden Meaning.] Veliko Tarnovo: University Publishing House "St. Cyril and Methodius."

Gotcheva, Venelina. 2001. "Вестникът, какъвтое." ["The Newspaper as it is."] In Lozanov, Georgi, Spassov, Orlin, and Iankov, Rossen (Eds.) *24 Часа – Вестникът*. [*24 Chassa –The Newspaper*.] Sofia: Trud Publishing House: 7–12.

Hiebert, Ray. 1999. "Transition: From the End of the Old Regime to 1996." In Aumente, Jerome, Gross, Peter, Hiebert, Ray, Johnson, Owen V., and Mils, Dean (Eds.) *Eastern European Journalism: Before, During and After Communism*. Cresskill, New Jersey: Hampton Press: 79–122.

Ianeva, Katya. 2018. *Моето защо. Радостина Константинова изследвания, репртажи и интервюта от три деситилетия*. [*My Why. Radostina Konstantinova: Investigations, reports and interviews from three decades*.] Sofia: Roprint

Iankov, Rossen. 2001. "Кратка история." ["Short History."] In Lozanov, Georgi, Spassov, Orlin, and Iankov, Rossen (Eds.) *24 Часа – Вестникът*. [*24 Chassa –The Newspaper.*] Sofia:Trud Publishing House: 13–24.

Ibroscheva, Elsa. 2008. "The Politics of Mediated Gender: Women Politicians in the Bulgarian Press." *Politics and Culture*, Issue 4. Accessed 10 January 2020. https://politicsandculture.org/2010/09/19/the-politics-of-mediated-gender-women-politicians-in-the-bulgarian-press/.

Jakubowicz, Karol. 2003. "Change in Polish Media: How far to go yet?" In Paletz, David and Jakubowicz, Karol. (Eds.) *Business as Usual. Continuity and Change in Central and Eastern Europe.* Cresskill, New Jersey: Hampton Press: 205–242.

Krastev, Ivan. 2001. "Критика на таблоидния разум." ["Critique of tabloid logic."] In Lozanov, Georgi, Spassov, Orlin, and Iankov, Rossen (Eds.) *24 Часа – Вестникът*. [*24 Chassa –The Newspaper.*] Sofia:Trud Publishing House: 79–88.

Lozanov, Georgi. 2009. "Кой как вижда невидимите." ["How do we see the invisible."] In *Бежанци и медии*. ["*Refugees and the Media.*"] (Ed.) Tabakova, Vessela. Sofia:Centre for Independent Journalism: 129–148.

Lozanov, Georgi. 2010. Bulgarian media expert. Face to face interview conducted by the author in August, 2010.

Lozanov, Georgi, Spassov, Orlin, and Iankov, Rossen. 2001. *24 Часа – Вестникът*. [*24 Chassa –The Newspaper.*] Sofia:Trud Publishing House.

Monova-Paneva, Totka. 1995. "Публикационна стратегия на местния печат по време на изборите 1991 г." ["Publication strategy of the local press during the election of 1991."] In *Журналистиката в тоталитарното и посттоталитарното общество*. [Journalism in Totalitarian and Post-totalitarian Society.] (Eds.) Karaivanova, Penka, Panaiotov, Phillip, Petrov, Milko, and Konstantinova, Zdravka. Sofia: Sofia University, Faculty of Journalism and Mass Communication: 155–166.

Monova, Totka. 2012. *Новият журнализъм на прехода*. [*The New Journalism of the Transition.*] Sofia:Pardox.

Naidenov, Dimitar. 1995. *Пресжурналистика (1989–1995)*. [*Press Journalism (1989–1995)*.] Sofia: Sofia University, Faculty of Journalism and Mass Communication.

Naidenov, Valeri. 2009. Former editor-in-chief of 24 Chassa. Face to face interview conducted by the author in August, 2009.

Nikolov, Iovo. 2009. Former crime and chief court reporter for 24 Chassa. Face to face interview conducted by the author in August, 2009.

Panaiotov, Phillip. 1995. "Национална съдба и журналистика." ["National Destiny and Journalism."] In *Журналистиката в тоталитарното и посттоталитарното общество*. [*Journalism in Totalitarian and Post-totalitarian Society.*] (Eds.) Karaivanova, Penka, Panaiotov, Phillip, Petrov, Milko, and Konstantinova, Zdravka. Sofia: Sofia University, Faculty of Journalism and Mass Communication: 9–13.

Raycheva, Lilia and Petev, Todor. 2003. "Mass Media's Changing Landscape in Bulgaria (1989–1999)." In *Business as Usual: Continuity and Change in Central and Eastern European Media*, (Eds.) Paletz, David, and Jakubowicz, Karol. Cresskill, New Jersey: Hampton Press: 73–109.

Roth, Klaus. 2010. "Between the Ottoman Legacy and the European Union: On the Utilisation of Historical Myths in Bulgaria." In *From Palermo to Penang. A Journey into Political Anthropology*. (Eds.) Ruegg, François, and Boscoboinik, Andrea. Berlin:LIT Verlag: 179–194.

Roudakova, Natalia. 2008. "Media-political Clientelism: Lessons From Anthropology." *Media, Culture & Society*, Vol. 30: 41–59.

Rowlands, Henry. 2009. "The Bulgarian Atrocity that Shocked The World." Novinite.com. 16 July. Accessed 1 Dec 2019. https://www.novinite.com/articles/105840/The+Bulgarian+Atrocity+that+Shocked+The+World.

Semov, Marko. 1995. Журналистика и народопсихология. [Journalism and National Psychology.] In *Журналистиката в тоталитарното и посттоталитарното общество*. [*Journalism in Totalitarian and Post-totalitarian Society*.] (Eds.) Karaivanova, Penka, Panaiotov, Phillip, Petrov, Milko, and Konstantinova, Zdravka. Sofia: Sofia University, Faculty of Journalism and Mass Communication: 9–13.

Spassov, Orlin. 2000. *Преходът и медиите. Политики на репрезентация (България 1989–2000)*. [*The Transition and the Media. Politics of Representation (Bulgaria 1989–2000)*.] Sofia: University Publishing House "St. Climent Ohridsky," Faculty of Journalism and Mass Communication.

Spassov, Orlin. 2001. "От политиката до гражданите." ["From politics to citizens."] In Lozanov, Georgi, Spassov, Orlin, and Iankov, Rossen (Eds.) *24 Часа – Вестникът*. [*24 Chassa –The Newspaper*.] Sofia: Trud Publishing House: 89–102.

Spassov, Orlin. 2004. "The 'Serious' Press, the Tabloid Context, and Qualities of the Public Sphere." In Spassov, Orlin. (Ed.) *Quality Press in Southeast Europe*. Sofia: Southeast European Media Centre (SOEMZ): 50–73.

Spassov, Orlin. 2010. Bulgarian media expert. Face to face interview conducted in August 2010.

Štětka, Vaclav. 2011. *Bulgaria – A country report for the ERC-funded project on Media and Democracy in Central and Eastern Europe*. Oxford: Media and Democracy in Central and Eastern Europe. Report downloaded by the author on 5 October 2011.

Stewart, James. 2013. A Suitable Case for Transplant? The BBC and public service journalism in post-communist Romania. *Journalism Practice*, Vol. 7 (3): 329–344.

Tomov, Tzvetozar. 2001. "Успелият вестник." ["The Successful Newspaper."] In Lozanov, Georgi, Spassov, Orlin, and Iankov, Rossen (Eds.) *24 Часа – Вестникът*. [*24 Chassa –The Newspaper*.] Sofia: Trud Publishing House: 157–164.

Trifonova Price, Lada. 2015. "Secrets, Lies and Journalist-Spies – the contemporary moral dilemma for Bulgarian media professionals. *International Journal of Press/Politics*, Vol. 20 (2): 185–203.

Tzankova, Svetla. 2018. *Съвременна българска преса. Пазарни и качествени трансформации*. [*Contemporary Bulgarian Press. Market and Quality Transformation*.] Sofia: UNSS.

Vaglenov, Stanimir. 2007. "24 Часа." ["24 Chassa."] In *Журналисти по теория, журналисти на практика*. [*Journalists in Theory and in Practice*.] Sofia: Sofia University, Faculty of Journalism and Mass Communication: 37–38.

Voltmer, Katrin. 2013. *The Media in Transitional Democracies*. Cambridge: Polity.

Vulkanov, Iliya, Antonova, Vesislava, Daskalova, Nikoleta, Bossev, Rosen, and Bozidarov, Diyan. 2019. "24 Часа – Исторически преглед и редакционна политика." ["24 Chassa – Historical Overview and Editorial Policy."] Bulgaria: Association of European Journalists. Accessed 17 January 2020. http://printmediareport.aej-bulgaria.org/24-chasa/.

Vulkanova, Veselina. 1995. "Графичен дизайн на Българските вестници преди и след политическата промяна от 10. IX. 1989." ["Graphic Design of Bulgarian Newspaper Before and After the Political Changes on 10. IX. 1989."] In *Журналистиката в тоталитарното и посттоталитарното общество*. [*Journalism in Totalitarian and Post-totalitarian Society*.] (Eds.) Karaivanova, Penka, Panaiotov,

Phillip, Petrov, Milko, and Konstantinova, Zdravka. Sofia: Sofia University, Faculty of Faculty of Journalism and Mass Communication: 117–185.

Wessler, Hartmut, Skorek, Malgorzat, Kleinen-von Königslöw, Katharina, Held, Maximilian, Dobreva, Mihaela, and Adolphsen, Manuel. 2008. "Comparing media systems and media content: Online newspapers in ten Eastern and Western European countries." *Journal of Global Mass Communication*, Vol. (1): 165–189.

Znepolski, Ivailo. 1997. *Новата Преса и Преходът*. [*The New Press and the Transition.*] Sofia:Druzestvo Grazdanin.

10 From baby bumps to border walls

Celebrity gossip magazines and the post-truth politic

Andrea McDonnell

Introduction

Media coverage of the 1977 death of Elvis Presley marked a critical shift in the relationship between mainstream news and tabloid journalism. When both ABC and NBC led their nightly news broadcast, typically devoted to politics, business, and international affairs, with coverage of The King's heart attack, it was clear that hard news and celebrity journalism could no longer be considered distinct and separate (Gregory and Gregory 1992). The influence of Elvis' death would extend even further, as the American tabloid press, especially the *Weekly World News* and *National Enquirer*, ran dozens of stories throughout the 1980s and 90s featuring "real" photos which allegedly revealed that 'The King' was, in fact, very much alive. An entire genre of stories, dubbed "Elvis Sightings", would become part of the pop culture lexicon thanks to the popularity of supermarket tabloids and the fantastical narratives they offered up (Newman 2014; Sloan 2001). In all of these ways, Elvis' death can be understood as a microcosm of developments in mainstream, tabloid, and celebrity journalism, which both reflected and helped to shape public understanding of truth and newsworthiness in the decades to follow.

This chapter considers these intersections in order to develop an understanding of tabloid culture's influence on conceptions of truth with regard to American politics throughout the twenty-first century. To do so, I trace the ways in which one particular tabloid genre, celebrity gossip magazines, has informed popular understandings and meaning-making processes around political news and information. Throughout the early 2000s, a cohort of magazines, including *Us Weekly, In Touch, Life & Style, Ok!*, and *Star*, gained prominence and popularity in the US market. They shared a core set of defining features, from their use of glossy, colour paparazzi photos, to their attention-grabbing headlines and imagery, to a highly speculative tone, which emphasized celebrity feuds, romance, and scandal (McDonnell 2014). These magazines drew from and expanded upon numerous existing tropes within tabloid and celebrity culture; they revelled in drama, innuendo, and intrigue, presented altered photographs as visual "proof", and encouraged readers to feel a sense of personal connection to celebrity figures (McDonnell 2014).

The celebrity gossip magazines that emerged in the early 2000s can best be understood not as a new or singular genre, but rather as an extension and reimagining of tabloid content dating back centuries. They reflect the penchant for the lurid and scandalous that defined the penny press in the nineteenth century. They mimic the storytelling and intimate access to the stars offered by fan magazines of the 1910s and '20s. They further the obsession with celebrity life cultivated throughout the 1980s in television programs like *Entertainment Tonight* and *Lifestyles of the Rich and Famous*. They are also very much a descendant of the tabloid fixtures of the 1980s and 90s. They extend public interest in celebrity scandal, made salient through the rapid expansion of court television and paparazzi photography, epitomized by the trial of football star O.J. Simpson and the untimely death of Princess Diana, both of which brought celebrity culture to the forefront of mainstream news. Finally, they draw upon themes established by supermarket tabloids, such as the *Globe, Weekly World News*, and *National Enquirer*, which, at their peak, reached some 12 million readers each week with their frenetic mix of celebrity gossip and fantastic narratives (Sloan 2001).

In his book, *I Watched a Wild Hog Eat My Baby!*, former *Star* and *Enquirer* editor Bill Sloan describes how tabloid papers covered the most sensational, unbelievable, even wacky stories, while also eventually focusing their lens on celebrity culture as a way of creating mass-market appeal (2001). Part of the lure of supermarket tabloids is their outrageousness, and the millions of readers who are drawn in by stories about Bat Boy, or Bigfoot's baby, angels, and aliens don't actually mind if what they are reading is true or not, so long as they are entertained (Bird 1992).

These publications' penchant for the implausible and the invented have also come to influence celebrity and mainstream journalism. In his book, *Newszak and News Media*, Bob Franklin argues that, throughout the 1980s and 90s, financial pressures, structural changes in media industries, and the blurring line between information and entertainment caused mainstream news organizations to adopt many of the tropes and techniques once reserved for the tabloid press. Journalism, he contends, has come to favour light-hearted, entertainment-based content, provided to audiences in short, digestible snippets, over investigative and critical reporting about those in power (Franklin 1997). In the twenty-first century, the rise of digital content, the instant accessibility of news and gossip on the Internet, and the sheer volume of unverified information circulating on social media, further eroded distinctions between news and entertainment, fact and fiction (Holmes 2006).

The editorial practices of celebrity gossip magazines have also influenced public perceptions around the truthfulness of journalists and encouraged scepticism towards mediated information. This chapter traces the ways in which these effects have contributed to a media environment in which the question of truth, what it is and who has a responsibility to tell it, has become central to our understanding of socio-political life. These practices also coincide with developments in the American political landscape, most notably the rapid shift from an information environment defined by "truthiness" during the George W. Bush administration, to a "post-truth" landscape under Donald J. Trump.

Speculation and editorialization in celebrity gossip

In 2001, *Us* magazine had a makeover. The former monthly entertainment magazine was transformed into a glossy weekly focused on celebrity news and gossip. By 2002, *Us Weekly* had achieved the tenth largest circulation growth amongst mass-market magazines, its newsstand sales were up 55.3 per cent, and the imprint was drawing over a million readers each week (Carr 2003). But it wasn't just *Us*. Looking to tap into this new market, Bauer Publishing launched *In Touch Weekly* in 2002 and sister-publication *Life & Style* in 2004, while *Ok!* and paper tabloid staple *Star* simultaneously tweaked their content to mirror the new format. This cohort of publications quickly became part of the zeitgeist of the early 2000s. Part adoring fan magazine, part tabloid scandal machine, with an image-heavy format made possible thanks to developments in high-quality digital photography and a burgeoning paparazzi industry, these magazines were soon fixtures at supermarket checkouts and pharmacy newsstands across the country (McDonnell 2014).

The rise of celebrity gossip magazines is especially noteworthy because it took place during a period in which print publications, including newspapers, were experiencing deep, industry-wide losses (Rose 2002). The information marketplace was increasingly saturated by a vast array of cable channels and a new stream of instant and, most financially damaging, free digital content. Print sales, news viewership, and advertiser revenue fell (Thompson 2016). To remain viable, producers had to be willing to compete, and competing meant covering stories that had once been considered too "soft" for mainstream journalism. It meant news outlets which had once prided themselves on their objectivity and seriousness had to run stories about hotel-heiress and paparazzi-darling Paris Hilton or the latest reality-competition contestant on *The Bachelor*. The already blurry line between celebrity and public affairs was becoming increasingly hazy.

In addition, this melding of news and gossip brought with it serious concerns about the nature of truthfulness in reporting. Whereas US journalism had, throughout the twentieth century, prided itself on its dedication to the pursuit of facts and aversion to bias (Franklin 1997), celebrity reporting revelled in speculation and exaggeration. Celebrity gossip magazines rely heavily upon the technique of editorialization, in which the publication takes a tiny tidbit of information, for example, a small detail of a photo, a quote from a source, or even a subtle gesture made by a star, and extrapolate an entire scenario based on that minutia. A 2011 feature on vice-presidential nominee Sarah Palin's daughter, Bristol, shows this kind of editorialization in action. The story, entitled "Knifestyles of the Rich and Famous", displays an older, "then" photo of Bristol who also starred in various reality television shows, alongside a newer, "now" image. From these two simple photos, the magazine speculates that

Bristol has lost weight, "gone rogue" with plastic surgery, and "made major life changes." The article cites a surgeon who, admittedly, has never treated Bristol, but nevertheless concludes that she "may" have had a chin implant and chemical peel, or "could" have undergone liposuction. Plus, her arched eyebrows "can also be due to conservative Botox injections" (*Star*, May 23, 2011, 55). While the reader may not know for sure, there is fun to be had in examining these two images and trying to decide for one's self what, if anything, Bristol has changed.

Stories written in winking, knowing prose further encourage readers to draw their own conclusions, to judge, and to speculate (McDonnell 2014). Editors use carefully chosen photos to suggest anger, resentment, or emotional turmoil. Brightly coloured arrows and circles overlaid on top of images draw readers' attention to a new ring (engaged?), a slightly different looking nose (surgery?), or a hand placed gently over a stomach (pregnant?). "Can you keep a secret?", asks a 2008 advertisement for *Star*, "neither can we" (*Star*, May 12, 2008).

Such techniques invite the reader to engage in what media scholar Joshua Gamson calls *believing games*. These games are designed and initiated by celebrity producers, who intentionally blend truth and fiction through a series of fabrication activities designed to mould, manipulate, and manage the celebrity image (Gamson 1994, 172). Audiences, in turn, take pleasure in a kind of game playing process, in which truthfulness is often a moot point. As Gamson writes in his book *Claims to Fame*, "rather than dwelling on either the inauthentic or the real, audiences simply go about the business of gossip without an overall concern for questions of authenticity" (1994, 173). According to this assessment, not only is it unnecessary for content to be accurate, it is also unnecessary that the audience *believes* what they are reading and discussing is true. As Elizabeth Bird writes about supermarket tabloid readers, while some believe that what they are reading is true, and others do not, all revel in the fantasy and possibility that the uncertainty of such texts offers up (1992, 119–123). In addition, gossip about celebrities is generally consequence free, and therefore more game-like than gossip about real-world acquaintances, co-workers, or family members.

Through polls, questions, and direct address, celebrity gossip magazines invite readers to change their opinion, speculate about the magazines' authority, or even contest the meaning of the content with friends and fellow readers (McDonnell 2014). Further, because these magazines follow the same cast of celebrity characters over years of coverage, readers may use the information they accumulate through their fandom to gather clues and draw informed conclusions. Through their engagement, they become a part of the narrative meaning-making process. "As in any game", Gamson notes, "the outcome is less important than the process" (1994, 180). Savvy consumers have become increasingly aware of and knowledgeable about the celebrity industry and its modes of manipulation, and use this knowledge as a kind of additional game-play tool (Gamson 1994, 180–181).

Yet these believing games are low stakes. If the reader, or the magazine, guesses wrong this week, there will be a new scandal and new judgement to be made when the next issue arrives. Misinformation and gossip about celebrities can be distributed in print and by word of mouth with very little consequence. In these ways, the celebrity gossip press both contributes to and benefits from the assumption that it is an unreliable source: trivial, tawdry, and trashy. "The pleasurable freedom of celebrity gossip", Gamson writes, "is built precisely on its freedom from but resemblance to truth" (1994, 177). But what happens when these techniques are applied to mainstream news and journalism? What happens when these believing games seep into the public sphere?

Truthiness

At the same time that celebrity gossip magazines began speculating about actors' alleged affairs, pregnancies, and cosmetic surgeries, the American public was also grappling with the question of truth as expressed through the politics of the George W. Bush administration. Bush had become the 43rd president of the United States in January 2001, following a highly contested recount of ballots in Florida and an electoral crisis of confidence that left many voters wondering if the winner could even be determined (Federal Election Commission 2000). But there was little time to consider this. By that fall, the American public faced a new crisis when nearly 3,000 people were killed in al-Qaeda terrorist attacks, when highjacked planes were flown into New York City's World Trade Center and the Pentagon, outside Washington, DC, and crashed in a field in Pennsylvania, in the most destructive act of terrorism ever committed on US soil.

During the months following 9/11, the Bush administration and its communications team encouraged speculation and uncertainty with inconsistent reports and vagaries. Some argued that the administration intentionally manipulated the American public, distracting with false information, fear tactics, and staged public relations stunts in order to garner support for the so-called "war on terror" (Rich 2006). Despite uncertainty, the alleged existence of weapons of mass destruction was a primary justification for the American-led invasion of Iraq, which began in March 2003. Two short months after troops had been deployed, Bush announced "the end of major combat operations in Iraq" from the deck of the USS *Abraham Lincoln*, flocked by military personnel and standing in front of a banner proclaiming "MISSION ACCOMPLISHED", but the enthusiastic certainty of the announcement was soon contradicted by the unmistakable reality facing the nation, as scepticism grew about the war and the so-called evidence that had been provided to justify it.

New York Times columnist and author Frank Rich wrote that the Bush administration's emphasis on deception and stagecraft to justify war had precipitated "the decline and fall of truth" in America (2006). Unburdened by facts, one aide reportedly told the press, "when we act, we create our own reality" (Rich 2006, 3). The U.S. Senate Select Committee on Intelligence ultimately found that Bush administration officials repeatedly made misleading statements, ushered the nation to war under false pretences, and deliberately presented the public with information that was known to be inaccurate, but by then, the damage was already done (2008).

During this period, Jon Stewart and Stephen Colbert rose to prominence, hosting satirical news shows on cable-network Comedy Central, during which they pointed out and poked fun at the onslaught of the Bush administration's contradictions. In 2005, Colbert coined the term "truthiness", referring to a form of truth that a person claims to know intuitively, emotionally, or "from the gut", without regard for evidence or logic. "Truthiness is tearing apart our country", Colbert said in a 2006 interview with *The Onion*'s culture site, 'the AV Club". "It used to be, everyone was entitled to their own opinion, but not their own facts. But that's not the case anymore. Facts matter not at all. Perception is everything. It's certainty" (Rabin 2006). The term quickly caught on and was named "Word of the Year" by the American Dialect Society and the Merriam-Webster dictionary. Colbert's delivery was humorous, but his message had serious implications for our national discourse.

It was in this political milieu and under the shadow of doubt in American politics, that celebrity gossip magazines thrived. Between 2002 and 2005, in the months following 9/11, celebrity-driven titles' newsstand sales rose 58 per cent, up nearly $200 million in less than three years (Davis 2005). By 2005, the celebrity gossip category would come to represent 30 per cent of total sales revenue within the magazine market (Davis 2005). Unlike coverage of politics and terrorism, which was frightening in its ambiguity, the uncertainty of celebrity gossip was fun and distracting. Maybe the latest story about Disney child-star-turned-tabloid-fixture Lindsey Lohan was true, maybe not, but it was fun to talk about. It was lighthearted and largely consequence free. Celebrity gossip offered a sense of comfort and an escape from color-coded terror levels. It made us feel confident in our opinions and knowledge during a period where political realities were increasingly uncertain, and it offered a much-needed reprieve from coverage of war (Douglas 2010, 250).

Occasionally, celebrity gossip magazines would also cover politics, and they did so by presenting the so-called ordinary lives of politicians alongside those of entertainment celebrities. In August 2000, while George W. Bush was on the campaign trail, *Us* ran an extensive, eight-page profile of soon-to-be First Lady Lara Bush, which described both her accomplishments and her "sparkly blue eyes" (August 21 2000, 68–75). During his time in office, Bush's daughters were also profiled in stories like "The Bush Twins Rock the Big Apple", which dished, "their dad came to town on business but the girls just want to have fun" (*Star*, September 20 2004, 36). Such stories were presented in the same way that stories about actors and models would be. For instance, Jenna Bush's wedding ceremony was featured in multiple publications, complete with photos of the venue, rings, dresses, and cake; *Star* described the nuptials as "A First Family Affair" (May 26 2008, 58–59). These stories treated political figures with the same gushing tone, glossy images, and gossipy reveals previously reserved for A-listers, thus rhetorically and stylistically erasing the line between star and politician. This coverage represented a new take on political news, one that was at once humanizing and celebratory.

Celebrities and politicians are typically considered distinct entities, but they share much in common and occupy many similar roles in mass media (Marshall 1997, 19). Celebrities have long played a part in public life, from singer Kate Smith's 1943 radio war-bond drive to the 1985 Live Aid concert, in which a star-studded roster of performers raised funds to support famine relief in Ethiopia. The tabloid press has also covered politicians such as the Kennedys and Ronald Reagan in the US or the British royal family, including Princess Diana, in the UK. By the early 2000s, stars like actor Arnold Schwarzenegger and reality show host Donald Trump were dabbling in politics, and presidential candidates were now blogging, appearing on *Saturday Night Live*, and even starring in their own reality TV shows (such as TLC's *Sarah Palin's Alaska,* which followed the failed Republican vice-presidential candidate and her family at home). At the crossroads of public and private, celebrity culture and politics had become inextricable in the twenty-first century (Wheeler 2013).

When we consider the legacy of the George W. Bush years, it may be tempting to dismiss the role of the gossip press, but as celebrity gossip magazines became increasingly profitable and visible fixtures of American popular culture, they also provided a roadmap, a kind of guidebook for deconstructing news stories, for using the information at our disposal to counter and question, to draw our own conclusions. Knowing readers cried "fake news" when dissecting the minutiae of celebrity narratives, scoffing at stories that strained credulity. Celebrity gossip magazines encouraged us to speculate and question. We learned how to sleuth out information and even found pleasure and excitement in doing so, but soon the American public would be applying these techniques to mainstream journalism, and "fake news" would come to take on a meaning far more sinister than Jennifer Aniston's latest alleged pregnancy.

Post-truth

In 2008, the Obama administration ushered in a new era for the Democratic party in the United States. Obama's team was the first to develop a robust social media presence and to use online content as a primary information delivery mechanism and tool for voter outreach (Cain Miller 2008). Unlike his predecessor, Obama projected dependability and a forthright plain-spokenness. Yet he and his administration were also criticized for obfuscating or misrepresenting the full story of what the US was doing around the world, including its use of drones, the nature of the attacks on the US facilities in Libya, and US Secretary of State Hillary Clinton's use of a private email server in handling classified information, among other scandals. The Republican base remained highly sceptical of Obama, fearful of his political and cultural influence. Led by Donald Trump, some even questioned his legitimacy as an American; "birthers", as they would be called, circulated conspiracy theories about Obama's country of birth in a racist attempt to undermine his stature as the first Black American president.

While the Bush family appeared on the pages of celebrity gossip magazines occasionally, the Obamas were routinely profiled. *Us Weekly* dedicated feature stories to Barack Obama's relationship with his daughters ("I Think I'm a Pretty Cool Dad", November 24 2009), he and first lady Michelle Obama's early days as a couple ("Couple of the Year", January 5 2009), and an entire spread even profiled the family dog, Bo ("Meet Bo Obama", April 27 2009). Like other celebrities featured in these magazines, Barack Obama was presented as being "just like us", and reports detailed "25 things you don't know about me", including the fact that the President is left-handed and had his first kiss outside a Baskin Robbins in his native Chicago (*Us Weekly*, November 12 2012). This coverage showed an American president not only as an ordinary person, but also as a celebrity. Of course, other US presidents, including Ronald Reagan and Bill Clinton, sought and found public appeal, even fame, but this was different. This was the first Black president of the United States being represented as a relatable, knowable individual who, like other celebrities of the twenty-first century, no longer seemed all that removed from the ordinary American experience.

Yet these rosy profiles were set against a news media landscape that was increasingly on edge. A decade of rapid technological change, including the widespread proliferation of smart phones, meant that social media were quickly supplanting print as sources of news and information. Platforms like Facebook and Twitter, available anytime, anywhere, encouraged users to publicly and continuously express their views and opinions. The moment-to-moment formatting of cable news, where partisanship continued to deepen, both fed on and fueled the real-time information availability and shareability of online news.

Celebrity gossip magazines were also deeply affected by these developments. Audiences didn't have to rely on a magazine to discover what their favourite stars were doing or wearing, and celebrities were no longer dependent on paparazzi or editors to communicate with fans and market their brand. Now, stars could speak directly to their audience, via websites, blogs, streaming video, and highly curated, instantly accessible social media accounts (Douglas and McDonnell 2019). Why wait an entire week for a magazine to break a story when you could see Kim Kardashian visit the dentist or hang with Chrissy Teigen on Snapchat in real time? Celebrity social media accounts provided audiences with a new level of access, and stars with a greater claim on authenticity. This dynamic, along with the alleged democratic potential of the Internet, has fed a sense that anyone with the right YouTube presence and careful editing could become a star. Sales of gossip magazines declined (Adams 2011).

These developments did not, however, lessen the power of fame: quite the opposite. In a digital landscape where everyone was competing for visibility, publicness and attention became highly valuable cultural capital. At the same time, individuals and their social media musings became newsworthy. Donald Trump took advantage of this in order to re-present himself to the American public.

Donald Trump can be described as the first American tabloid president. Prior to his presidential bid, Trump was a fixture in the tabloid press. His real estate deals, lavish spending, casino ventures, and playboy antics were routinely documented by the New York papers, including in the gossipy 'Page Six' column of the *New York Post*. As gossip columnist Susan Mulcahey writes, "if you worked for a newspaper in New York in the 1980s, you had to write about Trump" (2016). Trump courted the press, hosting lavish parties, injecting himself into the ranks of Manhattan's glitterati, and calling reporters to provide fodder that would ensure the details of his latest deal or divorce found their way into the tabloids (Mulcahey, 2016). He would even reportedly call journalists using pseudonyms, such as John Barron, and pretend to be his own publicist in order to spin his image and attract press attention (Cassidy 2018). By the late 1990s, however, Trump's wealth and fame were fading, until his reality television show, *The Apprentice*, thrust him back into the spotlight, casting him as lead dealmaker, wealthy mogul, and capable executive.

The Apprentice, as Patrick Radden Keefe wrote in the *New Yorker*, mythologized Trump. By the early 2000s, Trump was largely seen as a failing businessman, of little interest to those outside New York and Palm Beach social circles (2018). Suddenly, *The Apprentice* made Trump and his brand a household name. The show positioned Trump not as a "serially bankrupt carnival barker", but as a titan of business, a shrewd and commanding presence, all wrapped in unimaginable wealth. Though employees of the show would later tell the press that it was all a carefully stage-managed façade, it would be of little concern to the American viewing public, at the time enraptured by the burgeoning genre of reality television (Radden Keefe 2018).

Stories about *The Apprentice*, Trump, his family, and his wealth quickly began popping up in celebrity gossip magazines and throughout the Obama presidency became mainstays of the tabloid press. Reality TV provided a synergistic content pool for gossip magazines, seeking new tidbits for each week's issue (Meyers 2020). NBC regularly ran glossy, multipage advertisements for *The Apprentice* in gossip magazines, and editors created content that centered on the show's stars. One *Us Weekly* cover story, for instance, was dedicated to show's "catfights that won't stop". The four-page article featured large photos of an imposing Trump, wearing a suit, surrounded by lingerie-clad female contestants (April 19 2004, 44–47). The same magazine ran a story about "Trump's smart, sexy daughter," Ivanka, and her role on the show (*Us*, January 6 2007, 74), while *In Touch* polled readers on who they would rather work for, Donald Trump, or guest boss Martha Stewart, with 56 per cent replying that they would rather work for Trump (September 26 2005, 65). Meanwhile, the magazines devoted feature stories to Trump's personal life, his children, and his new fiancée, Melania, (*Star*, December 27 2004, 54–55).

The cumulative effect of this coverage was twofold. First, it reinforced Donald Trump's celebrity persona as a powerful, in-control, successful business tycoon for whom ordinary folks would be lucky to work. Second, it transformed Trump into a knowable individual, someone with whom readers could identify and feel close, someone who was authentic and who spoke directly "to us". Trump capitalized on this image in launching his new political career. Trump had flirted with political aspirations for decades, but he was always a celebrity first. His 2016 candidacy for president drew from and extended the tabloid persona that he had cultivated for more than 30 years.

By the time Trump announced his candidacy for the American presidency in June 2015, the reality TV genre was losing steam, but social media were on the cusp of surpassing newspapers as a top news source (Curry 2016). Mainstream news and politics at home and abroad were increasingly driven by social media content, including citizen journalism, captured online and shared through digital networks to activate social change, as evidenced in the Occupy Wall Street and Arab Spring movements of the early 2010s. Users could now create their own news, as digital connectivity allowed frustrated and sceptical citizens to instantly express and share their point of view with an interconnected audience of like-minded thinkers.

But while some (Gimmler 2001) have seen the potential of the Internet and social media to serve as a modern embodiment of Jürgen Habermas' public sphere (1991), through which citizens can freely share information, discuss, and debate in service of the public good, others have noted the potential anti-social and anti-democratic potential of these technologies (Klein 2017, 4). Despite the increased availability of a variety of information sources, audiences have been increasingly consuming news that conforms to their pre-existing beliefs, carefully tracked and targeted by algorithms in order to increase user engagement (Anderson and Rainie 2017). Meanwhile, the digital affordances that allowed us to connect and share were also creating a diffuse information environment in which anyone could edit, alter, and post their ideas and opinions, no matter how unfounded. False narratives weren't just being written about, they were also being represented with convincing visuals. Image manipulation strategies, a mainstay of the tabloid press epitomized by those aforementioned Elvis sightings, had become high quality and mainstream. Anyone with simple editing software could alter an image and, with the right tools and know-how, produce shockingly realistic forgeries. Soon, online activity was being linked to the rise of misinformation, conspiracy theories (Anderson and Rainie 2017), and hate groups (Klein 2017).

The sheer variety and specificity of news sources online were overwhelming, but instead of informed, the public felt confused and unsure where to turn. Even national newspapers, network television, and public radio, previously held up as bastions of reliability and neutrality, were called into question. By 2015, when Trump launched his campaign for US president, Americans' trust and confidence in the mass media "to report the news fully, accurately and fairly" had dropped to its lowest level in Gallup polling history. Only 32 per cent of respondents reported a great deal or fair amount of trust in the media and, among those who identified as Republicans, there was a 14 per cent decrease in trust reported over the previous year (Swift 2016).

Throughout his campaign for president, Donald Trump seized on this uncertainty, calling the media "fake news", lambasting the press, and deploying his surrogates to present "alternative facts", a term later made famous by Trump's advisor, Kellyanne Conway, on TV news. He used Twitter as a central tool to his campaign, blasting other candidates, expressing his grievances, and capitalizing on his pre-existing fame to cultivate an audience and generate attention-grabbing quips via his @realDonaldTrump handle. Trump dubbed his Democratic rival, Hillary Clinton, "crooked Hillary", and his Republican primary opponent, Ted Cruz, "lyin' Ted". Mainstream media bought into Trump's antics; sources estimate that Trump earned the equivalent of nearly $5 billion in media attention (termed 'unpaid media') in the lead-up to the election, allowing him to forego the massive advertising buys candidates traditionally had to make (Stewart 2016). The petty nicknames and rowdy jabs, which painted others as liars and himself as an unfiltered truth-teller, became embedded in the popular vernacular, in part because the public was already awash in a sea of contradictory reports.

Trump's own antics took off and were injected into a 2016 US presidential election campaign that was already taking place within a misinformation ecosystem. Fake and conspiracy-driven accounts published more than 6.6 million tweets, trolls and bots posted inflammatory content in order to stoke division, and Russia's Internet Research Agency coordinated the targeted spread of misinformation across social media (Knight Foundation 2018). Meanwhile, the political consulting firm Cambridge Analytica mined personal data from millions of Facebook users without their knowledge, coordinating with Trump advisor Steve Bannon, who used this data to target divisive ads to 2.1 million voters in 11 swing states (Hern 2018). All the while, at rallies and on his Twitter account, Trump told his followers of a vast "deep state" conspiracy to conceal incriminating information about Hillary Clinton's use of a private email server during her time as secretary of state, amongst numerous other conspiracy theories and innuendos. For all of these reasons, Trump was dubbed "the post-truth president" before he even took office (Tsipursky 2017) and, in 2016, Oxford Dictionaries chose "post-truth" as word of the year (Wang 2016).

It is important to note that this was not only a US phenomenon. During this period, similar changes were unfolding throughout political information economies globally, contributing to the Brexit movement, which pushed to have the United Kingdom leave the European Union, the 2018 election of Jair Bolsonaro in Brazil, and a marked increase for support of populist, nationalist candidates across Europe (Taylor 2019) and globally (Moffitt 2016). These movements, too, are reflective of and fueled by tabloid culture. A number of these populist candidates were established celebrities before running for office: Ukrainian President Volodymyr Zelenskiy was an actor and stand-up comic, Haitian President Michel Martelly was a singer, Slovenian Prime Minister Sarec was a comedian and satirist, and Pakistan's Prime Minister Imran Khan was a well-known cricket player (Etehad 2018). Those figures who achieved celebrity through their political visibility, such as UK Prime Minister Boris Johnson and US Senator (and two-time Democratic presidential candidate) Bernie Sanders, also benefitted from the cultural capital of celebrity, which allowed them "to articulate, and performatively enact, different versions of 'the people' to achieve cultural identification and electoral endorsement" (Nolan and Brookes 2013, 373).

Celebrity culture broadly, and tabloids in particular, have cultivated a sense that celebrities are authentic, and these narrative frames are activated when citizens consider the likeability and trustworthiness of celebrity populists. In this milieu, politicians can claim, like J-Lo (Jennifer Lopez) and Reese Witherspoon on the pages of *Us Weekly*, to be *ordinary* and *knowable*. Donald Trump, with his history as a tabloid fixture and his seemingly natural transition from reality television to mainstream politics, encouraged just this kind of seamless interpretation. Trump's claim to everyman-ness, in spite of his inherited wealth and pre-existing fame, was only possible in a media landscape where the billionaire Kardashians were plausibly represented as 'just like us'.

Indeed, throughout the Trump Presidency, coverage of the Trump family on the pages of gossip magazines has not only continued, but proliferated. The first three years of his administration saw unprecedented coverage of the first family, arguably propelled by the fact that David Pecker, a long-time Trump ally who used his control over the *National Enquirer* to "catch and kill" stories about Trump's sexual affairs during his campaign, now controlled the genre (Farrow 2019). Pecker is CEO of American Media, Inc., which, between 2011 and 2018, acquired all top-earning American celebrity magazines, with the exception of the long-running *People*. *Us Weekly*, for instance, was purchased by AMI in early 2017 and quickly began running numerous, flattering stories about the Trumps, including five back-to-back cover features that dubbed Ivanka "daughter in chief", gushed over the family's "gorgeous [Washington,] D.C. home", and empathized with Melania's emotional transition to first lady (Goldstein 2017; Ryan 2017). Tabloid coverage continues to 'celebrify' and humanize Trump and his family, even whilst his administration enacts undemocratic policies such as restricting travel of visitors from majority-Muslim countries and detaining and separating families of asylum seekers at the US-Mexico border.

Conclusion

In the 2006 *Onion* interview where he discussed the term "truthiness," Stephen Colbert further elaborated on the way in which politicians make use of ambiguity in order to consolidate power: "Truthiness is 'What I say is right, and [nothing] anyone else says could possibly be true.' It's not only that I *feel* it to be true, but that *I* feel it to be true. There's not only an emotional quality, but there's a selfish quality" (Rabin 2006). Looking back, Colbert's words from nearly 15 years ago serve as an eerie foreshadowing of what would come, a triumph of the personal over the political, the gut feeling over the fact, and the emotional over the institutional.

By attending to the technological, political, and popular cultural developments over the past two decades, this chapter has traced the rise of celebrity gossip magazines and the ways they both speak to and foreshadow the post-truth political economy in the United States. The American public's current relationship with news and information has been influenced by a rapidly evolving technological landscape and global economy. It has also been shaped by tabloid culture, which encourages audiences to accept ambiguous truthfulness as a pleasurable, entertaining, and agency-offering proposition. The editorial strategies popularized by celebrity gossip magazines in the early years of the twenty-first century primed the public's sceptical engagement with information, positioning news as subjective and open to debate.

References

Adams, Russell. 2011. "Magazine Sales Fall as Celebrity Titles Fade." *The Wall Street Journal*, August 10.

Anderson, Janna, and Lee Rainie. 2017. "The Future of Truth and Misinformation Online." Pew Research Center, October 19.

Bird, Elizabeth. 1992. *For Enquiring Minds: A Cultural Study of Supermarket Tabloids.* Knoxville, TN: The University of Tennessee Press.

Cain Miller, Claire. 2008. "How Obama's Internet Campaign Changed Politics." *The New York Times*, November 7.

Carr, David. 2003. "Gossip Goes Glossy and Loses Its Stigma." *The New York Times*, August 4.

Cassidy, John. 2018. "Trump's History of Lying, From John Barron to @realdonaldtrump." *The New Yorker*, April 24.

Curry, Kevin. 2016. "More and More People Get Their News from Social Media: Is That Good or Bad?" *The Washington Post*, September 30.

Davis, Baird. 2005. "Weeklies Up, Others Down." *Circulation Management* 20 (8), 24–30.

Douglas, Susan J. 2010. *Enlightened Sexism: The Seductive Message that Feminism's Work is Done.* New York, NY: Times Books.

Douglas, Susan J., and Andrea McDonnell. 2019. *Celebrity: A History of Fame.* New York, NY: NYU Press.

Etehad, Melissa. 2018. "From Comedians to Pop Stars, Some World Leaders Take Office with Little or No Political Experience." *Los Angeles Times*, August 20.

Farrow, Ronan. 2019. *Catch and Kill: Lies, Spies, and a Conspiracy to Protect Predators.* New York, NY: Hachette.

Federal Election Commission. 2000. "2000 Official General Election Results." http://www.fec.gov/pubrec/2000presgeresults.htm.

Franklin, Bob. 1997. *Newszak and News Media.* London; New York, NY: Arnold.

Gamson, Joshua. 1994. *Claims to Fame: Celebrity in Contemporary America.* Berkeley, CA: University of California Press.

Gimmler, Antje. 2001. "Deliberative Democracy, the Public Sphere and the Internet." *Philosophy & Social Criticism* 27 (4), 21–39.

Goldstein, Jessica. 2017. "Trump is Just Like Us Weekly's Favorite Celebrity." ThinkProgress, February 22. https://archive.thinkprogress.org/trump-is-just-like-us-weeklys-favorite-celebrity-5fc80b5898da/.

Gregory, Neal, and Janice Gregory. 1992. *When Elvis Died.* New York, NY: Scripps.

Habermas, Jürgen. 1991. *The Structural Transformation of the Public Sphere.* 6th ed.Cambridge, MA: MIT Press.

Hern, Alex. 2018. "Cambridge Analytica: How Did It Turn Clicks Into Votes?" *The Guardian*, May 6.

Holmes, Su. 2006. "Fame Simulation." In Su Holmes, and Sean Redmond, *Framing Celebrity: New Directions in Celebrity Culture*. London: Routledge.

Klein, Adam. 2017. *Fanaticism, Racism, and Rage Online: Corrupting the Digital Sphere*. New York, NY: Palgrave Macmillan.

Knight Foundation. 2018. "Seven Ways Misinformation Spread during the 2016 Election." October 4.

Marshall, P. David. 1997. *Celebrity and Power: Fame and Contemporary Culture*. Minneapolis, MN: University of Minnesota Press.

McDonnell, Andrea. 2014. *Reading Celebrity Gossip Magazines*. London: Polity.

Meyers, Erin. 2020. *Extraordinarily Ordinary: Us Weekly and the Rise of Reality Television Celebrity*. New Brunswick, NJ: Rutgers University Press.

Moffitt, Benjamin. 2016. *The Global Rise of Populism: Performance, Political Style, and Representation*. Stanford, CA: Stanford University Press.

Mulcahey, Susan. 2016. "Confessions of a Trump Tabloid Scribe." *Politico*, May/June.

Newman, Robert. 2014. "Elvis is Alive!" http://www.robertnewman.com/elvis-is-alive/.

Nolan, David, and Stephanie Brookes. 2013. "Populism in Theory and Practice: Analysing Celebrity Politics." *Media Asia* 40 (4), 373–383.

Rabin, Nathan. 2006, "Interview: Stephen Colbert. AV Club, January 26. https://tv.avclub.com/stephen-colbert-1798208958.

Radden Keefe, Patrick. 2018. "How Mark Burnett Resurrected Donald Trump as an Icon of American Success." *The New Yorker*, December 27.

Rich, Frank. 2006. *The Greatest Story Ever Sold: The Decline and Fall of Truth in Bush's America*. New York, NY: Penguin.

Rose, Matthew. 2002. "Magazine Sales on Newsstands Fell Again in '01." *The Wall Street Journal*, April 30.

Ryan, Erin Gloria. 2017. "Is Us Weekly Turning into a Trump Family Mouthpiece?" *The Daily Beast*, June 8.

Sloan, Bill. 2001. *I Watched a Wild Hog Eat My Baby!: A Colorful History of Tabloids and their Impact*. Amherst, NY: Prometheus Books.

Stewart, Emily. 2016. "Donald Trump Rode $5 billion in Free Media to the White House." TheStreet, November 20.

Swift, Art. 2016. "Americans' Trust in Mass Media Sinks to a New Low." Gallup, September 14.

Taylor, Paul. 2019. "Has Europe Reached Peak Populism?" *Politico*, September 5.

Thompson, Derek. 2016. "The Print Apocalypse and How to Survive It." *The Atlantic*, November 3.

Tsipursky, Gleb. 2017. "A Weird American in Trump's Post-Truth America." *Psychology Today*, April 29.

U.S. Senate Select Committee on Intelligence. 2008. "Senate Intelligence Committee Unveils Final Phase II Reports on Prewar Iraq Intelligence." June 5.

Wang, Amy. 2016. "'Post-Truth' Named Word of the Year by Oxford Dictionaries." *The Washington Post*, November 16.

Wheeler, Mark. 2013. *Celebrity Politics*. London: Polity.

11 Dispatches from *la Crónica roja*

Why sensationalism and crime still matter in the new Latin America media ecology

Marcela F. Pizarro and Jairo Lugo-Ocando

Introduction

Sensationalism was a key feature of crime reporting in the Latin American press from the 1930s until the mid-1980s (Brunetti, 2011; Parga, 1997) as crime reporting adopted several aesthetic formats that included genres such as the *Nota Roja* (Red Note) in Mexico, various aspects of television style (Hallin, 2000; Piccato, 2014), and news reporting of *sucesos* (events), as well as characteristics from the so-called *Crónica roja* (Red Chronicle) genre in newspapers. The coverage of crime in Latin America by mainstream newspapers can be compared in many ways to what is often referred as tabloid-style news (Kurtz, 1993).

To the extent that stories are often dramatized and provocative elements are deliberately highlighted to create shock and controversy, it is similar. As a genre, it also appeals to the poor and popular audiences by portraying itself to be 'the voice of the people' (Ramírez Tobón, 2001). Employing a gruesome display of morbid images alongside the use of local jargon, particularly in headlines, the genre narrates a series of events in chronological order. When doing so, journalists provide facts while expressing values and judgments on these events, often framing facts in terms of moral panics, personal drama, and, in cases, through hate speech against individual and social groups. These accounts are often serialized over a period of days and sometimes weeks. The stories follow one after the other at times with little or no context from previous days in ways that resemble television soap operas: "This incentivises readers to speak among each other in order to catch-up and discuss the stories in their daily conversations".[1]

Those working in the genre claim to be objective and factually based, even though facts are presented attached to hypothesis and opinion (Gargurevich, 1982; Gomis, 2008). While broadly based on a type of 'yellow journalism' that reports crime in explicit and gruesome details, the genre differs in having a grasp of storytelling that both reflects and appeals to its target communities. With the *Crónica roja*, the genre is defined by comprehensive yet accessible narratives, incorporating facts and drama using popular language and popular storytelling, including slang.

Featuring stories in the *Crónica roja* news genre became a key selling point for many newspapers and magazines, attracting millions of readers around the region (Ramírez Tobón, 2001; Saad, 2011). Such successes are not only due to language and style, but also the result of the low price of each copy, which in most cases is less than half the price of the 'serious' daily newspapers. Additionally, these tabloids expand their revenue through sales of dubious advertisements, including call-girl services, dodgy fortunes from tarot readers, and even offers of witchcraft to be directed towards lovers or against enemies. It was so successful that even papers of record incorporated this kind of content. All in all, newspapers that feature this genre of news story are among the highest-selling newspapers in the region. *Trome* in Peru, as an example, has been selling around 650,000 copies daily over the years (Mineo, 2014; Espinoza Olcay, 2019; Villagran, 2013), though many of the more serious outlets that carried this type of journalism have diminished (Corona-Berkin, 1997; Parga, 1997). This corresponds to a global trend in which the market for crime stories has declined dramatically and diminished as a tool with which to attract readers.

Even diminished, the genre continues to survive and even thrive in some markets, as with *Trome* in Peru or *El Gráfico* in El Salvador. Moreover, in light of the renewed war on drugs that has left thousands displaced and an equal number killed or disappeared, several titles featuring the genre have flourished in Mexico, with its own tradition called '*Nota Roja*'. One of these recently celebrated its centenary, and the tradition more broadly continues to grow in its own niche (Table 11.1).

The scholarly research around the *Crónica roja* genre can be broadly divided into two different approaches. One tendency frames the tabloid press as a mouthpiece of right-wing political interests, using sensationalism to divert poorer parts of society that make up the readership from more politically urgent issues by using a series of scaremongering tropes in an attempt to manipulate audiences (Lugo-Ocando, 2007, 2011; Williams and Dickinson, 1993). Another, influenced by reformulated structuralist readings and broadly located in the fields of linguistics and cultural studies, vindicates the genre as a space where popular urban culture is represented, with its own aesthetics, one which, in certain cases, can be subversive and critical (Conboy, 2006; Grabe, 1996).

In this chapter, we explore the survival of the *Crónica roja* genre across the continent and its adaptation to the new audiences and media platforms by arguing that, in the case of Latin America, approaches to understanding tabloids from the perspective of cultural studies offer a far more suitable explanatory

Table 11.1 Circulation of *Crónica roja* titles (adapted from Álvarez, 2016)

Newspaper	*Circulation*
La Prensa, Nicaragua	244,299
El Metro, Mexico	146,531
El Gráfico (Monday to Saturday), Argentina	138,291
Extra, Ecuador	120,031

theoretical framework to understanding this genre. In doing so, we argue that the genre is actually functional in representing segments of popular culture that are otherwise excluded, even when this is done at the expense of specific normative expectations of what journalism ought to be.

Society and *Crónica roja*

From an audience perspective, the *Crónica roja* genre was born out of contemplative cultural traditions around violence that remain very present today. These traditions date back to pre-Columbian societies (200 years pre-1492). However, the way this tradition plays out in the current media context owes more to the rigid system of censorship imposed by successive colonial and postcolonial governments in the region. Indeed, as many anthropologists and historians have recorded, pre-Columbian societies in Latin America paid particular attention to violence. Certainly, sacrifice as a voyeuristic spectacle and related forms of ritual violence were deeply rooted in cultural practices in these societies, linked to their own cosmology and interconnected to the exercise of power (Harris, 1991). In these communities, there was, and continues to be, an intimate relationship between political power and ritual violence (Spencer, 2012; Swenson, 2003). These rituals were performed in public and were effected in such a way that these events communicated power while fostering social cohesion. Contrary to common assumptions, this happened within a very complex and sophisticated pre-Columbian media ecology that incorporated theatre, news media, and other forms of communication to mass audiences (Beltrán et al., 2008; Forment, 2013).

The other important historical factor in this analysis is the role of authoritarian political power in imposing censorship over the press in Latin America. Although the region has had a dynamic and engaged civil society, even when under Spanish colonial rule (Forment, 2013), it is also true that its political life throughout most of its modern history has been defined and shaped by military rulers (Dix, 1994; Philip, 1980). Many of these societies have lived under frail democracies in the best scenarios, and these gave way to prolonged periods of dictatorship which tended to exercise an iron fist of censorship and control over the news media in each country (Lugo-Ocando, 2008; Matos, 2008). For most of the continent's republican history, access to the public sphere was restricted and freedom of expression has been an elusive, rather chimeric aspiration; a flashing light from a remote lighthouse that, more often than not, has been obscured by military juntas or opportunistic populists (Irwin and Micett, 2008; Mörner, 1960).

In this context, reporting crime became one of the very few ways in which news media could use their platforms to sell and connect with their audiences beyond politics. Authoritarian regimes mostly had a lax attitude towards this type of news reporting, as the resultant moral panics that came from newspapers' hyper-attention to crime and violence reinforced authoritarians' general cries for 'law and order'. Consequently, one could argue the *Crónica roja* genre was both a priority for the political economy of the news media and a way of communicating political power. Indeed, despite the apparent depoliticized nature of crime reporting as a news beat, it remains strongly linked to politically conservative agendas that use fear of crime to mobilize publics in their favour (Lugo-Ocando, 2007, 2011). These procedures are ascribed to larger discursive regimes in the press that legitimize the exercise of coercive power (Corona-Berkin, 1997) by using crime to promote fear and uncertainty.

The type of fear these stories elicit is further linked to the broader narrative which enables social control. In *Policing the Crisis; The State and Law and Order* (1978), Stuart Hall and colleagues (2013 [1978]) outlined these strategies, as a rising moral panic surrounding the relatively new (at the time) crime of mugging in the UK. Mapping news content of muggings, they argued that the state was able to justify hard crackdowns on perceived deviant groups and, in doing so, give the public a sense of emotional stability and deflect from its own political responsibilities. In Latin America, the *Crónica roja* developed its own particular procedures to articulate 'truth' when carrying out news reporting. In a continent riddled with poverty and inequality, with a long-standing tradition of populism, right-wing elites have appealed indirectly to the masses with the knowledge that presenting their real political agendas, based on neoliberal policies, would not guarantee electoral victory (Lugo-Ocando, 2020). Accordingly, the *Crónica roja* served as an important mechanism to control the agenda-setting process, bypassing debates on social issues in the public sphere and focusing instead on crime; a function it still fulfils today.

Selling sensationalism in the twenty-first century

The genre continues to maintain sales and reach large audiences in many places in the region. In Colombia, Guatemala, Mexico, Peru, and Paraguay, it continues to exercise an almost magical spell upon audiences, attracting them to news in the vein of the Pied Piper of Hamelin:

> You will find this genre in places that continue to be riddled with violence. Wherever you see violence on a certain scale, these titles will be present. In other places they have disappeared or are no longer as present because the violence is simply not there anymore, not at least on the scale that it used to be.[2]

Trome in Peru is an interesting example. The tabloid was launched in the late 1990s and continues to be the most widely sold paper in the Spanish speaking world. Raul Castro, a former journalist with the *El Comercio* conglomerate and one of the founders of *Trome*, recalls why the paper's business model worked at the time, and continues to do so now: "In strictly numerical terms, the impact of this paper was important because it entered into that area where it had no competition at the time. It had education, it had health, nutrition, women bought it".[3]

Castro attributes the newspaper's popularity not only to its news content, but also to the services it offers; services and products other media do not offer:

> We had a difficult situation in which there were ads in the middle of the paper – which were escort ads, so a lot of women complained and so we put them in the sports part of the ads, so we segmented the readership. It was complicated, there were pushes and pulls, but we had a great marketing department that was aligned with us. We ended up producing a good outlet.[4]

In Argentina, on the other hand, no outlet gets 'yellower' than *Crónica*. This publication began in the 1960s as a print outlet focused on gory sensationalism and morbid stories of bizarre killings. As Fernando Vázquez, crime reporter at *Crónica*, points out, "It's been said that *Crónica* doesn't have readers – it has fans. *Crónica* has developed a close relationship with the reader. The *Crónica* reader is from a working-class background so it's normal that they identify themselves with the paper".[5]

This last point is crucial in understanding the genre. It appeals to the working class in ways which reflect the entire community. By this we mean that in terms of topics, news agenda, language, and price, the newspaper manages to be sufficiently accessible. In Latin America, this is referred to as 'the popular', a concept not so much associated with 'popular culture' as it would be in the US and UK, but to the notion of 'subalternity' and providing a certain notion of belonging with the dispossessed and voiceless (Williams, 2002). Through this, we can associate this genre with enabling many communities to feel present in society via these media outlets. This is not only an issue of a market-driven editorial policy, but also a recognition of a reality that is often ignored or rendered invisible by the rest of the media:

> Obviously, you have to adapt yourself to the client [...] If you take a look Argentina's print history, you will see that the frontpage photos of dead people wasn't just something Crónica did, Clarín does it too – and they are really not the same kind of newspapers.[6]

Certainly, this final comment underscores an important aspect of the genre: despite similarities with tabloid cultures in the Global North and convergent agendas at times with their most serious mainstream newspapers, the *Crónica roja* press is distinctive. In reflecting 'subaltern voices' (Spivak, 2010 [1988]) and the realities of these communities in ways others do not, they are able to talk about what happens to the oppressed on a daily basis: "Many outlets have used the template because this is a business and you need to sell and so they all publish dead people on their front pages. The dead exist, violence exists, we don't hide it".[7]

Indeed, one of the key elements in the perennial success of this genre is how it engages the audience in ways that reflect reality as they experience it. When a newspaper publishes the pictures of a dead, pregnant young women, shot dead by her partner, it is at once performing a gruesome commercial exploitation by means of pornographic violence while, at the same time, bearing witness to the existence of the very person who was killed so she does not just become a statistic among a large pile of bodies lying at the local morgue. This is the *Crónica roja*'s appeal as part of the public imaginary of its own community, as Fernando Vazquez points out:

> There was a lot of violence, a lot of weird stories, and this made the audience feel close to the outlet. Crónica won loads of Martin Fierro awards[8] that showed how successful it was. And that was done with the support of the people, hence strengthening the relationship between the paper and the public.[9]

For these reasons, practitioners and scholars alike have argued for a more celebratory reading of the *Crónica roja*, one that acknowledges the deep flaws and problematic, commercially-exploitative nature in this type of reporting, while also highlighting its particular value, recognising the existence and daily life of an important segment of society. This new reading of the *Crónica roja* must also underline its success in reconciling factual reporting with compelling storytelling, as Raul Castro explains:

> Our genre is fundamentally journalistic and by no means is fake news. Fake news is the result of production mechanisms made by professional trolls. For example, Cambridge Analytics released information through influencers, bloggers, YouTubers that were not journalists. This is a part of the deprofessionalization of the production of news. The biggest traffic, the congestion is concentrated around viral phenomena which are made in factories that are made strategically set for political means. It's a strategy of disinformation that serves political agendas.[10]

Castro sees this as an example of their ability to uphold professional standards, while making clear the difference between 'proper' journalists and the new wave of bloggers and media influencers,

> These are not journalistic genres, they are informative strategies, which have other characteristics. This leaves a big challenge for journalism – but it also means we need to change the way we are packaging and reading things. Our genre is still valid because there is little point in producing serious content if no one is going to read us. It's a complex debate.[11]

In saying this, he is suggesting an even more important claim: this popular genre, for all its flaws, is still journalism and continues to be factual; it still complies with editorial standards around fact-checking; it still tells the truth, even though it does so in a sensational and grotesque manner. One example elucidates this point, a *Crónica roja* story from *Trome* in Peru:

> A young teen [...] climbed a high-voltage tower and threatened to jump into the void (...) [He] climbed to the top of the high-voltage tower without anyone being able to prevent him from doing so and for several hours he remained standing and silent.[12]

Elements that might seem speculative in this piece, such as the supposed 'fear' felt by the witnesses and the assertion that no one was able to prevent him from getting on top of the tower, were actually confirmed later by the police in their report. Examples from other news media outlets corroborate this. This shows that a story with a dramatic tone can nevertheless be accurate and fact based. A further example from *Crónica* (Argentina) in the following story:

> The father of Zoe Nerea Cortez, the 18-year-old girl who was shot dead in the head in the Buenos Aires town of Monte Grande while walking with a sister and friend, expressed his pain in social networks and asked for "forces" to his daughter to cope with the moment.[13]

Despite its emphasis on appealing storytelling, the *Crónica roja* genre succeeds by providing an interpretative but factual narrative of crime without falling into speculation. Even stories conveyed in sarcastic tones or employing scaremongering frames tend to be accurate. News stories about crimes rely on police reports and witnesses as even narratives that seem speculative are actually based on sources. One story illustrates this in the newspaper *El Gráfico* from El Salvador, which reported how a simple fight that started around a parking space ended up in a full shootout between the police and civilians:

> The fight ended in a shootout in the parking lot. Two federal police officers got involved in the struggle, which left one dead, four injured and six detained in Mexico City. The confrontation happened yesterday at 11 pm in the Bonanza sector of the Álvaro Obregón municipality.
>
> (Silva, 2020)

The tone of the story and its framing are sensationalist from start to finish but at all points the story is accurate and well-sourced. What we can draw from this single example is corroborated by scholarly work in this field, which despite comprehensive criticism towards the genre, nevertheless recognises that it is, broadly speaking, factual in its reporting (Barata, 2010; Brunetti, 2011; Corona-Berkin, 1997).

Despite the dramatic tone and the grotesque style, these stories are substantiated by facts. Journalists within the genre follow a specific deontology that requires both fact-checking and an accurate account of the events described in their stories. In all of the examples that we have examined, the case was the same; despite the dramatic tone and sensational narrative, these stories reflect the consensus of fact-based and accurate recounting of news.

Moving towards digital

As much as the *Crónica roja* genre continues, it is in overall retreat. Today, only specialized publications in crime and a few mainstream newspapers incorporating this genre continue to be widely read according to the Inter American Press Association (IAPA). Numbers for these titles continue to be robust and even, in some cases, growing.

However, sensationalism has increasingly moved to digital platforms and television formats. Newspapers' traditional readership, even when robust, is increasingly fragmented. In this sense, Fernando Vázquez warns that many of these media outlets are uncertain how to deal with these challenges, lacking the support and strategy needed to survive:

> There is a problem here … it's been hard for *Crónica* to adapt. Not in terms of operative issues … but in economic terms. There are people who won't put money into digital, they prefer to spend money on the print side, because you can touch it … and that tactile part tends to appeal more. It's trying to get up to speed with the present, but these are [just] the first steps.[14]

To be sure, even successful newspapers such as *Trome* are starting to see a decline in sales and revenue. Others are following suit, as they face the effects of audience fragmentation and digitalization and the abrupt fall in the ads market:

> People who go to *Crónica* want to read weird things, strange news items, crimes, but I think it is hard for those working in digital … there are no advertisers, the country is not in good shape, and if the papers has few ads … the web has less … the ads revenue is taken by Google. So, the transition we are going through at the moment … not just at *Crónica* but around the media landscape, is a big challenge for us all.[15]

Despite this lack of a coherent strategy to confront digital transformations in the media ecology, sales of many of the newspapers in the region that embrace the genre of *Crónica roja* still compete in a highly competitive media market. For some titles, they continue to be profitable as they depend less on advertisements and more on direct newsstand sales (Pichihua, 2014), and circulation figures, while declining, are robust in comparison to the US and Europe and national and local 'quality' competitors. Indeed, according to the IAPA, Latin American newspapers' circulation grew 6 per cent against a 23 per cent decline of their European counterparts in the same period (AFP, 2015). Coincidentally, *Crónica roja* papers' willingness to sell advertisements for escorts and witchcraft services meant that while large corporate advertisers left the mainstream media to head to Google and Facebook, less-reputable advertisers which found an outlet in the *Crónica roja* remained, to a point, and the genre remained healthy enough to continue with business as usual.

Redeeming the abject

Further explaining their continued fortune, over the years those newspapers that published *Crónica roja* stories have been able to ensure their success by creating social representations based on sensationalism, violence, and sexism (Parga, 1997; Vélez, Girlado, and Unás, 1998). In so doing, these media outlets foster a social imaginary characterized by a sense of immediacy, spectacle, chaos, 'machismo', fear, and overall uncertainty. Indeed, newspapers which subscribed to the *Crónica roja* model have thrived upon the simultaneous fear and pornography of violence.

However, the question remains: why, despite changes in media ecologies and audiences' habits, does the *Crónica roja* persist? The answer, according to Nelson Villagomez and Renata Patricia Ortiz Bahamonde (2002), can be found in the cultural and socio-economic context in which news on crime is disseminated among particular segments of the audiences; one which these authors refers to as 'news audience environment', a concept that links to the broader notion of 'news cultures':

> The red chronicle is not maleficent, what is frightening is the way in which media spectacle presents the events of reality. The red chronicle responds to people's daily lives, which are often ignored in schools of journalism, criticized on the altars of the academy and undervalued in the studies of communication.
>
> (Villagomez, et al., 2002: 21)

Furthermore, these newspapers create spaces for the community that are not often found in the mainstream public sphere:

> The red chronicle has become the social space that admits the existence of the vulnerable class, those recognized in this type of information, because it has been the only space that has given them a representation of their reality.
>
> (Villagomez et al., 2002: 17)

To understand its perennial appeal, therefore, we need to explore the communities that engage with this genre and that sustain a market for news stories that reflect, to many of them, the daily lives of people who coexist with violence in ways that foster an intimate relationship with it. Indeed, one of the key characteristics ascribed to the *Crónica roja* is its ability to foster communities by means of moral panics and the appealing storytelling around violence.

Instead of seeing this as a crude way of mobilizing the public using fear, as is the case of the narratives on immigration in Europe (Lugo-Ocando, 2007, 2011; Philo, Briant, and Donald, 2013), we need to consider it, at least in the case of Latin America, as a genre that brings together and reflects important areas of popular culture often excluded from the mainstream. It reveals a type of popular aesthetic that is often looked down upon but, nevertheless, is part of the broadest spectrum of those societies. In this regard, as violent crime continues to be such a widespread phenomenon in these communities, reporting it in elaborated ways by using data and statistics and providing policy related context, as has become the norm in most of the West (Lugo-Ocando, 2017), is not only unappealing but also excludes the nature of the readers' expectations. A reader recognizes that he/she exists as an individual. With high levels of crime in these countries, data are meaningless to these communities. Sensationalism, on the other hand, makes a crime story newsworthy because it at least acknowledges the existence of the individual as a person, in the sea of tragedies, mass graves, and assassinations.

As described by one of our interviewees, it is "a way of giving people something to talk about". José Enrique Contreras Sánchez, who worked as a reporter for *Mi Diario* daily in the city of Maracaibo in Venezuela (that ran as a daily for almost a decade between 2003 and 2011), adds:

> Some people used to look down on us and say that the type of journalism we did was not worth doing. They were very critical of the language we used both in our headlines and reports as well as the type of pictures we showed. But you know what? People read us at a time that they were not reading the traditional papers anymore.[16]

Contreras Sánchez takes pride not only in the outreach but also in the type of journalism that it was producing:

> Our newspaper sold five times more than the main newspaper, which was our parent company. And in 2008, we won the National Journalism Award for our coverage of floods in poor areas of the city, something that was ignored by the rest of the press.[17]

Indeed, this view evokes the debates around high culture and low culture to which Umberto Eco referred in his seminal work *Apocalyptic and Integrated* (Eco, 2011 [1964]). Society places certain values on different tastes and different types of consumption, and the hierarchical nature of those values is ultimately defined by power and ideology. Something is considered good or bad, inappropriate or not, because of the status it has in relation to 'class'; what is grotesque to some might be perfectly acceptable to others. Hence, beyond aesthetics and style, the accuracy of the content and its function in society remain crucial.

In this sense, the 'distaste' for particular cultural artefacts expressed by so many is not limited to the *Crónica roja*. Other cultural expressions such as much maligned, but widely consumed, *Reggaeton* music bear the brunt of classist disdain, which sees it as lower culture and almost pornographic given its explicit and sexualised lyrics (Cepeda, 2009; Torres, 2012). Both *Reggaeton* and the *Crónica roja* share morbid sensationalism around sex and violence and use common slang and obscene language, despised by some, but embraced by many for their expression and recognition of their language, culture, and ultimately, existence in society.

The use of a particular language, style, and news aesthetic in the *Crónica roja* is crucial in understanding why and how particular individuals and communities relate to this genre and why some professionals distance themselves from it. For journalists working in other outlets, scholars, and some experts, journalism is about delivering public service, and the grotesque presentation of news in order to satisfy the commercially-driven market has, for them, no place in that function. This obviates the fact that audiences and media communities that display loyalty and structure reading habits towards these news outlets are created around news that brings a sort of 'grotesque transparency' (Kitch and Hume, 2008; Nahon-Serfaty, 2017) to issues and events in society that other news genres do not, through common language and a more popular appeal.

For this genre, 'violence' is a cultural object that seems naturally embedded in the collective imaginary. This is because it is structured in the public imagination as both heritage of a colonial past in which the nation as such was forged under the brutal violence of conquest and slavery, and the daily life which has continued to suffer under the violence of dictatorships and widespread crime. As vindication of this claim let us not forget that six of the eight most violent cities in the world are in Latin America (Núñez et al., 1998). The very fact that a crime victim's identity and image are published is, for many readers, a recognition of their existence in a society in which their anonymity is self-evident, especially to those who die violently. The more dramatic the story, the more gruesome and grotesque the retelling, the more that memory will endure in the public imagination.

We can link this discussion to the aesthetic of celebrations of the Mexican holiday "The Day of the Dead". On this day, Mexicans remember friends and family members who have died, and celebrate death in order to support their spiritual journey. It is a celebration performed through an aesthetic ritual, with symbolism that is often misinterpreted in the West (Naggar and Ritchin, 1996). Despite the use of skeletons and other gruesome figures, at no point is this celebration intended to be scary. Rather, it acknowledges the simple fact that people die and that their bodies take that form in death. Contrary to idealised aesthetics in the West of spirits taking the form of the dead as they were in life, "The Day of the Dead" acknowledges and celebrates the dead as they are: grotesque (Brandes, 1998; Gonzalez, 2002).

In the same way, one can argue *Crónica roja* stories adopt violence as a cultural object that allows readers to uncover reality, bringing about transparency. Gruesome images are accompanied by a popular but explicit vernacular that is accessible to a particular target readership and inclusive of their own communities and language. Such tabloid language has the ability to create communities (Conboy, 2004, 2006, 2007) and serves as a mirror, even if it is distorted, of the people that no one else seems to talk about in the mainstream press. It is a genre that provides recognition to those living in poverty, the subaltern voices, even if it at times just makes them part of a market-driven dynamic to sell more copies. In doing so, the *Crónica roja* genre highlights their drama and the way common people in these countries coexist with violence as part of their daily life.

We can read into the *Crónica roja* a kind of rebellious aesthetic which, rather than bypassing the 'higher' form of journalistic discourse enshrined in the rhetoric of neutral objectivity and practical reason, adopts it under its own formats. This is achieved by underlining and exaggerating features of news events without subverting the notions around the social contract between journalists and society, one that states that journalists will have access to sources and protection as long as they perform the role of watchdogs. Indeed, reporters working for these newspapers need not sneak into crime scenes or neighbourhoods through the backdoor, as they are seen by many, if not most, as full members of the community; bringing celebrity status to all: police, criminals, and victims themselves alike and, in so doing, acknowledging their existence.

Conclusion

In times when mainstream traditional media face difficult challenges and economic decline, those segments of the media that engage the public by means of sensationalism continue to reach larger audiences than their counterparts. In this context, the *Crónica roja* genre continues to have great appeal in Latin America. Thanks to content about death, sex, and violence, it responds to the predetermined cultural frameworks and aesthetic expectations of its target audiences and communities. However, as discussed here, the reasoning for its seemingly perennial appeal goes beyond a pornographic, morbid appetite for violence and sex.

We can argue that there is something uniquely popular in this genre, as it links community and newspapers in ways that other genres do not; primarily, as in this specific context the 'popular' needs to be broadly understood as the inclusion of subaltern voices in the public sphere. If this tabloid style does indeed draw from the spectrum of populist demagogy, which remains politically appealing, it nevertheless does so while upholding accuracy and fact-checking. Journalists do depart from the ethics of neutrality, but not from the wider framework of professional standards. In so doing, the genre encourages reporters to "present themselves as themselves", as spokesmen for the entire society and standing in opposition to its enemies (Hallin, 2000: 41), whoever they are at a particular moment and therefore as part of an imagined community.

As a genre, it also challenges journalists by demanding they leave behind aesthetics expected of them by normative prescriptions, particularly from outside the region. Rather, journalists engaging within this genre use the appeal to the grotesque as a way of bringing about transparency, underlining the grief of everyday tragedies and crimes being reported to serve their publics (Kitch and Hume, 2008). They also do so professionally, and by this we mean that they uphold normative expectations in every other way. This is a crucial claim to make, and one that not all bloggers or social media influencers who might also want to be considered journalists can substantiate, as we saw in the interview with Castro.

News stories adopting *Crónica roja* aesthetics often speak about issues, people, and places that are invisible or anonymous in the rest of the news media, particularly in high-brow news media outlets that do not register the daily life of those in poverty nor the lives and deaths of those socially and politically excluded. To stigmatize the 'Red Chronicle' is to miss the point. In these places, journalists need to acknowledge the experience of common people in their daily storytelling, even when this seems to counterbalance generalized western assumptions and ideas of what news ought to be and how should it be presented (Vélez, Girlado, and Unás, 1998).

In this sense, scholarly research around this genre needs to broaden its scope at a time when the traditional Habermasian concept of what constitutes the 'public sphere' are becoming less tenable in other parts of the world. What creates publics, configures audiences, and ultimately articulates politics in Latin America is very different from what creates audiences and communities in Europe and the US. Hence, scholars might be better advised to treat this and other genres in the Global South as part of the political function of journalism, but one that varies among news cultures around the world.

Notes

1 Interview with journalist César Batiz on April 1st, 2020.
2 Interview with journalist César Batiz on April 1, 2020.
3 Interview with journalist Raul Castro on February 27, 2020.
4 Interview with journalist Raul Castro on February 27, 2020.
5 Interview with journalist Fernando Vázquez on February 28, 2020.
6 ibid.
7 Interview with journalist Fernando Vázquez on February 28, 2020.
8 The Martín Fierro Awards is the name of the most prominent awards for Argentine radio and television, granted by APTRA, the Association of Argentine Television and Radio Journalists.
9 Interview with journalist Fernando Vázquez on February 28, 2020.
10 Interview with journalist Raul Castro on February 27, 2020.
11 Interview with journalist Raul Castro on February 27, 2020.
12 See *Tromé* (2020). "Menor de edad subió a torre de alta tensión y amenazó con lanzarse al vacío en Los Olivos." https://trome.pe/actualidad/los-olivos-menor-torre-de-alta-tension-amenaza-rescate-policia-bomberos-noticia/?ref=tr [Accessed on March 11, 2020].
13 See *Crónica* (2020). "El padre de la chica asesinada en Monte Grande expresó su dolor en las redes." https://www.cronica.com.ar/policiales/El-padre-de-la-chica-asesinada-en-Monte-Grande-expreso-su-dolor-en-las-redes-20200310-0061.html [Accessed on March 11, 2020].
14 Interview with journalist Fernando Vázquez on February 28, 2020.
15 Interview with journalist Fernando Vázquez on February 28, 2020.
16 Interview with journalist José Enrique Contreras Sánchez on February 17, 2020.
17 ibid.

References

AFP. "Diarios Latinoamericanos Aumentan Circulación Pese Al Desafío Digtal." *ABC Color*, 2015.

Álvarez, Raúl "La Nota Roja Mexicana: Más De Cien Años Del Periodismo Más Escabroso Que Puedas Imaginar." Xataka, México: Revista Magnet, 2016. https://magnet.xataka.com/en-diez-minutos/la-nota-roja-mexicana-mas-de-cien-anos-del-periodismo-mas-escabroso-que-puedas-imaginar.

Awad, Isabel. "Communication and Inequality: The Media's Central Role in the Struggle for Recognitioncuadernos." *Cuadernos* 36 (2015): 10–11.

Barata, Francesc. "Retos Pendientes En El Periodismo De Nota Roja." *Chasqui: Revista Latinoamericana de Comunicación* 110 (2010): 54–61.

Beltran, L. Ramiro, Karina Herrera, Erick Pinto, and Esperanza Torrico. *La communicación antes de Colón: tipos y formas en Mesoamérica y los Andes*. La Paz: CIBEC, 2008.

Brandes, Stanley. "Iconography in Mexico's Day of the Dead: Origins and Meaning." *Ethnohistory*, 45 (2) (1998): 181–218.

Brunetti, Paulina. "Crónica Roja Y Sensacionalismo: Maneras De Hacer, Maneras De Ver." *Revista Oficios Terrestres* 26 (2011): 1–17.

Cepeda, Maria Elena. "Media and the Musical Imagination: Comparative Discourses of Belonging in 'Nuestro Himno' and 'Reggaeton Latino'." *Identities: Global Studies in Culture and Power* 16, no. 5 (2009): 548–572.

Conboy, Martin. *Journalism: A Critical History*. London: Sage, 2004.

Conboy, Martin. *Tabloid Britain: Constructing a Community through Language*. Abingdon, Oxfordshire: Taylor & Francis, 2006.

Conboy, Martin *The Language of the News*. Abingdon, Oxon: Routledge, 2007.

Corona-Berkin, Sarah. "México: Una Construcción De Verdad En La Crónica Policial." *Chasqui. Revista Latinoamericana de Comunicación* 60 (1997): 29–32.

Crónica. "El padre de la chica asesinada en Monte Grande expresó su dolor en las redes." (2020). https://www.cronica.com.ar/policiales/El-padre-de-la-chica-asesinada-en-Monte-Grande-expreso-su-dolor-en-las-redes-20200310-0061.html [Accessed on March 11, 2020].

Dix, Robert H. "Military Coups and Military Rule in Latin America." *Armed Forces & Society* 20, no. 3 (1994): 439–456.

Eco, Umberto. *Apocalípticos E Integrados*. Sevilla: Debolsillo, 2011 [1964].

Espinoza Olcay, Carlos. "Trome, el diario más leído del Perú cumple 18 años." *Publimetro* (2019). https://publimetro.pe/actualidad/nacional/trome-diario-mas-leido-peru-cumple-18-anos-114459-noticia/.

Forment, Carlos A. *Democracy in Latin America, 1760–1900: Volume 1, Civic Selfhood and Public Life in Mexico and Peru*. Vol. 1, Chicago, Illinois: University of Chicago Press, 2013.

Gargurevich, Juan. *Géneros Periodísticos*. Quito: Ciespal, 1982.

Gomis, Lorenzo. *Teoría De Los Géneros Periodísticos*. Barcelona: Editorial UOC, 2008.

Gonzalez, Rafael. *Día De Los Muertos*. San Jose, California: Dragonfly Press, 2002.

Grabe, Maria Elizabeth. "Tabloid and Traditional Television News Magazine Crime Stories: Crime Lessons and Reaffirmation of Social Class Distinctions." *Journalism & Mass Communication Quarterly* 73, no. 4 (1996): 926–946.

Hall, Stuart, Chas Critcher, Tony Jefferson, John Clarke, and Brian Roberts. *Policing the Crisis: Mugging, the State and Law and Order*. London: Macmillan International Higher Education, 2013 [1978].

Hallin, Daniel. "La Nota Roja: Periodismo Popular Y Transición a La Democracia En México." *América Latina, I loy* 25, no. 1 (2000): 35–43.

Harris, Marvin. *Cannibals and Kings: The Origins of Cultures*. New York: Vintage, 1991.

Kitch, Carolyn L., and Janice Hume. *Journalism in a Culture of Grief*. Abingdon, Oxfordshire: Routledge, 2008.

Kurtz, Howard. "The Tabloid Style." *American Journalism Review* 15, no. 7 (1993): 26–28.

Lugo-Ocando, Jairo. "The 'Changing' face of Media Discourses on Poverty in the Age of Populism and Anti-Globalisation: The Political Appeal of Anti-Modernity and Certainty in Brazil." *International Communication Gazette* 82, no. 1 (2020): 101–116.

Lugo-Ocando, Jairo. *Crime Statistics in the News: Journalism, Numbers and Social Deviation.* London: Palgrave, 2017.

Lugo-Ocando, Jairo "Media Campaigns and Asylum Seekers in Scotland." In *Anti-Racism and Multiculturalism: Studies in International Communication*, edited by Mark D. Alleyne. Abingdon, Oxfordshire: Routledge (2011): 95–128.

Lugo-Ocando, Jairo. *The Media in Latin America.* Maidenhead, Berkshire: Open University/McGraw-Hill Education, 2008.

Lugo-Ocando, Jairo. "A Tale of Donkeys, Swans and Racism: London Tabloids, Scottish Independence and Refugees." *Communication and Social Change* 1, no. 1 (2007): 22–37.

Matos, Carolina. *Journalism and Political Democracy in Brazil.* London: Lexington Books, 2008.

Mineo, Liza. "El Diario Más Vendido en el Mundo de Habla Hispana se Hace en Perú." *ReVista: Harvard Review of Latin America*, 2014. https://web.archive.org/web/20200927045052/https://revista.drclas.harvard.edu/book/el-diario-m%C3%A1s-vendido-en-el-mundo-de-habla-hispana-se-hace-en-per%C3%BA.

Naggar, Carole, and Fred Ritchin. *México through foreign eyes, 1850-1990: visto por ojos extranjeros.* New York: W.W. Norton, 1996.

Nahon-Serfaty, Isaac. "Towards a Theory of Grotesque Transparency: The Case of Hugo Chávez." *International Journal of Cultural Studies* 20, no. 6 (2017): 653–668.

Núñez, Pilar, María E. Noboa, Marta Vasallo, and Carmen Torres. *Prensa y Derechos Humanos. La Vida en amarillo.* Santiago de Chile: ISIS Internacional, 1998.

Parga, José Sánchez. "De La Crónica Roja Al Morbo Mediático." *Chasqui. Revista Latinoamericana de Comunicación* no. 60 (1997): 4–7.

Philip, George. "The Military Institution Revisited: Some Notes on Corporatism and Military Rule in Latin America." *Journal of Latin American Studies* 12, no. 2 (1980): 421–436.

Piccato, Pablo. "Murders of Nota Roja: Truth and Justice in Mexican Crime News." *Past & Present* 223, no. 1 (2014): 195–231.

Pichihua, Sofia "Diarios En América Latina Aún Mantienen Su Circulación." *Clases de Periodismo* (2014). https://www.clasesdeperiodismo.com/2014/06/10/diarios-en-america-latina-aun-mantienen-su-circulacion/.

Ramírez Tobón, William. "La Crónica Roja En Bogotá." *Historia Crítica* no. 21 (2001): 111–126.

Saad, Anuar Saad. "El Sensacionalismo O La" Insurrección" De Las Masas." *Razón y palabra* 16, no. 78 (2011).

Silva, Yara. "Riña Por Lugar De Estacionamiento Desata Sangrienta Balacera Entre Policías Y Civiles." El Gráfico (2020). https://www.elgrafico.mx/la-roja/rina-por-lugar-de-estacionamiento-desata-sangrienta-balacera-entre-policias-y-civiles-cdmx.

Spencer, Susan. "Detecting Violence in the Archaeological Record: Clarifying the Timing of Trauma and Manner of Death in Cases of Cranial Blunt Force Trauma among Pre-Columbian Amerindians of West-Central Illinois." *International Journal of Paleopathology* 2, no. 2-3 (2012): 112–122.

Spivak, Gayatri Chakravorty. "Can the Subaltern Speak?". In *Can the Subaltern Speak? Reflections on the History of an Idea*, edited by Rosalind Morris, 21–80. New York: Columbia University Press, 2010 [1988].

Swenson, Edward R. "Cities of Violence: Sacrifice, Power and Urbanization in the Andes." *Journal of Social Archaeology* 3, no. 2 (2003): 256–296.

Torres, Nora Gámez. "Hearing the Change: Reggaeton and Emergent Values in Contemporary Cuba." *Latin American Music Review* 33, no. 2 (2012): 227–260.

Tromé. "Menor de edad subió a torre de alta tensión y amenazó con lanzarse al vacío en Los Olivos." (2020), https://trome.pe/actualidad/los-olivos-menor-torre-de-alta-tension-amenaza-rescate-policia-bomberos-noticia/?ref=tr [Accessed on March 11, 2020].

Vélez, Luis Fernando, Julio C. Girlado, and Viviam Unás. "Crónica roja: hacia un periodismo del abrazo." *Chasqui: Revista Latinoamericana de Comunicación* 62 (1998): 58–61.

Villagomez, Nelson and Renata Patricia Ortiz Bahamonde. La Crónica Roja: Su Atractivo.. Quito, Ecuador: Universidad Internacional SEK 2002. Available at https://repositorio.uisek.edu.ec/handle/123456789/2483, accessed December 3, 2020.

Villagran, Lauren "The Best-Selling Newspaper in the Spanish-Speaking World." ZDNet/CBS Interactive (2013). https://www.zdnet.com/article/the-best-selling-newspaper-in-the-spanish-speaking-world/.

Williams, Gareth. *The Other Side of the Popular: Neoliberalism and Subalternity in Latin America.* Durham, North Carolina: Duke University Press, 2002.

Williams, Paul, and Julie Dickinson. "Fear of Crime: Read All About It? The Relationship between Newspaper Crime Reporting and Fear of Crime." *The British Journal of Criminology* 33, no. 1 (1993): 33–56.

12 The rise and fall of tabloid journalism in post-Mao China

Ideology, the market, and the new media revolution

Chengju Huang

Introduction

This chapter investigates the bumpy journey that tabloid journalism in post-Mao China has experienced. From being totally banned in the Mao era from 1950s to 1970s and heatedly debated in the 1980s, tabloid journalism in China flourished and enjoyed its golden decade from the mid-1990s to the mid-2000s. It has however rapidly declined since then and has ceased to exist in any real sense. This chapter argues that an investigation of the rise and fall of tabloid journalism in the People's Republic of China (PRC) may shed some new light on a better understanding of not just China's tabloid press sector itself, but also the country's journalism in general and even some of the common issues regarding the changing ecology of print journalism in diverse social contexts.

In the West, tabloid papers are conventionally compared to broadsheet/quality newspapers and both sectors are predominantly privately owned and free from government control. Very differently, in the Chinese context, tabloid titles are predominantly published by relevant state-owned press groups and used in comparison with their propaganda-oriented, state subsidized, and forced subscription-based sister Party organs. Despite these significant structural differences between Chinese and Western tabloids in the present, alongside the absence of press freedom in China, China's tabloid papers were once quite similar to their Western counterparts in terms of format and content preference. Two phenomena, the rise of China's tabloid press sector from the mid-1990s and its replacement of the Party organ sector as the new dominant force in the daily newspaper market by the early 2000s, have been described as "arguably the most significant structural changes in China's newspaper industry in the era of reform" (Huang, 2016: 654).

Tabloid journalism as a subject has attracted tremendous research interest among mainland Chinese media researchers and resulted in a huge amount of related publications. However, despite the important contribution made by these richly descriptive and factual accounts to our understanding of the tabloid sector in China, this body of work is composed primarily of reflective essays published in non-refereed trade or academic journals, and lacks systematic investigation and critical contextualization (Huang, 2016). In comparison, there has been a small but vibrant body of English-language literature on the subject (e.g., Huang, 2001, 2016; Wang et al., 2018; Wang and Sparks, 2018; Zhao, 1998, 2000). Three typical arguments have emerged from this scholarship: 1) media commercialization in general and the rise of tabloid journalism in particular have brought the media industry not only more journalistic and commercial opportunities but also greater editorial autonomy; 2) media marketization and tabloidization under one-party rule in China have in fact helped repackage and popularise official propaganda and sell it for profit and thus ultimately reinforce the Party–state's authoritarian rule; and 3) tabloid journalism in China had peaked by the mid-2000s and has since entered into an era of stagnation. Despite such insights, more up-to-date information and knowledge is needed to better understand the most recent developments of the sector, particularly in the era of Xi Jinping since 2012. Before focusing on this, it is important to first have a look at China's tabloid journalism from a historical perspective.

Four decades without a tabloid press

Before it was banned in 1952, tabloid journalism had been present in China's major coastal cities for half a century, from late Qing to the early 1950s. In Shanghai, for example, between 1897 and 1952, there appeared 1,266 different kinds of tabloid titles, accounting for 70.88 per cent of total newspaper titles published in the city during this period. While most of these tabloids were short-lived and non-news oriented, some of them lasted for decades and remained journalistically influential (Xi, 2017). Despite its diverse and important social functions and cultural value in its own right, tabloid journalism was historically discriminated against within the dominant elitist tradition of modern Chinese journalism (Li, 2006; Xi, 2017; see also Cheek, 1989). As elaborated below, this historical, ideological, and moral prejudice against tabloid journalism was later inherited by Chinese Communists within a new and radical Marxist revolutionary rhetoric, and such prejudice still lingers among press regulators and certain journalists and media critics alike today and can become emphatic on occasion.

With the founding of the new Communist regime under Mao in 1949, tabloid journalism was quickly and effectively banned. The last tabloid title was closed in 1952, perceived as part of the 'morally rotten' old bourgeois culture that was not just useless but also poisonous to Communist China's revolutionary course. Journalistically, tabloid papers were also seen as direct threats to the propaganda-oriented Party journalism and the Communist press ideology at large. It would be difficult to imagine Maoist Communist puritans tolerating such sensational stories as "A Poet, A Social Butterfly, and A Masseur" (Li, 2004) from one of the "old" Shanghai's tabloid titles. During this period, there were about a dozen evening papers across the country that served as supplements to morning Party organs, providing readers with some politically "correct" and morally "healthy" soft news and materials. However, these were hardly tabloids and rather were merely less propaganda-oriented and more reader-friendly Party newspapers (Xi, 1995: 32). Even these titles were later forced to close down during the Cultural Revolution (1966–1976), having been accused of voicing a bourgeois lifestyle (Ding and Zhou, 1999). Moreover, long before the Cultural Revolution began, there had been a growing hostility towards any human-interest based, popular journalistic practice in an increasingly conservative political-ideological environment. In this context, sometimes even an ordinary feature story could be deemed as sensational and immoral.

A notable example of this situation occurred in early 1957 with Shanghai-based *Liberation Daily*. On March 24th of that year, a reprinted feature story on a famous Shaoxing opera actress' love story entitled, "My husband, my honeymoon", which was an invited, self-narrated piece by the actress, appeared in the newspaper. It caused a huge stir. The newspaper received hundreds of letters from readers complaining that the story was "bourgeois", "yellow journalism" that had damaged the newspaper's reputation as a Party organ. Based on their reading of the story, it was reported that the commanders in the headquarters of the Eastern Fleet of the Chinese navy based in Shanghai even suspected that there might have been an anti-revolutionary incident happening in the newspaper and prepared to encircle its building. Both the actress and her husband were heavily criticised. Her husband who happened to be a journalist was suspended from duty and investigated. It was not until Mao was told about the incident and shrugged it off in early April while at a Party conference in nearby Hangzhou that the uproar calmed down (Li, 2017).

Mao's tolerance of the story was, however, largely based on a temporary tactical consideration, rather than any ideological approval. This was demonstrated by the fact that the story was harshly criticized again later during the Cultural Revolution (Li, 2017). The story was published at a critical time during the Hundred Flower Campaign that Mao had launched 11 months previously for the supposed purpose of offering the public an opportunity to voice their opinions about the new Communist regime. However, at the time the story was published, no one, perhaps except Mao himself, knew that in less than a month, the campaign would be dramatically turned into a ruthless Anti-Rightist Campaign against the regime's critics. Compared to the love story, Mao and his regime had greater concerns to deal with now. In journalism academia, their biggest enemy was Wang Zhong, the late journalism professor of Fudan University in Shanghai who remained active in voicing his reformist journalistic ideas during the Hundred Flower Campaign (Xu, 2006: 30). Wang advocated bringing back the commercial-professional journalistic mechanism that had been widely practised pre-1949 and incorporating it into the new socialist press system. Wang was soon labelled a "bourgeois" and "anti-Party" scholar, suffered bitter, public attacks, and was humiliated for months before being purged as a "rightist" in early 1958. Among others, the primary "crime" Wang committed was criticising the propagandization of China's socialist press and maintaining an appreciation of and emphasis on the idea of "newsworthy", including the "human interest" value of a news story (Wang, 2004; Xu, 2006).

The ideological root of the anti-popular journalism mentality in China's Communist press history can be traced back to the Yan'an Rectification Campaign during 1942–1944 that aimed to further strengthen Mao's authority as the CCP's undisputed leader and Marxist theorist against his political rivals within the Party and, more broadly, Yan'an's liberal intellectuals. As an integral part of this move, Mao mobilized a comprehensive press reform campaign, aiming to transform the Party's media network into more centrally controlled and propaganda-oriented Party organs. The ideological consequence of the campaign was the rise of a Maoist Party press doctrine as a Sinicized Leninist interpretation of a proletarian press (Fudan University, 1985; Stranahan, 1990; Wang, 1992). Being heavily influenced by Lenin's (1901) well-known statement that "[a] newspaper is not only a collective propagandist and a collective agitator, it is also a collective organizer", Mao and his followers argued that a proletarian press consisted of a series of key characteristics. They included, among others, the "class character" according to which all media had their class affiliation, meaning that the proletarian press should serve the interest of the working class, just like the bourgeois, privately-owned press served the interest of the rich/ruling class; "Party character" in which all media were essentially controlled by certain political parties, and the proletarian media must accept the Communist Party's absolute leadership; "propaganda character" through which all media served as the propaganda tool of a certain class and political party and according to which the proletarian press was the mouthpiece of the Communist Party; and "educational character" which emphasized the proletarian press' role in remoulding the masses' thinking and worldview (e.g., see Liberation Daily, 1942; Liu, 1948; Lu, 1943; Mao, 1942, 1948).

None of these characters had anything to do with journalism, particularly the idea of "human interest". As Mao characteristically warned in his influential 1942 "Talks at the Yan'an Forum on Art and Literature" that would dominate the CCP's cultural policy for decades to come, in China's Communist movement there was no room for "love", "freedom of speech", "art-for-art", "individualism", "sectarianism", "human nature", and other "bourgeois", "petty-bourgeois", or "anti-Communist" theories or viewpoints. This was because "all culture, all art and literature belong to definite classes and follow definite political lines" (1942: 104, 109, 115). Echoing Mao, Lu Dingyi (1943), a leading Maoist media ideologue, openly expressed his deep distrust of Yan'an's liberal journalists who were seen as coming from the "old society" and being influenced by "dishonest" and "unscientific" "old theories of journalism" (Lu, 1943: 165). Lu argued that there was no such thing as common interest in journalism for even "interest has a class nature … news of interest to workers … may be of no interest to the exploiting classes" (Lu, 1943: 166). After the CCP took power in 1949, this propaganda-oriented Yan'an Party press doctrine became the official press ideology of the newly established PRC and caused widespread concerns and controversies in the journalistic community, as mentioned earlier.

With Mao's death and the introduction of Deng Xiaoping's reforms and opening up policy, in the early 1980s a heated debate on how "newsworthy" could be defined emerged between reformist and conservative media critics. For reformist scholars, newsworthiness was a classic and well-defined concept, based on five values: timeliness, importance, proximity, prominence, human interest; and it was commonly accepted and practised by the journalistic community around the world and thus there was no point redefining it (e.g., Fudan University, 1985). Conservative critics, however, argued that China's journalists should go further to also look at an event's "proletarian" news values or propagandistic values, assessing its ability to: reflect the Party's political line and relevant policies; promote productive forces and social progress; influence the nation's political life and social progress; reflect the masses' work efforts, studiousness, and lives in general; and provide people with new knowledge and enrich their spiritual lives (see Zhao et al., 2005: 266). Despite the growing popularity of the common Western understanding of "newsworthiness", as reflected in the re-emergence of evening papers in the 1980s, the idea of tabloid journalism tied to a full-fledged market-driven and sensation-oriented journalistic philosophy still remained largely an ideologically and morally taboo issue. Meanwhile, the call for press freedom through journalistic institutional reforms during the two major democratic movements in 1986 and 1989 almost exclusively focused on the political function of the press and left little room for any possible tabloid journalistic practice (e.g., Hsiao and Yang, 1990; Hu, 1989; Liu, 1990; Sun, 1986).

The golden decade

It was not until the mid-1990s, four and a half decades after the founding of the PRC and 15 years after Deng's reforms, that tabloid journalism emerged, rapidly developing for a decade until the mid-2000s. Aimed at bringing China out of its post-Tiananmen political-economic recession, Deng Xiaoping's call for further reforms and opening up in early 1992 led to the CCP's formal adoption of the "socialist market economy" policy later the same year. For Chinese journalism, this paved the way for media commercialization and the rise of an influential tabloid press sector from within China's state-run press industry. After a few years of experimentation, the first string of mass-appeal daily newspaper titles emerged in the mid-1990s. Named after a commonly used family name *dushi bao* (metro paper), these tabloids brought fresh journalistic and business initiatives to China's otherwise dull, Party-organ dominated, and state-subsidized press sector. Initiatives included a profoundly reader-oriented and sensational editorial approach, a fully-fledged market-driven and self-sufficient business model, an independent distribution network, a performance-based competitive personnel policy, the introduction of sensational writing styles and layout, a strong focus on local news, crime stories, gossip, celebrity, and sports news, complemented by subsidiary sections packed with soft news and entertainment materials (Huang, 2001; Zhao, 1998). As both the orthodox Party press and liberal-oriented press were marginalized in the age of media commercialization, politics and ideology were at least temporarily sidelined. All the creativity of the press community that had been repressed for decades was now channeled to chase sensational stories and improve circulation and revenue.

By the late 1990s, the explosive growth of tabloid metro papers had profoundly transformed China's press landscape. For traditional evening papers facing market pressure from metro papers, they had little choice but to join a collective defection to the tabloid wonderland by adopting metro papers' sensational editorial approach and even changing their publication time from afternoon to morning. This development indicated that competition in the daily newspaper market between metro papers, evening papers, and Party organs had by now drawn to a close and tabloids had triumphed (Huang, 2001). This tabloid press renaissance reached its climax in the early and middle 2000s following China's WTO entry in 2001. For example, in 2005, the tabloid press sector comprised 287 titles, compared with the Party organ sector's 438 titles. Despite having 151 titles fewer, in the same year, the former accounted for more than 40 per cent of total copies of newspapers printed and more than 60 per cent of total sheets of newsprint used nationwide, compared with the latter's share of 22.1 per cent and 18.1 per cent in both categories respectively. In terms of its financial performance, the tabloid sector shared nearly 47 per cent of the press industry's overall revenue and 50 per cent of its total pre-tax income, compared with the Party organ sector's share of 32 per cent in both categories (NPPBC, 2007a, 2007b, 2007c, 2007d). Among the 19 daily newspapers whose turnover passed the RMB500 million mark in 2005, 14 were tabloid titles (NPPBC, 2007d: 94–95). In the same year, 25 tabloid titles recorded an average circulation of 500,000 copies or higher (NPPBC, 2007c: 53, 56). Strictly speaking, the two sectors were virtually incomparable, given the fact that tabloid titles were financially self-sufficient, sold predominantly by private subscription and retail sale, while Party organs relied overwhelmingly on state-subsidy and forced official subscription. This effectively prefigured the journalistic death of the Party organ sector, as it had nearly nothing to do with ordinary readers' everyday news consumption.

However, just as the rapid development of the sector peaked, the tabloid sector's hidden concerns and challenges started looming large. Since then, tabloids have been experiencing a long and painful period of journalistic and business stagnation and circulation decline.

The decade of stagnation

The growth of China's tabloid-dominated daily newspaper sector's circulation, readership penetration, and particularly advertising income started slowing down from the mid-2000s (NPPBC, 2007c). At the time, there were nearly 300 tabloid titles following an almost identical journalistic approach and business model, boosting circulation and advertising by playing the sensationalism card. As they had been in a comfortable position in the marketplace for years, they were also losing both their creative edge and reformist spirit and suffered from a high degree of mimetic-isomorphism in terms of both genre and funding. Meanwhile, the fast growing new-media sector was imposing growing pressure on print media. The unfolding technological revolution and a new media-savvy younger generation, with major purchasing power, increasingly lost interest in print media, and in the early 2010s the average newspaper reader was more than 42 years old (Yao, 2013: 90). In response, tabloid titles joined the "go online" campaign, adopting a practice of offering free online PDF copies of their print editions. While this opened up new opportunities online, it had a further impact on printed tabloid titles' circulation and advertising income. The exaggerated money-driven tabloid culture also brought lots of criticism of tabloids' professional and ethical standards, from press regulators, media critics, and ordinary readers (e.g., see Rui, 2007; Wu, 2005; Zheng and Chen, 2004). For nearly a decade, tabloids' practice of selling sensational 'soft news' for profit was tacitly approved by authorities who were keen to chase a high GDP and, accordingly, a more self-sufficient press industry. However, such "freedom" was never guaranteed as the Party-state's press censorship regime remained intact. While this political hurdle had been temporarily forgotten at the height of media commercialisation, it re-emerged in the early 2000s in the form of a conservative ideological turnaround in Chinese politics in general and journalism in particular. This change put tabloid journalism under stricter ideological-moral scrutiny. Notably, in October 2003, the Hu Jintao-led new CCP leadership launched a nationwide "Marxist view of journalism" education campaign that required news organisations to "use a Marxist view of journalism to guide journalistic work" and "stick to the Party principle of journalism". They were also required to follow and promote "healthy", "socialist" moral values (Xinhua, 2003).

In this situation, the tabloid sector's approach to boosting circulation and advertising through emphasizing sensational content increasingly became untenable. In response, the sector started a high-profile "towards a mainstream press" campaign, designed to transform their tabloid titles into supposedly superior "mainstream" quality papers. By the end of the 2000s, the majority of China's tabloid titles had proudly declared that they had completed the upgrade. Encouragingly, together with a few influential news magazines such as *Southern Weekly* (http://www.infzm.com/), *Caixin Weekly* (http://weekly.caixin.com/), and *Caijing Magazine* (http://www.caijing.com.cn/), a handful of tabloid outlets such as the *Beijing News* (http://www.bjnews.com.cn/) and *China Youth Daily* (http://zqb.cyol.com/html/2020-02/28/nbs.D110000zgqnb_01.htm) experimented with what Huang (2016) called a Chinese-style "broadloid", or what Wang et al. (2018) called an "infotainment", approach. They attempted to combine tabloid and quality/watchdog journalistic ideas and techniques, playing the sensationalism card on the one hand and pushing the boundaries of China's media censorship regime on the other. However, lacking the willingness and/or political and journalistic resources to follow this broadloid/infotainment path, the overwhelming majority of tabloids ended up taking a still largely sensational, but increasingly restrained and non-aggressive, approach.

Despite these insights regarding the situation of China's tabloid journalism, there is a gap in knowledge about the details and implications of some significant recent changes in the past five years. Based on a close reading of leading Chinese tabloid titles' coverage, including their websites, together with observation of broader political and journalistic developments in China in recent years, those changes are identified below and will be further analysed in the last section of this chapter.

The death of tabloid journalism and its online limits

Since 2015, the market crisis of the sector has become more evident than ever before. Slowing down gradually in the previous decade, the sector has since experienced a free-fall decline in circulation and advertising income. This has forced major tabloid titles to shift resources further away from their print editions. Unfortunately, and despite this, few have managed to become online journalism leaders. This double failure has had further negative impact on the sector's overall journalistic performance and quality, leading to a vicious journalistic-business cycle. According to a recent report on China's media development, the tabloid-dominated newspaper industry's annual circulation income and advertising income peaked in 2011 (RMB26.7 billion RMB and RMB45 billion, respectively), but has since declined sharply, especially since 2013. By 2018, the industry's circulation income had declined to RMB10.2 billion, down 62 per cent from 2011, and its advertising income declined to RMB7.6 billion, a staggering 83 per cent drop from 2011 (Cui et al., 2019). Data from similar surveys also show the collapse of China's newspaper circulation. In 2015, newspaper circulation through retail sales dropped 46.5 per cent overall, and 50.8 per cent when it came to the tabloid sector compared to the previous year. In the same year, subscriptions of tabloid titles also fell 40 per cent from 2014. In the meantime, the country's newspaper readership penetration rate decreased from 65.7 per cent in 2011 to 38.4 per cent in 2015 (Chen, 2017).

During their "golden age" from the mid-1990s to the mid-2000s, tabloids commonly published 40 to 50 pages per issue, with numerous sensational stories and commercial advertisements. A tabloid nowadays typically has about 10 to 20 pages per issue, filled with rather ordinary and often boring stories and extremely limited and sometimes no advertisements, suggesting the sector's rapidly fading popularity among readers and advertisers. It seems their real market "value" is to remind people of their past glory or tactically keep a physical face for news organisations whose real journalistic and business interests have shifted online, even away to other media or non-media industries. Dozens of loss-making tabloid titles have closed their doors in recent years. In particular, when *Beijing Times* shuttered at the end of 2016, it sent a shockwave across the sector. Established in May 2001, this was once a creative and influential tabloid that dominated Beijing's morning newspaper market and was among the world's 100 most circulated newspapers in 2010 (Zhang, 2017).

Hand in hand with the commercial decline of the tabloid press sector has been the severe degeneration of its journalism in recent years. We now see a Chinese tabloid press sector largely in name or form only, as one can read little tabloid journalism in leading tabloid titles' daily coverage. When I say the journalistic "degeneration" of the sector, I mean the loss of the strong sensational spirit and considerable critical edge that the sector was once extremely proud of and which the overwhelming majority of its readership endorsed. Its loss of core tabloid journalistic characters has made it little more than a dead-man-walking, from a tabloid perspective. The dramatic changes which the Chengdu-based *West China City News* underwent in recent years offers a prime example of this extraordinary loss of identity. According to Huang et al. (2002), as the very first tabloid title in post-Mao China, the paper was once hailed as a creative and energetic tabloid champion in terms of both journalistic excellence and market performance in the 1990s. Adopting an exaggerated and eye-catching layout and a sensational writing style, its daily news coverage was once full of human interest stories, "man-bites-dog" news, and soft news material. Huang et al. found in one sample week between November 13 and 19, 1998, there were 262 stories published in the newspaper related to robbery, kidnapping, juvenile crime, people trafficking, domestic violence, murdering, deadly car and other accidents, food poisoning, underage marriage, bikini shows, and political and business corruption. Investigative crime stories in the paper remained particularly popular. According to one source cited in the study, the newspaper once spent RMB400,000 on an investigative reporting campaign on missing children, which was a serious societal problem in China at the time. Another extremely "successful" case was the paper's consecutive coverage of an eight-day police campaign to rescue a group of young prostitutes from the hands of gangsters. In the first year of its publication (1995–1996), the paper launched 15 such investigative reporting campaigns. Some of their stories were reprinted by dozens of other media outlets across the country. Even influential national state media such as the China Central Television and the Xinhua News Agency took part in the paper's investigative campaigns. Though the paper's critical reports focused largely on political and business corruption, social issues, and environmental concerns at the local level and avoided questioning China's one-party political system and high-ranking officials, this "beating the flies and leaving the tigers" strategy was not entirely without watchdog journalism merits (Huang et al., 2002). Since then, the paper has sadly become a mediocre title with nearly all these features disappearing. Like most other tabloid titles in China today, being politically "correct", ideologically "harmonious", and morally "appropriate" with little surprise and excitement, *West China City News* now serves as merely a very basic and ordinary information bulletin board. At the same time, it worth noting that the web platforms of China's tabloid titles do not feature much tabloid journalism either, also reflected with the *West China City News* website (http://www.huaxi100.com/). The passionate, dynamic, and exciting newsroom culture for journalistic excellence from a popular press perspective that China's tabloid sector once proudly upheld and cherished is now largely gone.

Finally, though tabloid journalism has penetrated online through commercial web portals and online platforms such as blogs, forums, and social media, it has been constrained by the same rigid media censorship policy that showed little tolerance of the state-owned tabloid press sector. As a result, any online tabloid journalism has manifested in a scattered manner that is by no means able to fill the tabloid journalism vacuum left by the dying tabloid press sector. For example, China's privately-owned leading web portals such as Sina (https://www.sina.com.cn/), NetEase (https://www.163.com/), Sohu (https://www.sohu.com/), and Tencent (https://www.qq.com/) are essentially news aggregators rather than formal news organisations. Not only are they not allowed to collect and publish original hard news, they also have little autonomy to practise tabloid journalism. Despite their coverage of soft news topics, including sport, entertainment, fashion, lifestyle, travel, food, shopping, and finance and investment, it far from matches China's tabloid press sector's once systematic coverage of a whole range of tabloid news and those tabloid techniques that had been built up over nearly two decades from the mid-1990s. Strictly speaking, web coverage of soft news can be hardly seen as tabloid journalism in a traditional sense.

China's tabloid journalism crisis: reasons and lessons

The reasons and implications behind China's tabloid journalism crisis are multiple and complex. This concluding part of the chapter discusses how the interplay of ideological, technological, and media market changes, combined with the tabloid sector's response to such changes, have had an impact upon the sector and the possible lessons that can be drawn from this case.

First, the collapse of tabloid journalism in China resulted primarily from the conservative revisionism in the CCP's political-journalistic ideology in the era of Xi Jinping. Post-Mao China has remained a one-party state despite policies of reforming and opening up since 1978. However, the degree of actual political control of media under the same political system has varied depending on the CCP's leadership's ideological mindset. Arguably the two best periods for journalism in post-Mao China were the mid-1980s, when media reforms focused on the issue of press freedom, and the 1990s when tabloid journalism grew under media commercialisation and when Deng Xiaoping's pragmatic political ideology prevailed. Starting from the era of Hu Jintao and particularly since Xi came to power in 2012, the regime has become, to an increasing extent, politically and ideologically conservative (Cheek and Ownby, 2018; Lam, 2015; So, 2019). This shift has inevitably spilled over into journalism. In 2013, the conservative "Marxist view of journalism" approach was included in *Journalists' Training Textbook* (Liu and Jiang, 2013), the PRC's first official textbook for the nationwide journalistic continuing-education program. In the same year, about 25,000 journalists across the country were, for the first time, required to pass a professional test that included questions on the "Marxist view of journalism" to be eligible to renew their press cards (People.cn, 2013). In his inspection tour of China's top official media outlets in 2016, Xi declared that

China's state-run media were the Party's "propaganda fronts" that "must have the party as their family name", and "love the party, protect the party, and closely align themselves with the party leadership in thought, politics and action" (Guardian, 2016). These and other similar speeches on the instrumental use of media for Party propaganda were later collected in *Lectures on Xi Jinping's Journalistic Philosophy* (The Writing Group, 2018). Xi's "journalistic" philosophy however had nothing to do with journalism and offered nothing new, even from a media propaganda perspective, as it merely reemphasized the same familiar propaganda-oriented Maoist press discourse. The new quasi-Yan'an Rectification Movement based on thought moulding, order, and punishment under Xi has worried many China observers (Cheek and Ownby, 2018; Lam, 2015; So, 2019). Similarly, the return of the ghost of the Yan'an Maoist Party press doctrine has largely killed not only China's emerging investigative journalism (Gao, 2018; Hernández, 2019), but also the far less politically oriented tabloid journalism in the country.

Second, the demise of tabloid journalism occurred in the context of growing propagandization of China's journalism under Xi. Propagandistic use of the media is, to varying extents, a worldwide phenomenon, and the relationship between journalism and propaganda can be complex and complicated in practice. Nevertheless, this gives one no excuse to conceptually mix up the two concepts. Until recently, this distinction had been recognised by most Chinese media scholars, representing a significant outcome from a decade of fierce debate between reformist and conservative critics on the matter in the 1980s (e.g., Gan, 1982; Wang, 2004). However, in recent years, this distinction has come under growing political-ideological pressure. For example, Chen Lidan, arguably China's most influential establishment Marxist press scholar at Renmin University of China, referred to the "Marxist view of journalism" as the ideological principle behind Chinese journalism, as "a certain set of principles, concepts, and guidelines by which the Party-led journalism and communication industry as well as the Party-led wider cultural industry should politically comply with" (Chen, 2006: 1). This confusing and controversial definition was later adopted in a nearly identical form by the official *Journalists' Training Textbook*. Similarly, Chinese journalists and university journalism students have been under growing pressure to identify themselves, first and foremost, as the Party-state's propagandists rather than truth-seekers (e.g., see Liu and Jiang, 2013; see also Xu, 2018). Historically, the significance of the rise of tabloid journalism in the mid-1990s lay exactly in its determined and effective breaking away from this powerful propagandistic tradition of China's Marxist/Communist journalism originating in Yan'an. As the CCP under Xi turned more conservative in recent years, it has inevitably and visibly affected tabloid journalism.

Third, the fall of China's tabloid press sector is also partly rooted in its state ownership structure. The overwhelming majority of China's tabloid titles were originally published by their parent Party organs in China's metropolitan areas in the 1990s. Most of them later came under the control of relevant state-run press groups often named after their parent Party organs, as they were strategically expanded as press conglomerates around China's WTO entry in 2001. In other words, China's tabloid titles have always existed in the shadow of their parent Party organ-based press groups and lacked independence of ownership. They have always been essentially state entities despite their market orientation, being politically and ideologically controlled by their parent press groups as an integral part of the Chinese Party-state's political-ideological apparatuses. When the overall political-ideological situation remained stable, people tended to forget the hidden implications of this institutional arrangement. However, when political-ideological turbulence did come, the weakness of the system made the tabloid sector highly vulnerable.

Fourth, the decline of tabloid journalism can be partly attributed to the sector's panic and poor response to political-ideological and market pressures beginning in the 2000s. The challenge imposed by new media on print media was real. The growing political-ideological pressure for a "clean" tabloid journalism was also clear. However, media did not have to panic when facing such challenges and could have responded more strategically. The tabloid sector's "towards a mainstream press" campaign that started in the mid-2000s was, overall, poorly conceptualized and a misreading of the situation. The campaign took a rather simplistic approach, calling for the transformation of hundreds of tabloids into watchdog-spirited serious titles, failing to foresee the enormous political and journalistic challenges of doing so or considering the diverse needs of the country's huge consumer market for news. A media reform program that did not carefully consider media economics together with political, professional, and technical constraints was likely to fail. To its own disadvantage, the tabloid sector somewhat strangely took an ideologically self-shaming approach by looking down on its decade-long successful practice of tabloid journalism in contrast to a supposedly superior serious press. Similarly, the sector's "go online" shift has hardly been a success story. Most tabloid titles rushed to set up their web platforms without a long-term strategy. As a result, they have ended up being unable to compete with privately-owned, more technologically experienced, and financially powerful emerging web portals and new media corporations on the one hand, and have lost their print-version-based traditional readership and advertisers on the other. Though the newspaper industry, including the tabloid sector, is suffering a severe decline globally in the age of digitization, compared with many of their western counterparts, China's tabloid titles, as the dominant force in the daily newspapers market, have failed to perform and deliver vibrant tabloid journalism both offline and online. Even worse, they have also awkwardly ended up practising neither serious nor popular journalism, as they have lost their old identity while failing to create a new one.

Last, it can be argued that the ecological situation of tabloid journalism in China and perhaps elsewhere may be seen as a reflection of the overall health of its national political-media system at large. One does not have to glorify tabloid journalism. However, individual media outlets' and audiences' right to choose "dumbing down" must be respected. It may be safe to say that a society without tabloid journalism is likely to be a boring place. In the case of China, together with a Chinese-style broadloid journalism as I suggested elsewhere (Huang, 2016), a real tabloid journalism may return and refresh itself in the near future in a more mature political, journalistic, and market environment.

References

Cheek, Timothy. 1989. "Redefining Propaganda: Debates on the Role of Journalism in Post-Mao Mainland China." *Issues & Studies* XXV (2): 47–75.

Cheek, Timothy, and David Ownby. 2018. "Make China Marxist Again." *Dissent*. Accessed May 21, 2020: https://www.dissentmagazine.org/article/making-china-marxist-again-xi-jinping-thought.

Chen, Guoquan. 2017. "China Newspaper Industry Development Report." *Sina Finance*. Accessed May 21, 2020: https://cj.sina.com.cn/article/detail/2151768482/163990.

Chen, Lidan. 2006. *The Thought System of Marxist View of Journalism*. Beijing: China Renmin University Press.

Cui, Baoguo, Lijun Xu, and Mai Ding, eds. 2019. *Chinese Media Industry Development Report. Beijing*: Social Sciences Publishing. Accessed May 21, 2020: https://zhuanlan.zhihu.com/p/79737687.

Ding, Fazhang, and Shengling Zhou. 1999. "50 Years of China's Socialist Evening Newspapers." *News Front*. http://www.cqvip.com/qk/81222x/199910/1004421063.html.

Fudan University, ed. 1985. *A Concise Course in China's Journalism History*. Fuzhou: Fujian People's Publishing.

Gan, Xifen. 1982. *Theoretical Foundation of Journalism*. Beijing: China Renmin University Press.

Gao, Helen. 2018. "The Demise of Watchdog Journalism in China." *The New York Times*. Accessed May 22, 2020: https://www.nytimes.com/2018/04/27/opinion/watchdog-journalism-china-oppression.html.

Guardian online. 2016. "Xi Jinping Asks for 'Absolute Loyalty' from Chinese State Media." 19 Feb. Accessed May 22, 2020: https://www.theguardian.com/world/2016/feb/19/xi-jinping-tours-chinas-top-state-media-outlets-to-boost-loyalty.

Hernández, Javier C. 2019. "'We're Almost Extinct': China's Investigative Journalists Are Silenced Under Xi." *The New York Times*. Accessed May 22, 2020: https://www.nytimes.com/2019/07/12/world/asia/china-journalists-crackdown.html.

Hsiao, Ching-Chang, and Mei-Rong Yang. 1990. "Don't Force Us to Lie: The Case of the World Economic Herald." In *Voices of China: The Interplay of Politics and Journalism*, edited by Chin-Chuan Lee, 111–121. London: The Guilford Press.

Hu, Jiwei. 1989. "There Will Be No Genuine Stability Without Press Freedom." *World Economic Herald*, 8 May.

Huang, Chengju. 2001. "China's State-Run Tabloids: The Rise of 'City Newspapers'". *International Communication Gazette* 63 (5): 435–450.

Huang, Chengju. 2016. "Towards a Broadloid Press Approach: The Transformation of China's Newspaper Industry since the 2000s." *Journalism* 17: 652–666.

Huang, Chengju, Alan Knight, and Chris Lawe Davies. 2002. "Beyond Party Propaganda: A Case Study of China's Rising Commercialized Press." *Ejournalist* 2 (1): 1–21.

Lam, Willy Wo-Lap. 2015. *Chinese Politics in the Era of Xi Jinping: Renaissance, Reform, or Retrogression*. New York and London: Routledge.

Lenin, Vladimir. 1901. "Where to Begin?". In *Lenin Collected Works* (Vol. 5), 13–24. Moscow: Foreign Languages Publishing House.

Li, Junna. 2017. "Fang Ruijuan Died: The Saga of a 'Yellow Journalism' Case 60 Years Ago." *Shanghai Observer*, February 17. Accessed May 22, 2020: https://www.jfdaily.com/news/detail?id=45027.

Li, Nan. 2004. "Tabloids and Culturati in Late Qing and Republic of China." Shanghai Archive Network. Accessed May 22, 2020: http://www.archives.sh.cn/shjy/scbq/201203/t20120313_6033.html.

Li, Nan. 2006. *Tabloids in Shanghai in Late Qing and Republic of China.* Beijing: Renmin Literature Publishing.

Liberation Daily. 1942. "The Party and Party Organs." September 22.

Liu, Binjie, and Jianguo Jiang, eds. 2013. *Journalists' Training Textbook.* Beijing: People's Press.

Liu, Binyan. 1990. "Press Freedom: Particles in the Air." In *Voices of China: The Interplay of Politics and Journalism*, edited by Chin-Chuan Lee, 132–139. London: The Guilford Press.

Liu, Shaoqi. 1948. "A Talk to the North China Press Corps." In *Selected Works of Liu Shaoqi*, (Vol. I, 1981), 393–404. Beijing: Foreign Languages Press.

Lu, Dingyi. 1943. "Our Basic Viewpoints on Journalism." *Chinese Sociology and Anthropology* XVIII (3/4): 164–173.

Mao, Zedong. 1942. "Talks at the Yenan Forum on Art and Literature." In *Mao Tse-tung on Art and Literature* (1960), 75–122. Beijing: Foreign Languages Press.

Mao, Zedong. 1948. "A Talk to the Editorial Staff of the *Shansi-Suiyuan Daily*." In*Selected Works of Mao Tse-tung* (Vol. IV, 1960), 241–245. Beijing: Foreign Languages Press.

NPPBC (National Press and Publication Bureau of China). 2007a. "The Development of the Newspaper Industry Remains Stable." In *2007 Chinese Newspaper Industry Development Report*, edited by Jiang Lin and Yuming Feng, 4–22. Beijing: Social Sciences Publishing.

NPPBC. 2007b. "Major Indexes of the Newspaper Industry Remained Stable." In *2007 Chinese Newspaper Industry Development Report*, edited by Jiang Lin and Yuming Feng, 23–42. Beijing: Social Sciences Publishing.

NPPBC. 2007c. "Progress Achieved across Different Sectors of the Newspaper Industry." In *2007 Chinese Newspaper Industry Development Report*, edited by Jiang Lin and Yuming Feng, 43–86. Beijing: Social Sciences Publishing.

NPPBC. 2007d. "The Overall Financial Situation of the Newspaper Industry Remains Healthy." In *2007 Chinese Newspaper Industry Development Report*, edited by Jiang Lin and Yuming Feng, 87–110. Beijing: Social Sciences Publishing.

People.cn. 2013. "Renew Reporter Pass by Passing the Exam." Accessed May 22, 2020: http://media.people.com.cn/n/2013/1012/c120837-23174737.html.

So, Alvin Y. 2019. "Neoliberalism and the Rise of Authoritarianism in China in the Early 21st Century." *International Review of Modern Sociology* 45 (1). Accessed May 22, 2020: https://www.academia.edu/38681953/Neoliberalism_and_the_Rise_of_Authoritarianism_in_China_in_the_early_21st_century.

Stranahan, Patricia. 1990. *Moulding the Medium: The Chinese Communist Party and the Liberation Daily*. New York and London: Sharpe.

Sun, Xupei. 1986. "On Socialist Press Freedom." *Journalism Law Bulletin* (supplement issue).

The Writing Group, ed. 2018. *Lectures on Xi Jinping's Journalistic Thought.* Beijing: People's Press and Learning Press.

Wang, Haiyan, and Colin Sparks. 2018. "Chinese Newspaper Groups in the Digital Era: The Resurgence of the Party Press." *Journal of Communication* 69 (1): 94–119.

Wang Haiyan, Colin Sparks, and Yu Huang. 2018. "Popular Journalism in China: A Study of *China Youth Daily*." *Journalism* 19 (9-10): 1203–1219.

Wang, Jin. 1992. "The First Media Reform in the History of Party Organs." *Journalism Research Materials* 57: 132–154.

Wang, Juan. 2009. "Imagining Citizenship: The Shanghai Tabloid Press, 1897–1911." *Twentieth Century China* 35 (1): 29–53.

Wang, Zhong. 2004. *Collected Works of Wang Zhong*. Shanghai: Fudan University Press.

Wu, Guping. 2005. "The Practice of False Journalism Is Worsening." *Journalism Review*10.

Xi, Po. 2017. *Shanghai: Untold Stories*. Shanghai: Shanghai Social Sciences Academy Press.

Xi, Wenju. 1995. "New Thinking of New Evening Newspapers." *Press Circles* 5: 31–33.

Xinhua. 2003. "The Central Propaganda Department Called for a Comprehensive Educational Campaign on Three Important Issues on the Journalistic Front." Accessed May 22, 2020: http://www.people.com.cn/GB/14677/14737/22039/2158087.html.

Xu, Jian. 2018. "The Return of Ideology to China's Journalism Education: The 'Joint Model' Campaign between Propaganda Departments and Journalism Schools." *Asia Pacific Media Educator* 28 (2): 1–10.

Xu, Peiding. 2006. *An Academic History of Chinese journalism*. Chongqing: Chongqing Press.

Yao, Lin. 2013. "An Analysis of 2012 China Newspaper Advertising Market." In *Blue Book of China's Media*, edited by Baoguo Cui, 82–91. Beijing: Social Sciences Publishing.

Zhang, Zhuping. 2017. "Towards a Market-Oriented Press Reform: The Case of the *Beijing Times*." *Radio & TV Journal* 2. Accessed May 22, 2020: http://media.people.com.cn/n1/2017/0220/c410918-29093795.html.

Zhao, Kai, Fazhang Ding, and Zhixiao Huang, eds. 2005. *China's Social Sciences in the 20th Century* (Journalism Volume). Shanghai: Shanghai People's Press.

Zhao, Yuezhi. 1998. *Media, Market, and Democracy in China*. Urbana and Chicago: University of Illinois Press.

Zhao, Yuezhi. 2000. From Commercialization to Conglomeration: The Transformation of the Chinese Press within Orbit of the Party State. *Journal of Communication* 50 (2): 3–26.

Zheng, Baowei, and Xuan Chen. 2004. "Media Workers' Attitude on 'Paid Journalism.'" *Journalism Review* 5.

13 Reclaiming and tabloidizing "truth" in Turkey

Mine Gencel Bek

Introduction

"Post-truth" and fake news have become buzzwords of our era, one in which we have also witnessed the rise of global right-wing populism. "Post-truth" is not the same as "classic deception" or even "lies". As Dahlgren explains: "Rather, it signals an emerging new epistemic regime, where emotional response prevails over factual evidence and reasoned analysis" (Dahlgren, 2018). It is not surprising to see that right-wing populist leaders and the media which support them and their policies often employ tabloidization, with its emphases on personalization and emotional reporting and infotainment (Reinemann et al., 2012). Such media forms continue to play a vital role in both hindering as well as enabling "civic culture" (Dahlgren, 2018). This chapter focuses on how this hindering process takes shape through analysis of news verification or fact-checking organizations in Turkey. We have witnessed, especially in the last decade, the rise of the fact checking or news verification organizations which are supposed to push back against authoritarianism and disinformation. This chapter tries to show how we can see tabloidizing elements even in those operations that may appear to promise anti-tabloid strategies. It argues that not only is journalism "complicit with populism's rise" (Zelizer, 2020: 84) but so too are those operations which reclaim truth, including by being involved in the processes of sharing and circulating these values within their sensational and tabloidized format and content.

The chapter will briefly introduce and discuss the rise of organizations reclaiming truth in the Turkish political and communication context. It will then trace the tabloidizing elements through the personalization of politics and foregrounding the human side of politics as well as humorous representation. Finally, the chapter, again by tracing textual content, discusses how these organizations which are dedicated to establishing facts actually serve to reinforce and function in line with the oppressive governments with nationalist and religious references.

Reclaiming "truth" in changing Turkey?

Turkey, "as a subject of academic research, has found itself caught in an intellectual and theoretical 'no-man's land', located somewhere between south-eastern

Europe and the Middle East" as Christensen rightly notes (2007: 180). Some descriptions of Turkey in the research literature, as quoted in Küçük and Özselçuk, (2019), describe competitive authoritarianism (Levitsky and Way, 2010; Akkoyunlu and Öktem, 2016), authoritarian neoliberalism (Bruff, 2014), authoritarian capitalism/populism, and corporate nationalism (Madra and Yılmaz, 2019). Bilge Yeşil (2016) also uses the term "authoritarian neoliberalism". Concerning the media system, she argues that the Turkish system is a *hybrid* system based on a symbiotic relationship between commercial and statist imperatives. This type of system is similar to those in European countries with their commercial nature, to those in Latin American and Asian countries with their clientelism, and to systems in Middle Eastern and Southeast Asian countries with their strong state tradition and links between the media, the military, and political Islam, as can be seen in Egypt and Pakistan (Yeşil, 2016: 70–71). To an extent, the European Union (EU) candidacy process affected Turkey at the end of the 1990s and the beginning of the 2000s. However, a trend of de-Europeanization has dominated after 2011, as Yılmaz (2016) discusses in relation to deterioration of media freedom. The socio-political transition process from Kemalist laicism to Islam-dominated politics (Farmanfarmaian et al., 2018) increased in intensity during this period and triggered these characteristics, "serving as an instrument of state, as well as a projector of values that consistently have defined Turkish identity: the family, the nation, and the conservative moral framework of community" (Farmanfarmaian et al., 2018: 122).

Fact-checking and news verification organizations were established as a solution to 'polarization', mainly on social media from 2016. Polarization and populism continue in the actions and discourses of leaders globally (see Baybars Hawks and Uzunoğlu, 2019 for a comparative analysis of discourses of leaders Theresa May, Donald Trump and Recep Tayyip Erdoğan) as well as newspapers in the following periods as well (for textual analysis of Turkish newspapers coverage of populism in different cases such as the constitutional referendum in April 2019, see Şen, 2019; Turkey-Netherlands diplomatic crisis in March 2017, see Doruk Şahin, 2019). Moreover, as this chapter demonstrates, these discourses are reproduced even by the news verification organizations themselves. Established in 2016, *teyit.org* ("teyit' meaning verification or confirmation in Turkish) was the first news verification organization in Turkey. It is one of two[1] organizations to be a signatory to the International Fact-Checking Network's Code of Principles and is also a partner of First Draft News. Another organization called *Malumatfuruş* (meaning a person who pretends to be knowledgeable) focuses on editorials and columns in the news media. In addition to these, other news organizations work openly as apparatchiks of the government, as will be explained later.

Atakan Foça explains the rationale for teyit.org in a piece entitled "*teyit*.org in the age of Pinocchio" (Atakan Foça, 2016). According to him, we encounter distorted news and fictionalized information being shared in social media mainly as a result of news sites' priorities of getting more clicks and the corresponding emotional reactions, anger, and polarization. The organization *teyit.org* describes itself as a "group of data-volunteers with mostly journalist backgrounds" stepped into action, taking responsibility to uphold the accepted values of objectivity, truth, transparency in order to prevent the Internet becoming a rubbish bin of information.

Murat Uluk (2018) conducted a content analysis of fake news from June 2015 to January 2018, announced on *teyit.org*. His approach focuses on technology in an apolitical way, in line with the news verification organization itself. According to this analysis, ordinary people's participation and use of web technology and their motives for looking for 'likes' have created ethical problems. This research relies on data based on a selection from *teyit.org*: material tagged as fake by *teyit.org* includes items from social media platforms (181 from a total of 305), from websites and social media together (71 from a total of 305), and from websites only (40 of 305) (Uluk, 2018: 113). Research based on already chosen material from *teyit.org* confirms that fake news is often a product of social media or websites.

Neslihan Yolçu's piece entitled "Fact-Checking Websites as New Media's New Gatekeepers: The Example of 'Teyit.org'" provides further research into the issue and the role of *teyit.org*. According to Yolçu: "As trust towards the traditional media gradually decreases, users are more likely to be exposed to fake news as they are directed to alternative media and especially to social media" (Yolçu, 2019: 203).

The questions being asked here are as follows:

- Why did trust in traditional media decrease?
- Why have users moved to alternative media and social media?
- What is the evidence that, through these channels, users are exposed to fake news?
- How can these issues be analyzed without looking at the AKP, the state–media relationship, authoritarianism, and contextual information?

Media users, it must be stressed, turn to social media and alternative media because no trusted mainstream or legacy media remain. More than 90 per cent of the media has been purchased with AKP-supporting capital investment.[2] The claim that social media produce fake news is also a much-used discursive strategy of Erdoğan's.[3] Why is this happening? The author Neslihan Yolçu argues that this represents the fast-changing political agenda, in an unfortunate way: "In particular, [in] countries where the political agenda changes so rapidly, such as Turkey, neither citizens nor journalists follow up on the cases" (Yolçu, 2019: 219). Following diagnosis of the issue, Yolçu's solutions are conceived as technical and apolitical, in accordance with the news verification channels presented above. These are: developing new media literacy education and the relevant skills to be a fact-checker; the mainstream news media developing joint projects with civil enterprises; the traditional news media having their own verification tools and fact-checking services; and removing restrictions on the freedom of the press (Yolçu, 2019: 220). The suggestion of media literacy should be considered carefully in the Turkish context, since these literacy initiatives can be linked and used by and/or with the already nationalist, sexist, and conservative values. In Yolçu's recommendations, the last statement is a core matter. In fact, according to a report quoted in Yolçu's work, there is a connection between fake news and media literacy, and resilience against fake news is not low because of education performance but rather is related to a "very low media freedom score.[4]"

Reclaiming truth with tabloidization: the human side of politicians and humorous representation

Turning to *teyit.org*, it has been active on Facebook and Twitter, and has recently focused on developing digital content including visuals and video and expanding its social media presence, first to Instagram and then to YouTube, in order to reach younger media users. Its series of *They Lied to Us* YouTube videos are products of its attempts to reach a wider public and increase the social impact of their work (Atakan Foça, 2019). The series started on October 5, 2019, as a partnership between *teyit.org* and journalist Mirgün Cabas. The first four episodes of *They Lied to Us* are analyzed here.

In October 2019, four episodes of *They Lied to Us*, each running between 10 and 15 minutes, were posted on the 'Boşlukları Doldur' YouTube channel. The videos were viewed between 100,000 and 200,000 times. The presenter of the programs, Mirgün Cabas, is a former news anchor with NTV news. He described the aim of the program in the first video as "covering suspicious-looking news stories, infiltrating the public agenda as well as our minds." (October 5, 2019, Boşlukları Doldur).[5]

What *teyit.org* offers in this video, with Cabas at the helm, in an attempt to reclaim truth, is in fact a form of tabloidization of truth, demonstrated, for example, in the personalized and humorous coverage of politicians. Personalization and emotional reporting are frequent indicators of tabloidization, linked to infotainment (Reinemann et al., 2012), and these characteristics might be able to express political issues at the level of everyday life (Gencel Bek, 2004; Van Zoonen, 2012; Wasserman, 2008) beyond the polarized discourses of politicians. However, there are significant limitations to such approaches, as discovered in the study of TV news noted previously (Gencel Bek, 2004), as it can tend towards portraying politicians in an amusing and even sympathetic way, suggesting politicians who represent different positions are alike, as if no policy differences existed between them. The news verification programme *They Lied to Us* thus becomes a medium of populism itself, as demonstrated below.

In the first episode, published on October 5, 2019, and seen by around 200,000 viewers, the main topic is coverage of the newly elected mayor of Istanbul, Ekrem Imamoğlu. The selection of this topic is not surprising, as the victory of Imamoğlu as a candidate from the main opposition party CHP was the subject of a series of targeted fake news stories. Interestingly, though, the episode tabloidizes this situation in *teyit.org*'s chosen coverage with the title,

"You suffered so much." The phrase "You suffered so much" ("Ne çektin be" in Turkish) is borrowed from the Turkish sitcom Yalan Dünya (Lie/Fake World). The audience is reminded of this wording in a short clip from the sitcom written by Gülse Birsel, the script writer and actress in the sitcom. Arguably, by using humour and references to fictional television programming, this video minimizes and trivializes more profound concerns of fake news attacks on political opponents. The video highlights all manner of relevant fake news, including Imamoğlu wearing a cross necklace around his neck, having his picture taken with Fethullah Gülen, who is the head of Islamist Gülen, or Hizmet, movement and current enemy of the AKP and Erdoğan after the claim that he attempted the failed military coup of July 15, and having his photograph taken while buying the Turkish alcoholic drink *rakı* from a supermarket. While the photo was a fake, we can see it as a problematic photo with specific political implications, as buying *rakı* rankles those in favour of the increased İslamization of everyday life, while pushing back against the photo as fake suggests there is something wrong with buying *rakı*, again feeding into the trend of increased İslamization of everyday life.

In a way, it is apparent what is going on by showing these fake news items. However, it is not made clear why they are produced or shared. The programme often shows individual users from Twitter as agents of fake news, and agency and motivation for producing fake news are therefore attributed to individuals and their lack of "social media literacy skills," a point clearly made in the programme. The solution, according to the program, is to: "check before sharing it." A similar explanation can be found in another video, from October 12, with Mirgün Cabas describing these as the result of 'truth-telling men', saying: "I must be the one to share it first. The funniest analysis must be mine. I won't let anyone else get those likes". The solution is simple according to him: "check things before sharing them, we are not only appreciated, but also ridiculed. To me, it is not worth it. If you doubt it, check it. If you don't, doubt it." (October 12, Boşlukları Doldur). On October 26, Cabas expands on his view on why these stories are being shared, answering the following questions: "Could it be because we like fabricated stories that suit us? Could we be caring less about fact-checking if that false information supports our existing opinions and beliefs? I think so" (October 26, Boşlukları Doldur).

Humorous listing of fake news on politicians is also evident in other examples. Melih Gökçek, former mayor of Ankara for the AKP and a populist right-wing Islamist politician, is shown in the programme with an extract from tabloidized coverage of him from another TV channel. This is not to deny the possibility of humour being used to inform and even provide critiques of political, economic, or social affairs and of people in power as seen in news satires and news parodies (Tandoc et al., 2018: 141–142). However, what is at stake is a separate matter, and it is not simply nor only a tabloid strategy of blending other popular media trends into a truth verifying programme which is supposed to be outside the tabloid news world. Rather, it opens a space to already powerful right-wing populism.

According to the presenter, while sharing Melih Gökçek's social media post and a fake video it includes (October 19, Boşlukları Doldur): "A lot of people, including Melih Gökçek, rushed to share the video, only to regret it later." Further coverage is then shown of Gökçek saying, "later do not say I have deserved whatever happened to me, I am the one responsible" (broadly translated from a popular Turkish song entitled "kendim ettim kendim buldum" or "I am sending you a song"). A video follows of Gökçek on Kanal 3 Hilal TV playing a song by Neset Ertaş, the late popular singer. Ertaş' lyrics are mostly about rural peasant life, good and naïve humans, and are liked by many different people from across the political spectrum and from both urban and rural areas. The song is accompanied by Gökçek's "smiling" face. Here, again, *They Lied to Us* represents these political figures as ordinary people sharing fake news, even portraying them as nice human beings and normalizing the sharing of fake news. We know that, during his long standing as Ankara mayor, Gökçek's was heavily involved in spreading fake news and in information pollution and propaganda. It is impossible to accept that representation without taking a critical stance not only as journalists or academics but as citizens.

US president Donald Trump, another populist right-wing leader, features heavily in this video series as well, particularly with his use of fake news. It is interesting that Trump is not an object of criticism as one might expect from a fact-checking news verification channel. With his "angry populism" and populist discourse and rhetoric, he embodies, employs, and seeks broad appeal (Wahl-Jorgensen, 2018). In fact, whatever he performs sensationally is being reproduced and circulated uncritically. For example, on October 19, the program shows a social media post which states that the US secretary of state Mike Pompeo was allegedly given a pack of dog food by an Italian journalist as a show of protest on Kurdish issues, with the message that he could become kind and loyal in the same way as dogs are very loyal creatures. The programme enlightens us by relying on an article published online. The package, which was passed from hand to hand, contained parmesan cheese and not dog food, to protest against tariffs imposed on European food products. Additional customs duties had recently been imposed by the US, so journalists asked for the cheese to be given to Trump.

Trump was again a theme in the videos on October 26, this time in relation to mozzarella cheese: "This week, we have mozzarella on the Trump menu. Don't think that we are covering these stories for advertising cheese – we are not. The stories themselves come 'cheesy.' And what is more, they come through big news websites". Readers then learn the correct story behind the fake news about Trump: "Donald Trump had called the Italian President 'mozzarella.' So, we sat down in excitement to watch the entire press conference on YouTube. The result? The man does not say mozzarella. He says Mattarella, which is the name of the Italian president." However, as a result of this discussion, the programme tabloidized the truth while depoliticizing the debates.

Reclaiming "truth" with tabloidization: nationalism and Islamicization

In the YouTube series *They Lied to Us*, the following emphases were quite common: these things which reference negative events not only happen in Turkey and not only now. Emphasis on the traceability not of fake news but bad news in other countries and from earlier periods in Turkish history arguably also works to decontextualize and hide the political and economic dynamics at hand. The programme does not list such news but does produce answers to questions such as: "Is Turkey the only country, as being claimed, taxing their citizens' international travel on departure?" "No, Iran and the Philippines also," the presenter replies, "There is no such thing as nowhere in the world but in Turkey." The presenter links this with other news stating that smoking in private cars is prohibited in other countries too, especially when there is a child in the car, and that this regulation was not something new but had started to be applied recently in Turkey (October 5, 2019). "This is not the first time we see this," argues the presenter, who then jumps to another issue and asks why fake news multiplies in times of war, answering, "because war distorts truth." The second episode (October 12, 2019, also viewed by 200,000 viewers) deals with the "bombardment of fake news about the Turkish Armed Forces" in relation to operation *Peace Spring* in Syria. It is striking that all the chosen images and videos were shown with the emphasis that, "these are not *our* war planes. This aircraft is not *ours*." These, in actual fact, belong to the Dutch Air Force and are sampled from film called *Medal of Honor*. In the third episode on October 19, 2019, the videos shown on social media were, it was argued, not videos belonging to Turkish forces of operation *Peace Spring* or civilians injured in Turkish air raids. It has been claimed that a video of a flying tank: "It is not even *ours*. It is an Israeli flying tank." In the second episode, the war is connected to earthquakes demonstrating that fake news emerges not only in relation to war. In a way, the presenter equates war, which is a human product preventable and able to be ended, with a natural disaster. While humorous representation can hardly be expected here, in asking about the owner of the company responsible for spreading fake news about the claimed predictions of earthquakes, the programme uses the words of Erdoğan, "Who [do you think] you are huh?" (translated from: 'Sen kimsin ya, siz kimsiniz ya?'), with a montage of views of him accompanied by cheerful techno music. This is highly problematic not only because of the humour directed towards a serious issue but also because of the softening of the angry words and attitudes expressed by Erdoğan. Indeed, autocratic Islamist leader Erdoğan uses this same question in his hateful, populist, and polarizing discourses against opposition political party leaders, critical intellectuals, and sometimes those in Europe, whoever is constructed as the other.

Under the AKP government, and despite increasing pressure, opposition and dissent continue to make themselves visible in different ways. Women and feminist organizations are examples of dissenting groups. In particular, every year on March 8, International Women's Day, they organize a big parade, defending women's rights and condemning the government for its policies against women. In 2019, following March 8, the pro-government newspaper *Türkiye* published fake news that demonstrating women booed the Islamic call to prayer and behaved disrespectfully. Traditionally, and particularly in recent years, concerts in public and other public events have stopped when the call to prayer starts and continued after it ends. However, it is unreasonable to expect this during a protest which is, first, already so loud that the call to prayer can hardly be heard and, second, not scheduled in the same fashion as concerts or other public events. This news was used as propaganda for Erdoğan in his ongoing populist and Islamist politics, further reinforcing 'us' versus 'them' divisions. Erdoğan raised this in a public speech and complained about feminist women to the "public": "They disrespected the *ezan* (call to prayer) by slogans, booing and whistling".[6] Later, although *Türkiye* corrected the fake report, *teyit.org*, on March 13, 2019, posted on its Facebook page and stated that they were still searching for evidence of the claim of booing.[7]

Thus, *teyit.org* worked to verify news that was already revealed as fake, and reenergized a discussion of whether it is a crime or disrespectful to chant slogans when *ezan* has started. Why was such news published? When we consider that *teyit.org* is the most prestigious, serious source, emphasizing its independence compared to other information channels, the implications of their sensationalizing already debunked fake news are alarming.

As well as *teyit.org*, another initiative claims to address columns and editorials, rather than the news. In reality, it reacts to whatever is found on the web, pushing back against any narratives in opposition to those favoured by the government and its supporters, while claiming fact-checker status. This initiative is called *Malumatfuruş*. [8] As with *teyit.org* and *They Lied to Us*, we see evidence of tabloidized content, for example, looking at verified content during the month of October 2019, it includes: creatures from space, confirmation of encyclopaedic information such as Zurich not being the capital of Switzerland, the city of Hakkari being in the Southeast of Turkey, and hippo milk being beige, not pink. At the same time, the initiative uses Twitter very effectively and includes entries which make us think that they are operating to justify and legitimize the government and pro-governing forces. For example, on October 31, *Malumatfuruş* argues that this news does not emanate from *Yeni Akit* newspaper but from a parody account using the *Yeni Akit* name. The falsified "news" is translated as follows: "a DNA test of a mummy in Egypt revealed that, in their last breath, the mummy made a *kelime-i şahadet*", referring to the Islamic prayer before dying to ask forgiveness from God. This reflects tabloidization in the context (a sensational story related to a mummy), which reinforces the rising Islamic values of "new" Turkey by suggesting its last breath was an Islamic prayer. Pro-government mouthpiece newspapers such as *Yeni Akit* often work like government weapons with lynching campaigns against anyone thinking differently from the government. *Malumatfuruş* can respond to this by tweeting: "Oh, what an imagination dear." "Those who declare that 'in our soil there are no Fethullahists who can live. Here is Izmir,' cannot unknow that those FETOists who attempted a military coup have grown from Izmir" (@Malumatfuruş, December 21, 2019).

In these examples, there is no information on news, dates, or channels. In practice, *Malumatfuruş* has nothing to do with news verification at all. These examples should be read in the context of tabloidization within everyday values of the new Turkey, in line with Nagehan Tokdoğan's (2018) analysis on affective politics and neo-Ottomanism. *Malumatfuruş* challenges the CHP in the context of *kayyum* (local governors assigned by Erdogan and replacing elected officials) assigned to the Urla (the secular Aegean town home to CHP voters and not many AKP voters) mayor by the AKP, justified by FETÖ (using the claim to almost any person and voice as part of their fascist Islamic totalitarian regime), and challenges their reaction that there is no FETÖ in İzmir.[9] It reinforces a dynamic of mainstream media working as "the apparatchiks of Erdoğan's post truth regime" (Gencel Bek, 2020a) through demonizing, criminalizing and defaming 'them' (which can be anyone and any group not keeping silent in the face of this autocracy) while monopolizing the perspective of 'nation'. Islam has been a very important parameter in the construction of this ideal nation and exacerbated polarization, a trend that began with the fake news on the Gezi park protestors drinking alcohol in mosques or attacks on veiled women in 2013. Thus, *Malumatfuruş* uses the sensational appeal of certain story types to weave in a more politicized message regarding Islamization and the 'new' Turkey. There are many other examples of how Islam has been a repeatedly circulated reference in this supposedly truth verification organization. While *Malumatfuruş* claims at the beginning that they analyze newspaper columns, in fact they also take into their coverage whatever they find on social media. What results is the systematic dissemination of rising Islamic values in a tabloidized, sensational way, under headlines such as:

- Column writers who cannot say *Selamün Aleyküm* correctly (Islamic greeting) (December 8, 2015, *Malumatfuruş*).
- The writers interpreting the sign of *Besmele* (Islamic greeting) on the cover page of Immanuel Kant's PhD thesis (October 18, 2019, *Malumatfuruş*)
- The claim of the first building of the earth being *Kabe* (September 7, 2019, *Malumatfuruş)*
- The claim that the Kuran had already encrypted the date of the human kind going to moon for the first time (September 23, 2019, *Malumatfuruş)*
- The claim of a famous rapper being Muslim (April 6, 2019, *Malumatfuruş*)
- The myth of Neil Armstrong heard *ezan* (Islamic call for pray) on the moon and become Muslim (January 7, 2019, *Malumatfuruş*)
- The picture claimed to be holy grave of Prophet Muhammet is a picture of Mevlana's holy grave. (April 10, 2019 *Malumatfuruş*)

The result of such content is *Malumatfuruş* arguably inverts journalistic norms by threatening factual truth with power; a dynamic that Hannah Arendt (1968: 227) described in terms of power threatening truth, particularly "factual truth."

Formal or rational truths, according to Arendt, such as "two plus two equals four" are not as vulnerable as factual truths because "facts and events – the invariable outcomes of men living and acting together – constitute the very text of the political realm." (Arendt, 1968: 227) Factual truth is very vulnerable to politics.

While *Malumatfuruş* jumps between tabloidized news, factual truth, and pro-government or pro-Islamic material, it still sometimes refers to more "liberal" organizations such as *teyit.org*. However, the overview of news verification organizations in Turkey is even more worrying if we extend the discussion to allegedly pro-government groups aiming for the international arena as a tool of "soft power." These include *Günün Yalanları* ("The Lies of the Day"), a project of Bosphorus Global which aims to defend "Turkey" on the global stage, not only in Turkish but also in Arabic and English. They openly defend the interests of the government, in Turkey and beyond, with other related initiatives. Like the previous examples, they do so by mixing sensational tabloidized appeal in the stories they emphasize, alongside a more specific politicized message. For instance, the pinned tweet atop the account for *Günün Yalanları* follows a similar approach to those discussed on the YouTube videos from *teyit.org*. In the October 9, 2019, tweet, they both amplify the already falsified claim that Turkish armed forces targeted children, while debunking it by instead arguing that this followed a bomb attack in rural Idlib by Assad's regime. In a way, we see similarities between more liberal news verification channels and *Günün Yalanları*, [10] as they converge on the issue of national interest, and when doing so defending the agenda of the government by calling out perceived manipulation, aspersions, and lies. However, *Günün Yalanları* goes further and has a different section examining the lies of the foreign press[11] and showing connections to another project on Islamophobia and discrimination from other parts of the world.[12] It calls this the "chronicles of shame", and links to a website which can be translated as "one body".[13] *Günün Yalanları* emphasizes a connection to another "kardeş" ('brother' or 'sister' in Turkish) project called *Factchecking Turkey* (in English and in Arabic) which aims to monitor "the factual accuracy of various news and claims about Turkey",[14] and in doing so reinforce the overall government's message. Yet rather than pushing back against 'fake news', these sites use the sensational appeal of attacks on Turkey, and the types of stories that attract attention that we have already discussed, to become "amplifier[s] of misinformation" (Valenzuela et al., 2019: 803), and contribute to the threatening media situation in Turkey by acting as part of the propaganda machine of the government in Turkey and beyond.

Conclusion

It is important to explore the impact of news verification organizations in reducing fake news, and the dynamics of tabloidization that come into the practices of communicating facticity and falsity in the Turkish context in order to seat this discussion in a wider understanding of tabloidization and media.

According to analysis of fake news in local elections in 2019 by *teyit.org*, 77 per cent of fake news stories are still in circulation and have not been corrected, edited, or removed.[15] According to scholarly research conducted with *teyit.org* data from June 2015 to January 2018, nine in ten pieces of fake news are not removed, edited, or corrected on publication channels (Uluk, 2018). This contributes to suspicion about the impact of more serious and professional-looking news verification channels in defending truth in Turkey and Turkish news media. It also shows the complicated relationship between efforts at debunking fake news, and working within a media ecology that both spreads and supports such misinformation.

The ongoing case of *teyit.org* reinforces this, as they are about to launch a program called Factory that will combine innovative technology, enterprise culture, and business with their ongoing work.[16] As Johan Farkas and Jannick Schou (2020: 137) argue, while companies such as Facebook and Google are often described as villains of the post-truth era, political, journalistic, and academic elites simultaneously portray these companies as potential saviours. At the same time, the links between these tech companies and media organizations have become blurry, especially when their priorities seem to work against one another. Case in point, *teyit.org* has been collaborating with Facebook since May 2018, so that when material is tagged on Facebook as not true, it is then automatically transmitted to *teyit.org*. At the same time, and paradoxically, the algorithms of Facebook and the operation of Google AdSense and Google Page Rank have been shown to contribute to the process of spreading populism and fake news (Flew and Iosifidis, 2019). As a result, the infrastructures of these media platforms work against their other initiatives, including those with *teyit.org*. Adding to this, in Turkey current developments and tendencies amplify the already existing situation, including Google's innovative news support being provided to the Demirören group, a pro-government media group.[17] It forces the question, regarding the civic aims of news verification and the sensational appeal of misinformation and fake-news stories, in the context of Turkey: what is happening at a civic level and between pro-government, pro-nationalism, and pro-global capital?

In this chapter I have tried to show the negative issues affecting news verification organizations in Turkey in relation to civic culture, particularly regarding their use of a tabloidized and sensational style. Among the arguments posed, I have tried to demonstrate where these sensational, tabloidized approaches to verification can at once promote, while trying to deconstruct, problematic 'fake' or politicised content. While global market-driven media and journalism are arguably infotainment and sensationalist spectacles (Thussu, 2007; Vettehen et al., 2006), and this is also the case for news verification organizations, these trends highlight paradoxes in their ambitions. While a trend of 'post-truth' messaging in politics is one of the drivers of populism and a threat to democracy (Flew and Iosifidis, 2019; Iosifidis and Wheeler, 2018), this study shows news verification channels are far from challenging this and, in fact, risk adding to authoritarian populism when they use sensational appeal and tabloidized approaches that can spread, even while debunking, fake news.

What is needed, it seems, is an interrogation-and-demand system asking for citizen participation and giving journalists a key role: "the fundamental role of journalism in democracy is to link citizens to political life" (Dahlgren, 2009: 150).

Although autocracy continues with intensity, other sources of hope are nevertheless apparent in the AKP's post-truth era. These include media incorporating reflections and continuity through aesthetic and creative protests in digital and offline spaces (Özdüzen, 2019), alternative media (Akser and McCollum, 2019), or even arguably the digital spaces of diaspora (Gencel Bek, 2020b). The news verification and fact-checking organizations discussed here undoubtedly cannot be sources of hope and challenge for civic against authoritarianism on their own, or perhaps even at all. The urgent task, if truth matters to us at all, is not opening up another initiative but seeing the destructive effect of a pressured political environment which does not tolerate any alternative ideas, lynching and criminalizing all others and polarizing society while favouring nationalism, populism, and Islam. In order to realize this, constraining legal and non-legal conditions over all forms of critical knowledge production, including but not limited to media, and incorporating academics, civic rights defenders, artists, and students, must be lifted.

Notes

1 The other organization, *Doğruluk Payı* was established even earlier, in 2014. However, as it focused directly on the truth claims of politicians, not on the media, it falls outside the scope of this chapter. The authors Bengi Ruken Cengiz and Koray Kaplıca (2019) analyze Doğruluk Payı as a case study and argue that fact-checking is a new type of citizen activism as well as being a journalistic practice.

2 Licali, Mahmut (2019) "'AKP medyanın yüzde 95' ini kontrol ediyor'". *Cumhuriyet*, 4 March. Accessed 4 December at: https://www.cumhuriyet.com.tr/haber/akp-medyanin-yuzde-95ini-kontrol-ediyor-1277808..

3 While writing this article, Erdoğan described social media as total rubbish with no control. https://www.hurriyet.com.tr/gundem/cumhurbaskani-erdogan-sosyal-medya-tam-bir-copluk-41444433.

4 https://osis.bg/wp-content/uploads/2018/04/MediaLiteracyIndex2018_publishENG.pdf.

5 All videos are cited by date, and can be found at the time of writing at the following YouTube channel: https://www.youtube.com/channel/UC8m7_g8NqFDhzp5lSHmYKsg

6 "Erdogan accuses women's march of disrespecting Islam". https://www.reuters.com/article/us-womens-day-turkey-erdogan/erdogan-accuses-womens-march-of-disrespecting-islam-idUSKBN1QR0JT.

7 https://www.facebook.com/teyitorg/posts/658642387900959.

8 In the interview with Sarphan Uzunoğlu, it is interesting that interactions take place between this and more technology-oriented blog writers: https://journo.com.tr/malumatfurus-kose-yazarlari-yanlis-bilgi-paylasiyor.

9 https://twitter.com/malumatfurusorg/status/1208469427781541898?s=20 21 December 2019.

10 https://gununyalanlari.com/

11 https://gununyalanlari.com/etiket/dis-basin

12 http://utancgunlugu.com/

13 http://yekvucut.com/
14 http://factcheckingturkey.com/.
15 https://teyit.org/wp-content/uploads/2019/05/Rapor-YS-2019-1.pdf.
16 https://factory.teyit.org/.
17 https://journo.com.tr/google-demiroren-gni-fund.

References

Akkoyunlu, Karabekir and Kerem Öktem. 2016. "Existential Insecurity and the Making of a Weak Authoritarian Regime in Turkey." *Southeast European and Black Sea Studies*. 16 (4): 505–527.

Akser, Murat and Victoria McCollum. 2019. *Alternative Media in Contemporary Turkey. Sustainability, Activism, and Resistance*. London: Rowman and Littlefield.

Arendt, Hannah. 1968. *Between Past and Future*. New York: Viking Press.

Atakan Foça, Mehmet. 2016. "Pinokyolar Çağında teyit.org." teyit.org. 26 October. https://teyit.org/pinokyolar-caginda-teyit-org/.

Atakan Foça, Mehmet. 2019. "Gerçeklerin Değersizleştiği Bir Dönemde Hakikat Arayışı." teyit.org. 26 October.https://teyit.org/gerceklerin-degersizlestigi-bir-donemde-hakikat-arayisi-teyit-uc-yasinda/.

Baybars Hawks, Banu and Sarphan Uzunoğlu, 2019. "Populist Leaders and International Organizations: A Comparative Analysis." In Banu Baybars Hawks and Sarphan Uzunoğlu (eds.) *Polarization, Populism, and the New Politics: Media and Communication in a Changing World*. Newcastle upon Tyne: Cambridge Scholars Publishing.

Bruff, Ian. 2014. "The Rise of Authoritarian Neoliberalism." *Rethinking Marxism*. 26 (1): 113–129.

Christensen, Christian. 2007. "Breaking the news. Concentration of ownership, the fall of unions and government legislation in Turkey." *Global Media and Communication* 3 (2): 179–199.

Dahlgren, Peter. 2009. "The Troubling Evolution of Journalism." In Barbie Zelizer(ed.) *The Changing Faces of Journalism Tabloidization, Technology and Truthiness*. New York: Routledge.

Dahlgren, Peter. 2018. "Media, Knowledge and Trust: The Deepening Epistemic Crisis of Democracy." *Javnost – The Public* 25 (1-2): 20–27.

Doruk Şahin, Özlem. 2019. "Media Populism in Turkey: Analysing the Turkey-Netherlands Diplomatic Crisis and Populist Discourse in the News Media from a Discourse-Historical Perspective." In Banu Baybars Hawks and Sarphan Uzunoğlu (eds.) *Polarization, Populism, and the New Politics: Media and Communication in a Changing World*. Newcastle upon Tyne: Cambridge Scholars Publishing.

Farkas, Johan and Jannick Schou. 2020. *Post-Truth, Fake News and Democracy. Mapping the Politics of Falsehood*. New York: Routledge.

Farmanfarmaian, Roxane, Ali Sonay, and Murat Akser. 2018. "The Turkish Media Structure in Judicial and Political Context: An Illustration of Values and Status Negotiation." *Middle East Critique*. 27 (2): 111–125.

Flew Terry and Petros Iosifidis. 2019. "Populism, globalisation and social media." *The International Communication Gazette* 82 (1): 1–19.

Gencel Bek, Mine. 2004. "Research Note: Tabloidization of News Media, An Analysis of Television News in Turkey," *European Journal of Communication* 19 (3): 371–386.

Gencel Bek, Mine. 2020a. "Collective Myths and Decivilizing Politics in Turkey." In Stefan Kramer and Peter Ludes (eds.) *Collective Myths and Decivilizing Politics* (pp. 142–157). Volume 5 of The World Language of Key Visuals: Computer Sciences, Humanities, Social Sciences. Münster: LIT Verlag.

Gencel Bek, Mine. 2020b. "Questioning/Contesting Home, Nation and Beyond: Digital Space of New Migrants from post-gezi Turkey" In Daniel Stein, Cathy C. Waegner, Geoffroy de Laforcade, and Page R. Laws (eds.). *Migration, Diaspora, Exile: Narratives of Affiliation and Escape*. London: Lexington Books.

Iosifidis, Petros and Mark Wheeler. 2018. "Modern political communication and Web 2.0 in representative democracies." *Javnost – The Public* 25 (1-2): 110–118.

Krämer, Benjamin. 2018. "Populism, Media, and the Form of Society." *Communication Theory* 28 (4): 444–465.

Küçük, Bülent and Ceren Özselçuk. 2019. "Fragments of the Emerging Regime in Turkey: Limits of Knowledge, Transgression of Law, and Failed Imaginaries." *South Atlantic Quarterly* 118 (1): 1–22.

Levitsky, Steven and Lucan A. Way. 2010. *Competitive Authoritarianism: Hybrid Regimes after the Cold War* (Problems of International Politics). New York: Cambridge University Press.

Madra, Yahya M. and Sedat Yılmaz. 2019. "Turkey's Decline into (Civil) War Economy: From Neoliberal Populism to Corporate Nationalism." *South Atlantic Quarterly* 118 (1): 41–59.

Özdüzen, Özge. 2019. "Bearing Witness to Authoritarianism and Commoning through Video Activism and Political Film-making after the Gezi Protests." Aidan McGarry, Itir Erhart, Hande Eslen-Ziya, Olu Jenzen, and Umut Korkut (eds.) *The Aesthetics of Global Protest: Visual Culture and Communication* (pp. 191–210). Amsterdam, NL: Amsterdam University Press.

Reinemann, Carsten, James Stanyer, Sebastian Scherr, and Guido Legnante. 2012. "Hard and soft news: A review of concepts, operationalizations and key findings." *Journalism* 13 (2): 221–239.

Ruken Cengiz, Bengi and Koray Kaplıca. 2019. "Journalistic Practice or Citizen Activism? Fact-Checking in a Changing World". In Banu Baybars Hawks and Sarphan Uzunoğlu (eds.) *Polarization, Populism, and the New Politics: Media and Communication in a Changing World* (pp. 145–161). Newcastle upon Tyne: Cambridge Scholars Publishing..

Şen, Fulya. 2019. "The Mediatization of Politics: The Construction of Populist Discourses in Turkish News Media". In Banu Baybars Hawks and Sarphan Uzunoğlu (eds.) *Polarization, Populism, and the New Politics: Media and Communication in a Changing World*. Newcastle upon Tyne: Cambridge Scholars Publishing.

Tandoc, Edson C.Jr., Wei Lim, Zheng, and Richard Ling. 2018. "Defining 'Fake News.'" *Digital Journalism*, 6 (2): 137–153.

Thussu, Daya K. 2007. *News as Entertainment: The Rise of Global Infotainment*. London: Sage.

Tokdoğan, Nagehan. 2018. *Yeni Osmanlıcılık. Hınç, Nostalji, Narsisizm*. İstanbul: İletişim.

Uluk, Murat. 2018. *Hakikat Sonrası Çağda Yeni Medya & Yalan Haber*. Eskişehir: Dorlion Yayinlari.

Valenzuela, Sebastián, Daniel Halpern, James E. Katz, and Juan Pablo Miranda. 2019. "The Paradox of Participation Versus Misinformation: Social Media, Political Engagement, and the Spread of Misinformation." *Digital Journalism* 7(6): 802–823.

Van Zoonen, Liesbet (2012). "I-pistemology: changing truth claims in popular and political culture." *European Journal of Communication* 27 (1): 5667.

Vettehen, Paul Hendriks, Koos Nuijten, and Johannes W.J. Beentjes. 2006. "Research Note: Sensationalism in Dutch Current Affairs Programmes 1992–2001." *European Journal of Communication* 21 (2): 227–237.

Wahl-Jorgensen, Karin. 2018. "Media coverage of shifting emotional regimes: Donald Trump's angry populism." *Media, Culture & Society*. 40 (5): 766–778.

Wasserman, Herman. 2008. "ATTACK OF THE KILLER NEWSPAPERS!" *Journalism Studies*, 9(5): 786–797.

Wasserman, Herman. 2010. *Tabloid Journalism in South Africa: True Story!*Indiana: Indiana University Press..

Yeşil, Bilge. 2016. *Media in New Turkey. The Origins of an Authoritarian Neoliberal State.* Oxfordshire: University of Illinois Press.

Yılmaz, Gözde. 2016. "Europeanisation or De-Europeanisation? Media Freedom in Turkey (1999–2015)." *South European Society and Politics*, 21 (1): 147–161.

Yolçu, Neslihan. 2019. "Fact-Checking Websites as New Media's New Gatekeepers: The Example of 'Teyit.Org.'" In Nigar Pösteki (ed.) *Critical Thoughts on Contemporary Turkish Media* (202–223). Newcastle Upon Tyne: Cambridge Scholars Publishing.

Zelizer, Barbie. 2020. "*Why Journalism Needs to Change*." Media and Populism, 1st Lisbon Winter School for the Study of Communication. https://www.ascmediarisk.org/wp-content/uploads/2020/01/Media-and-Populism-Ebook-Versao-Final.pdf. pp. 81–92.

Quoted websites:

http://factcheckingturkey.com/

http://utancgunlugu.com/

http://yekvucut.com/

https://gununyalanlari.com/

https://gununyalanlari.com/etiket/dis-basin

https://journo.com.tr/google-demiroren-gni-fund

https://osis.bg/wp-content/uploads/2018/04/MediaLiteracyIndex2018_publishENG.pdf

https://teyit.org/gerceklerin-degersizlestigi-bir-donemde-hakikat-arayisi-teyit-uc-yasinda/

https://teyit.org/bize-yalan-soylediler-1-bolum-yayinda/

https://teyit.org/wp-content/uploads/2019/05/Rapor-YS-2019-1.pdf

https://twitter.com/malumatfurusorg/status/1208469427781541898?s=20 21 December 2019

https://www.facebook.com/teyitorg/posts/658642387900959

https://www.reuters.com/article/us-womens-day-turkey-erdogan/erdogan-accuses-womens-march-of-disrespecting-islam-idUSKBN1QR0JT

Index

For Product Safety Concerns and Information please contact our EU representative GPSR@taylorandfrancis.com
Taylor & Francis Verlag GmbH, Kaufingerstraße 24, 80331 München, Germany

www.ingramcontent.com/pod-product-compliance
Lightning Source LLC
LaVergne TN
LVHW021126300926
849160LV00010B/873